STOCK EXCHANGES, IPO'S AND MUTUAL FUNDS

Stock Exchanges, IPO's and Mutual Funds

E. Klein
(Editor)

Nova Science Publishers, Inc.
New York

For permission to use material from this book please contact us:
Telephone 631-231-7269; Fax 631-231-8175
Web Site: http://www.novapublishers.com

LIBRARY OF CONGRESS CATALOGING-IN-PUBLICATION DATA:
Available Upon Request

ISBN: 1-59454-173-6

Published by Nova Science Publishers, Inc. ✢ New York

CONTENTS

PREFACE

In Chapter 1, the authors conduct time series comparison of the number of trades, volume, and average trade size for NYSE-listed stocks that trade on the NYSE and the regional stock exchanges from 1993 through 2002 (we include NASDAQ as a regional exchange). They find that the percentage of volume that the NYSE executes is fairly constant over the ten-year time period. Daily trading activity on the exchanges is significantly related to market movements, interest rate changes and Mondays. Overall, there is a strong negative correlation for trading activity between the NYSE and regional exchanges.

The landscape of stock exchanges has undergone changes in the recent times. Most of the exchanges are currently for-profit organizations with diversified activities. The authors of Chapter 2 start by analyzing what functions a stock exchange in this new setting has. Next, they characterize the key factors of competition for order flow and for listing such as liquidity, transaction costs, listing fees, price discovery, regulation and accounting standards. The most interesting feature of trade is that two contrary forces seem to co-exist simultaneously: Consolidation fostered by economies of scale and network externalities, and fragmentation, a consequence of informational frictions, heterogeneity of investors and informational advantages.

As discussed in Chapter 3, widespread use of derivatives can cause the relationship of market fundamentals to price of a stock to be distorted. When the index was only an indicator of general price movement, there was no trading of the underlying securities. Then, came the advent of S&P500 Mutual Funds. With the ability to invest in indexes, demand for shares can be unrelated to the changes in the fundamentals. Therefore, demand became a function of fundamentals and index related demand.

The importance of equity markets as a vehicle for capital formation is well recognized. However, the role of secondary equity markets in providing economically valuable governance services is equally significant. Chapter 4 examines the impact on market liquidity of two significant U.S. Securities and Exchange Commission (SEC) regulatory reforms applied to The Nasdaq Stock Market: SEC's 'trade reporting' rules of 1992, and SEC's "order handling" reforms of 1997. The chapter concludes that public policies that increase market transparency and efficiency — such as "trade reporting" requirements and better "order handling" rules — promote the effectiveness of the secondary equity markets in delivering corporate governance through increased market liquidity.

As an explanation for the historically positive level of initial returns, the theory of partial adjustment of offer prices with respect to both private and public information has held up relatively well. In Chapter 5, the author tests six hypotheses related to the cognitive errors of conservatism and anchoring biases, finding that evidence in the IPO market is consistent with this alternative explanation. Specifically, he finds that the original estimate of the offer price (i.e., the midfile price) is set at a relatively low level and adjustments to this file price, particularly upward adjustments, are insufficient, which implies that offer prices are also downward biased.

A principal purpose of an IPO is to gain access to a liquid market. However, post-IPO liquidity may be impaired by the information asymmetry between outsiders and the firm's founders and early investors. Consequently most IPOs feature "lockups" that prohibit insider share sales for six months. In Chapter 6 the authors present the first detailed analysis of the liquidity consequences of lockups, by examining liquidity changes around the expirations of 1,497 IPO lockups in the period 1995-1999. They find substantial increases in market depth as measured by quote depth, average trade size, and number of trades. They find no material increase in the asymmetric information component of the spread, nor do we find other expected signatures of information asymmetry.

Hedge funds are becoming available to a broader spectrum of investors through funds of hedge funds and investible hedge funds indices. There is no formal official of the strategies applied but each database providers defines its own strategies, which can count as much as 20 different strategies. The study reported in Chapter 7 aims at analysing hedge fund strategies and determining so many different hedge fund strategies that exists by analysing into details the correlation patterns that exists between theses strategies. This study proves that investible hedge funds indices segregated per strategy are strongly correlated. The authors have also determined that the correlation between investible hedge funds indices is much higher than the average correlation between the individual funds of each hedge fund strategy.

As discussed in Chapter 8, due to the multiple-share-class structure of mutual funds, the entry decisions by fund families include two separate decisions: the introduction of new (single-share-class or multiple-share-class) portfolios and the introduction of new share classes for existing portfolios. The two decisions are based on very different considerations and lead to very different share class compositions. In addition, fund families starting new multiple-share-class portfolios appear to follow a very risky introduction strategy.

In: Stock Exchanges, IPO's and Mutual Funds
Editor: E. Klein, pp. 1-20
ISBN 1-59454-173-6

Chapter 1

A COMPARISON OF NYSE AND REGIONAL TRADING (1993-2002)

Bonnie F. Van Ness, Robert A. Van Ness and Richard S. Warr*
University of Mississippi
*North Carolina State University

ABSTRACT

We conduct time series comparison of the number of trades, volume, and average trade size for NYSE-listed stocks that trade on the NYSE and the regional stock exchanges from 1993 through 2002 (we include NASDAQ as a regional exchange). We find that the percentage of volume that the NYSE executes is fairly constant over the ten-year time period. The Cincinnati, Pacific and Philadelphia Stock Exchanges lose a substantial percentage of the trading volume in the NYSE-listed securities, while NASDAQ substantially increases its percentage of trades in NYSE-listed securities. Daily trading activity on the exchanges is significantly related to market movements, interest rate changes and Mondays. Overall, there is a strong negative correlation for trading activity between the NYSE and regional exchanges.

INTRODUCTION

Although regional stock exchanges are an important facet of our market system, few studies document regional activity. Furthermore, previous research focuses primarily on the competitiveness of the regionals' quoting behavior or on the impact of fragmentation on market quality. For example, Lee (1993), Blume and Goldstein (1997) and Bessembinder (2002) examine price competition between the NYSE and the regional stock exchanges and find that the NYSE has the best prices and executions. Arnold, Hersch, Hulheron, and Netter (1999) examine regional stock exchange mergers over time and the effect that these mergers have on attracting order flow and narrowing bid-ask spreads. These studies all encompass short time spans– from one month to two years.

Chordia, Roll and Subrahmanyam (2001), examine NYSE liquidity and trading activity for 11 years (1988 through 1998) and find increases in trading activity over time and decreases trading costs (spreads, effective spreads). While, Chordia et al., only focus on NYSE trades, we expand upon their analysis and provide the first long-term study of competition between the NYSE and regional stock exchanges for volume in NYSE-listed stocks.[1] The time period of our study runs from 1993 to 2001. This extensive time series allows us to examine the impact of not only rule changes and tick size reductions on the overall competitiveness of the regional markets, but also, the performance of different market structures under a variety of market conditions. The 1990s were a particularly active period in the history of the regional markets characterized by one of the longest bull markets in history, the advent of alternative trading venues such as ECNs and the prevalence of preferenced order flows. There have been significant structural changes in the markets during our study time period. In 1997, the SEC enacted new order handling rules for NASDAQ, and the minimum tick size was reduced to \$1/16 from \$1/8 in 1997 and to 1¢ in early 2001.[2] We expect that the change in tick sizes will have significant impact on the ability of the regional exchanges to compete with the NYSE if the NYSE is the most cost efficient market place. Further, tick size reductions may significantly reduce the ability of the regional stock exchanges to purchase order flow from retail order takers. Our study also examines the day-to-day competition between the NYSE and regional exchanges.

Our results indicate that the time period studied is characterized by a steady increase in trades on the NYSE that comes largely at the expense of the regionals. Tick size reductions also serve to benefit the NYSE. On a daily basis, there are considerable fluctuations in the proportion of trading activity handled between the NYSE and regionals. These changes appear to be driven by the overall return on stocks, Mondays, and changes in key interest rates. Our study also raises several interesting questions regarding the role of retail traders in intra-day trading activity and the importance of market design during periods of declining prices.

DATA

Data for this study are obtained from the New York Stock Exchange TAQ (trades and quotes) database. We examine data from January 1993 through December 2002 (ten years). We limit our examination to only NYSE common stocks (as designated in the "mast" file of the TAQ database). We adjust our sample each month and eliminate trades out of sequence, trades that occur before the open, and trades that occur after the close of regular NYSE trading hours. We aggregate the number of trades, the average trade size and total volume for each day. We supplement the data set with market data from CRSP and the dates of key macroeconomic data releases.

---

1 For the purpose of our study, NASDAQ is considered a regional stock exchange as it competes for off NYSE volume with the other regionals.

2 See Barclay, Christie, Harris, Kandel, and Schultz (1999) for a discussion of these order handling rules and empirical findings of the resulting changes. Bessembinder (1999) examines the effect of the reduction in minimum tick size change to 16ths. For decimalization studies see: Bacidore, Battalio, and Jennings (2002) and Chakravarty, Wood, and Van Ness (2002).

RESULTS AND ANALYSIS

Aggregating Trading Activity

Table 1 presents aggregate summary statistics for the sample. In panel A we report the number of firms in the sample. As the number of firms within our sample varies from year to year, we focus on percentages rather than absolute values. In panel B we report the percentage of the number of trades between the exchanges. These data are also presented monthly in Figure 1. The proportion of trades handled by the NYSE is relatively stable at around 60% until 2001 when the percentage increases to 73%, and then to 76% in 2002. Lee (1993), Blume and Goldstein (1997), and Bessembinder (2002) find that the NYSE generally quotes the best prices when compared with the regional stock exchanges. Therefore, our results are consistent with the previous work. We believe it would be interesting is to know why the proportion of trades handled by the NYSE increases so dramatically after 2000. Most of these trades appear to come from NASDAQ where the percentage of trades drops from about 17% to 12.7% and 12.6% in 2001 and 2002 respectively. The percentage of trades executed on the remaining regional exchanges all decline during the last years of the sample. The percentage of trades on the Cincinnati, Pacific and Philadelphia exchanges all decline to less than 1% by 2002 from highs ranging from 3.9% (Philadelphia) to 7.7% (Chicago). The decline in these markets is dramatic but we should note that these exchanges may have substituted the loss in NYSE volume with activity from other sources.

Turning to panel C, which presents the percentage of volume for each exchange, we see that the NYSE is consistent over time in maintaining about 83 to 85% of the overall volume. Further, NASDAQ experiences an increase in volume from 6.4% in 1993 to 9.47% in 2002. The reason for this increase can be seen in panel D which presents trade sizes. From 2001 forward the average NASDAQ trade exceeds the average NYSE trade. Each of the remaining regional exchanges gets less than 5% of the volume during any year of the study. The Pacific and Philadelphia stock exchanges also lose noticeable market share in terms of volume. Monthly volume data is also presented in Figure 2, while monthly trade sizes are presented in Figure 3.

A possible explanation for the observed declines in regional market share maybe an overall decline in retail order flow, which would manifest itself in a decline in the smaller trade sizes on the regionals. This decline in retail order flow may be due, in part, to the overall market decline from April 2000, and the impact of tick size reductions, which served to reduce the ability of regional market makers to purchase order flow from retail brokers.

Table 1. Summary Statistics of Trades, Volume and Trade Size for NYSE and Regional Stock Exchanges from 1993 to 2002

Exchange	1993	1994	1995	1996	1997	1998	1999	2000	2001	2002
Panel A: General Statistics										
Number of Firms	2362	2563	2686	2842	3035	3092	3046	2931	2755	2745
Average Price	27.05	25.84	25.49	26.55	28.83	27.75	25.11	24.38	23.74	25.31
Panel B: Percentage of the Number of Trades										
NYSE	58.92%	60.37%	57.30%	59.97%	62.52%	62.54%	59.49%	60.69%	72.91%	76.27%
Boston	3.55%	3.32%	3.61%	2.66%	3.07%	4.12%	4.85%	4.97%	4.25%	4.50%
Chicago	8.75%	8.10%	7.38%	6.39%	6.75%	8.03%	8.80%	8.93%	9.37%	4.81%
Cincinnati	3.85%	4.76%	5.97%	5.18%	3.69%	2.53%	2.62%	3.46%	1.95%	0.76%
NASDAQ	13.32%	13.03%	15.59%	16.31%	15.79%	15.91%	17.56%	16.80%	12.72%	12.59%
Pacific	7.74%	7.03%	7.17%	6.62%	5.73%	5.02%	5.06%	3.51%	0.75%	0.44%
Philadelphia	3.87%	3.40%	2.97%	2.86%	2.45%	1.85%	1.63%	1.65%	1.04%	0.63%
Panel C: Percentage of Volume										
NYSE	83.65%	84.14%	83.21%	83.96%	84.85%	84.23%	82.98%	83.70%	84.99%	83.31%
Boston	1.28%	1.18%	1.26%	1.08%	1.05%	1.41%	1.66%	1.57%	1.64%	2.39%
Chicago	3.73%	3.36%	3.21%	2.85%	3.04%	3.63%	3.90%	4.00%	3.83%	3.73%
Cincinnati	1.30%	1.58%	1.80%	1.49%	1.17%	0.84%	0.88%	1.17%	0.81%	0.49%
NASDAQ	6.40%	6.59%	7.47%	7.69%	7.22%	7.58%	8.30%	7.86%	7.97%	9.47%
Pacific	2.42%	2.03%	2.02%	1.96%	1.81%	1.65%	1.70%	1.11%	0.29%	0.20%
Philadelphia	1.22%	1.12%	1.04%	0.97%	0.86%	0.64%	0.58%	0.58%	0.47%	0.41%
Panel D: Average Trade Size										
NYSE	1,863.65	1,890.79	1,945.94	1,949.09	1,824.77	1,691.22	1,701.58	1,692.42	1,260.47	978.17
Boston	760.92	780.46	791.99	935.03	765.55	780.25	789.22	837.72	749.06	792.08
Chicago	782.98	851.58	913.35	956.25	964.85	926.58	892.04	933.71	1,002.87	1,000.21
Cincinnati	746.29	734.42	656.42	640.61	697.72	717.78	723.77	729.61	755.50	849.99
NASDAQ	1,582.97	1,710.50	1,456.69	1,424.14	1,319.92	1,380.67	1,333.04	1,307.06	1,399.22	1,429.34
Pacific	569.87	567.85	571.25	594.00	600.56	617.68	630.50	660.46	915.51	565.68
Philadelphia	627.39	707.94	755.97	778.51	799.46	817.40	776.55	885.42	1,105.09	1,118.97

Note: This table shows the number of firms and average price for each year (1993 through 2002) for the sample of NYSE listed stocks (panel A). Panel B the percentage of the number of trades that occurs on each of the exchanges that trade NYSE listed stocks (NYSE, Boston, Chicago, Cincinnati, NASDAQ, Pacific, and the Philadelphia Stock Exchanges). Panel C shows the percentage of volume that each exchange receives for each of the nine years in the sample. Panel D shows the average size of a trade that occurs on each of the exchanges that trade NYSE listed stocks from 1993 through 2002.

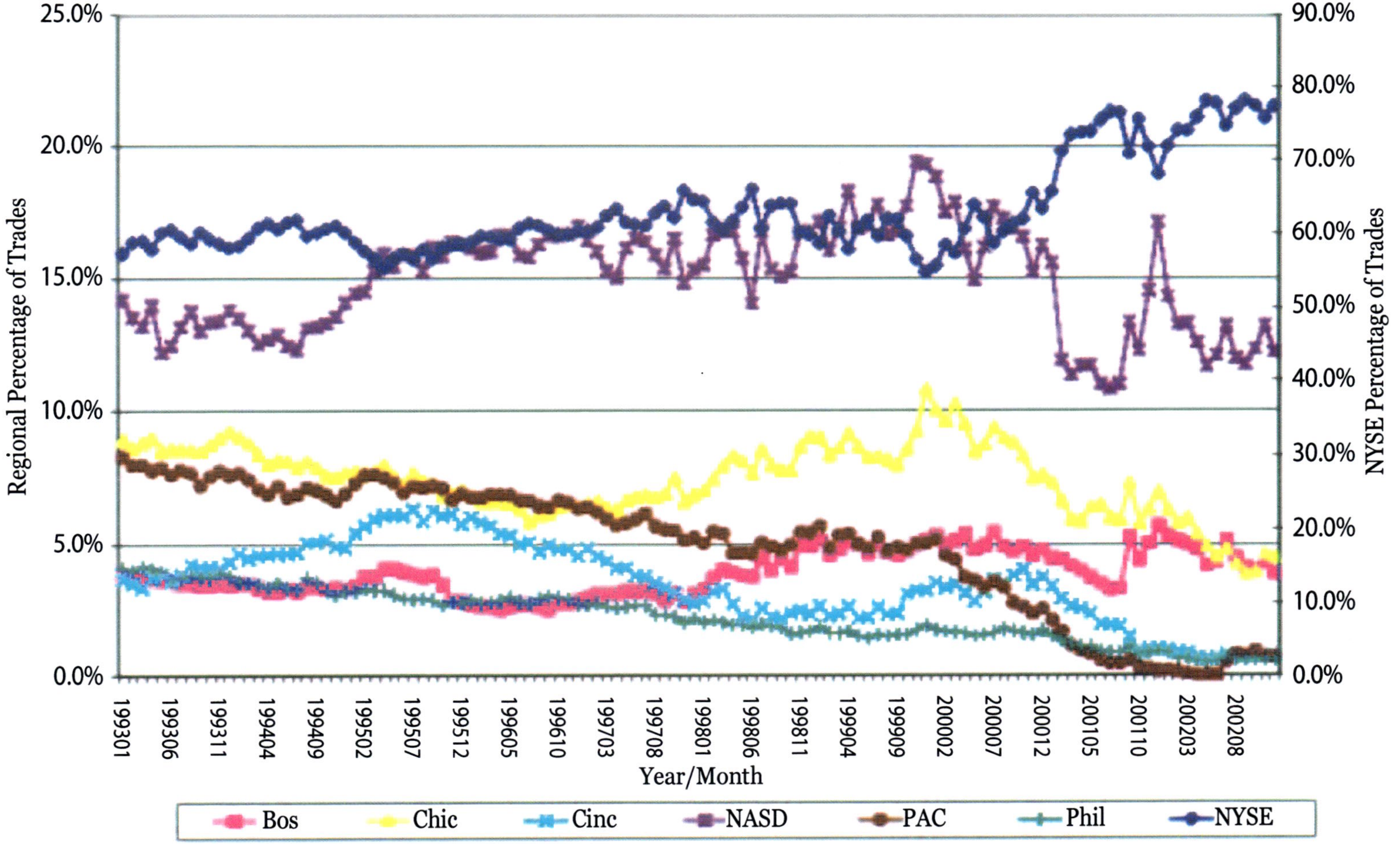

Figure 1. Percentage of Trades on NYSE and Regionals.

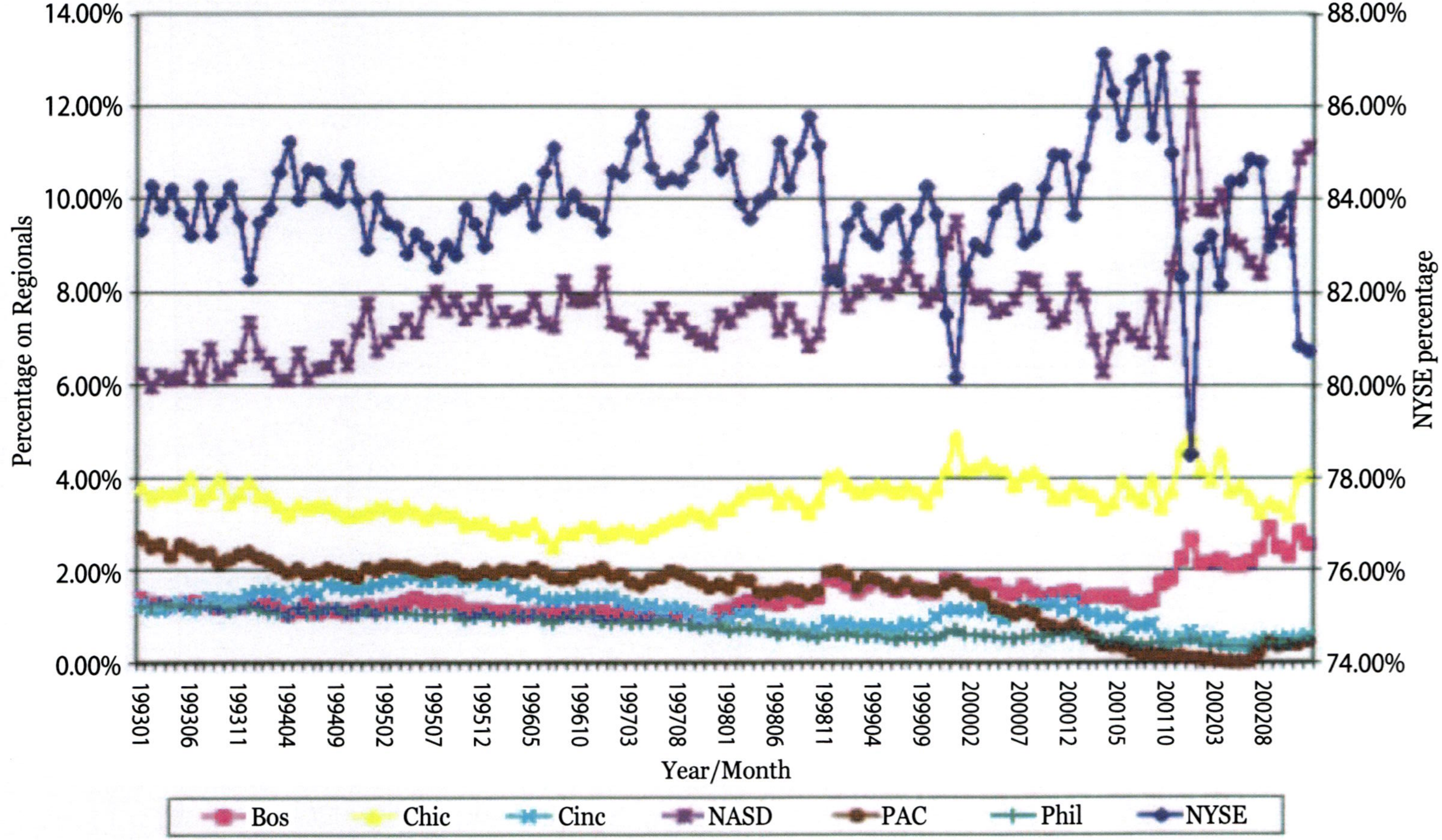

Figure 2. Percentage of Volume of NYSE.

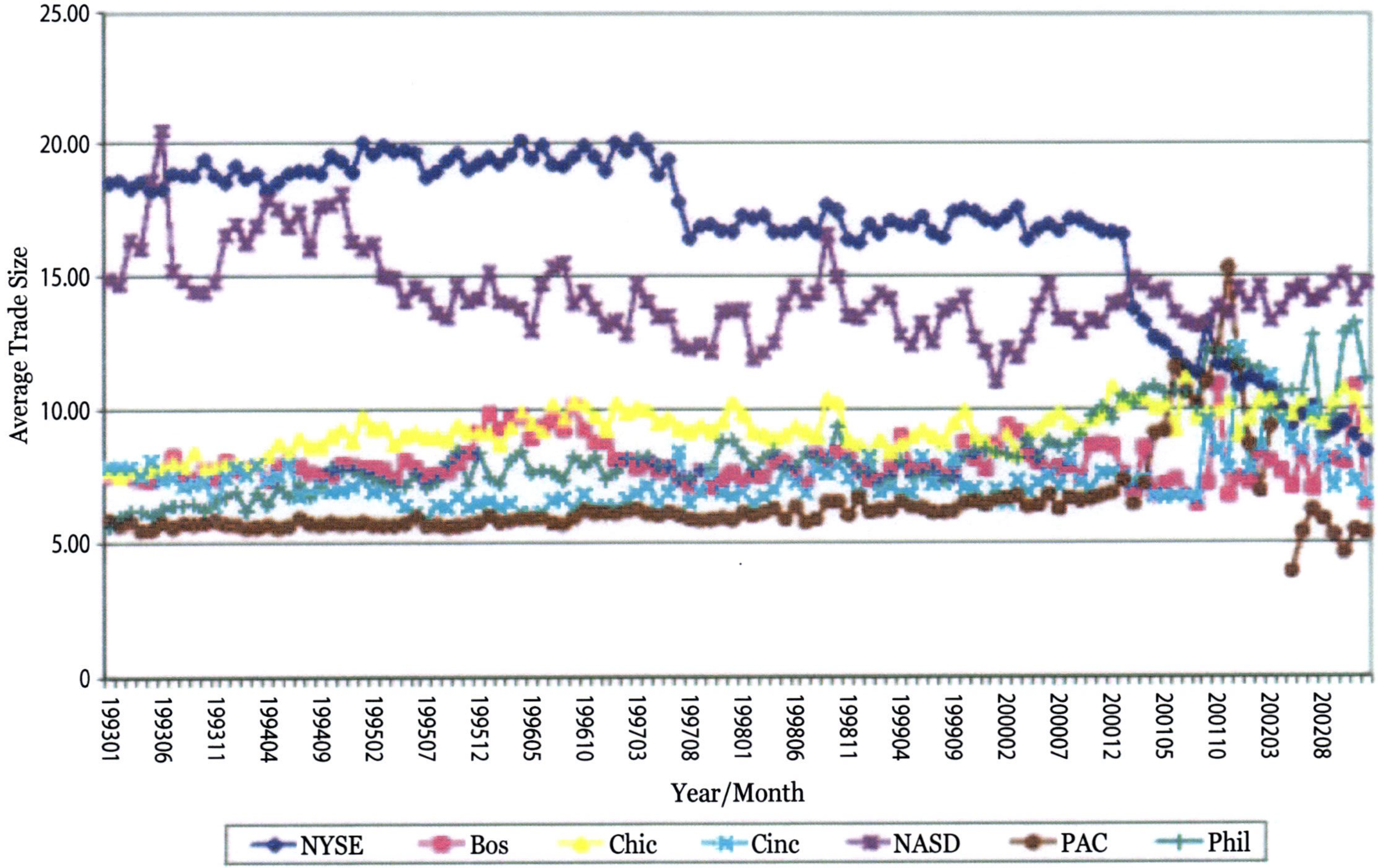

Figure 3. Trade Size on NYSE and Regionals.

Table 2. The Number and Percentage of Firms Trading on Each Exchange

Exchange	1993	1994	1995	1996	1997	1998	1999	2000	2001	2002
Panel A: Number of firms with trades on each Exchange										
NYSE	2362	2563	2686	2842	3035	3092	3046	2931	2755	2745
Boston	1697	1874	1923	1988	1942	1795	1676	1600	1644	1342
Chicago	2149	2345	2499	2634	2800	2879	2879	2754	2541	2434
Cincinnati	666	651	688	620	682	599	757	915	746	643
NASDAQ	2341	2553	2679	2838	3029	3090	3044	2930	2755	2722
Pacific	1337	1407	1620	2105	2321	2368	2345	2253	1783	2117
Philadelphia	1971	2213	2338	2441	2573	2545	2242	2033	1710	1504
Panel B: Percentage of Firms trading on each Exchange										
NYSE	100.00%	100.00%	100.00%	100.00%	100.00%	100.00%	100.00%	100.00%	100.00%	100.00%
Boston	71.85%	73.12%	71.59%	69.95%	63.99%	58.05%	55.02%	54.59%	59.67%	48.89%
Chicago	90.98%	91.49%	93.04%	92.68%	92.26%	93.11%	94.52%	93.96%	92.23%	88.67%
Cincinnati	28.20%	25.40%	25.61%	21.82%	22.47%	19.37%	24.85%	31.22%	27.08%	23.42%
NASDAQ	99.11%	99.61%	99.74%	99.86%	99.80%	99.94%	99.93%	99.97%	100.00%	99.16%
Pacific	56.60%	54.90%	60.31%	74.07%	76.47%	76.58%	76.99%	76.87%	64.72%	77.12%
Philadelphia	83.45%	86.34%	87.04%	85.89%	84.78%	82.31%	73.60%	69.36%	62.07%	54.79%
Exchange	1993	1994	1995	1996	1997	1998	1999	2000	2001	2002
Panel C: Percentage of Firms that Trade on Each Exchange or More										
1 Exchange	0.85%	0.23%	0.19%	0.11%	0.20%	0.10%	0.20%	0.03%	0.07%	0.73%
2 Exchanges	4.36%	3.59%	2.76%	2.85%	2.31%	2.49%	2.99%	3.38%	5.19%	6.16%
3 Exchanges	9.35%	8.86%	8.45%	8.06%	8.96%	9.73%	12.11%	13.10%	16.62%	14.43%
4 Exchanges	14.98%	16.15%	15.19%	13.02%	13.90%	14.91%	14.97%	15.22%	15.90%	20.15%
5 Exchanges	17.10%	18.92%	19.02%	15.02%	16.57%	19.79%	20.06%	18.80%	16.84%	18.18%
6 Exchanges	26.62%	28.29%	30.34%	39.76%	36.80%	34.54%	26.07%	21.29%	20.22%	18.29%
All 7 Exchanges	26.75%	23.96%	24.05%	21.18%	21.25%	18.43%	23.60%	28.18%	25.15%	22.08%

Note: This table shows the number of NYSE listed securities. Panel A shows the number of firms that trades on each of the exchange (NYSE, Boston, Chicago, Cincinnati, NASDAQ, Pacific, and Philadelphia Stock Exchanges). Panel B shows the percentage of firms that have trades on each of these exchanges.

Numbers of Firms on Exchanges

Table 2 presents the number of firms trading on the various exchanges. As can be seen from the aggregate numbers (panel A of table 2) and the percentage of NYSE-listed firms (panel B of table 2) NASDAQ is the most dominate of the regional exchanges in terms of the number and percentage of NYSE-listed securities traded. The Chicago Stock Exchange maintains trading around 90% of the NYSE-listed securities over the entire ten year time period. The Cincinnati Stock Exchange hovers around twenty percent. The Boston and Philadelphia stock exchanges show a dramatic decline in trading NYSE-listed securities, while the Pacific Stock Exchange shows an increase over the ten year time period. Panel C presents the percentage of stocks that trade on one or more exchanges. In all years, less than 1% trade only on one exchange, which by construction must be the NYSE. Therefore, virtually all NYSE stocks can be traded in venues outside of the NYSE – despite the evidence of the decline in the importance of the other exchanges for NYSE stocks during our sample time period.

Table 3. Spearman Correlations of Trades and Volumes for the NYSE and Regional Exchanges

	NYSE	Boston	Chicago	Cincinnati	NASDAQ	Pacific	Philadelphia
Panel A: Number of Trades							
NYSE	1.0000						
Boston	0.0742†	1.0000					
Chicago	-0.7368†	0.3048†	1.0000				
Cincinnati	-0.7572†	-0.4768†	0.2877†	1.0000			
NASDAQ	-0.6544†	0.2524†	0.4405†	0.2727†	1.0000		
Pacific	-0.8632†	-0.4495†	0.4933†	0.7993†	0.2934†	1.0000	
Philadelphia	-0.7299†	-0.5135†	0.4097†	0.7860†	0.0468*	0.9136†	1.0000
Panel B: Volume							
NYSE	1.0000						
Boston	-0.4447†	1.0000					
Chicago	-0.5831†	0.4852†	1.0000				
Cincinnati	-0.1698†	-0.5598†	-0.2805†	1.0000			
NASDAQ	-0.7114†	0.6665†	0.4235†	-0.3526†	1.0000		
Pacific	-0.2094†	-0.5682†	-0.2103†	0.6869†	-0.4197†	1.0000	
Philadelphia	-0.1620†	-0.5356†	-0.2469†	0.7636†	-0.4342†	0.8030†	1.0000

*Statistically Significant at the 5% level.

†Statistically Significant at the 1% level.

Note: This table examines the correlations of NYSE listed stocks and the exchanges in which they trade (NYSE, Boston, Chicago, Cincinnati, NASDAQ, Pacific, and the Philadelphia Stock Exchange). Panel A shows the correlation of the percentage of trades between each exchange. Panel B shows the correlation of the percentage volume between each exchange.

Correlations between Exchanges

Table 3 examines the correlations between the percentage of trades on the NYSE and regionals (panel A) and the percentage of volume on the NYSE and regionals (panel B). First, looking at the percentage of trades; with the exception of Boston, all of the regionals have a strong negative correlation with the NYSE. Looking at the percentage of volume in panel B we see that the negative relation is consistent across all the regionals, although the magnitude of the correlation varies substantially with NASDAQ having the greatest negative correlation and Cincinnati and Philadelphia having the smallest. The correlations between the regionals are more mixed with NASDAQ having a positive correlation with Boston and Chicago and a negative correlation with the Pacific and Philadelphia exchanges.

The striking result of table 3 is that there is strong evidence of volume going between the regionals and the NYSE. What is not clear is what causes this movement. We seek to examine this issue further in the following section.

Determinants of Changes in Trading and Volume between the NYSE and Regionals

In order to examine factors that might determine the volume on the NYSE versus the regional exchanges, we employ the methodology of Chordia, Roll and Subrahmanyam (2001) who examine the impact of market wide and macroeconomic factors on market liquidity and trading activity. Chordia et al. find that the overall market return, the day of the week, holidays, and the change in the level of key interest rates significantly affect traded and effective spreads and overall market activity, however, their paper examines only NYSE stocks traded on the NYSE. We modify their regression model as follows:

$$
\begin{aligned}
[\text{Dependent}_{it}] &= b_0 + b_1\,\text{MKTUP}_{it} + b_2\,\text{MKTDN}_{it} + b_3\,\text{MA5MKTUP}_{it} \\
&+ b_4\,\text{MA5MKTDN}_{it} + b_5\,\text{MA5}|\text{MKT}_{it}| + b_{6\text{-}9}\,\text{Day of the week Dummies}_t \\
&+ b_{10}\,\text{Holiday}_t + b_{11}\,\text{Short Rate}_t + b_{14}\,\text{Short Rate}_t + b_{15}\,\text{Term Spread}_t \\
&+ b_{16}\,\text{Quality Spread}_t + b_{17}\,\text{GDP(1-2)}_t + b_{18}\,\text{GDP(0)}_t + b_{19}\,\text{UNP(1-2)}_t \\
&+ b_{20}\,\text{UNP(0)}_t + b_{21}\,\text{CPI(1-2)}_t + b_{22}\,\text{CPI(0)}_t + \varepsilon_{it}
\end{aligned}
$$

where Dependent_{it} is either the daily change in percentage volume or percentage number of trades. Our goal is to examine what market wide factors might impact the movement of trades or volume to and from the NYSE. The independent variables are those used by Chordia et al. (2001) and are: MKTUP_t, the CRSP equally weighted daily return if positive and zero otherwise; MKTDN_t, the CRSP equally-weighted return if negative and zero otherwise; MA5MKTUP_{it} is the CRSP index return for the past five days if it is positive, 0 otherwise; MA5MKTDN_{it} is the CRSP index return for the past five days if it is negative, 0 otherwise; $\text{MA5}|\text{MKT}_{it}|$ is the average of the absolute value of the past five day's CRSP index returns; days of the week dummies (Thursday is excluded); a holiday dummy that takes the value of 1 if the preceding day is a holiday; Short Rate_t, the change in the daily Federal Funds rate; Term Spread_t, the change in the difference between the 10-year Treasury rate and the Fed Funds rate; and Quality Spread_t, the difference between the average yield on Moody's Baa rated corporate bonds and the 10-year Treasury rate; GDP(0) is 1 on the day of a GDP announcement, 0 otherwise; GDP(1-2) is 1 on the two days prior to a GDP announcement, 0 otherwise. UNP and CPI are defined as GDP for unemployment and consumer price index announcements, respectively.

Table 4. Change in Percentage Number of Trades

	NYSE	Boston	Chicago	Cincinnati	NASDAQ	Pacific	Philadelphia
Intercept	-0.0020	0.0001	0.0017	-0.0003	0.0004	0.0002	-0.0001
	(1.53)	(0.17)	(4.28)*	(1.51)	(0.58)	(0.89)	(1.42)
MKT +	-1.1531	0.1893	0.2839	0.1076	0.4411	0.0898	0.0416
	(11.35)*	(7.55)*	(8.83)*	(6.77)*	(8.14)*	(4.50)*	(5.07)*
MKT –	0.8016	-0.1330	-0.2056	-0.0806	-0.3092	-0.0544	-0.0188
	(8.55)*	(5.75)*	(6.93)*	(5.50)*	(6.18)*	(2.95)*	(2.48)*
MA5MKT+	0.0745	-0.0109	-0.0199	-0.0089	-0.0211	-0.0076	-0.0063
	(1.87)	(1.11)	(1.58)	(1.43)	(0.99)	(0.97)	(1.95)
MA5MKT-	-0.1274	0.0172	0.0389	0.0102	0.0428	0.0120	0.0063
	(2.84)*	(1.55)	(2.74)*	(1.45)	(1.79)	(1.37)	(1.74)
MA5|MKT|	0.7366	-0.1071	-0.1883	-0.0616	-0.3102	-0.0553	-0.0142
	(4.78)*	(2.81)*	(3.86)*	(2.55)*	(3.77)*	(1.82)	(1.14)
Monday	-0.0032	0.0004	0.0011	0.0004	-0.0001	0.0010	0.0003
	(2.09)*	(1.13)	(2.28)*	(1.72)	(0.08)	(3.36)*	(2.46)*
Tuesday	0.0091	-0.0011	-0.0053	-0.0001	-0.0015	-0.0013	0.0002
	(6.22)*	(2.96)*	(11.48)*	(0.47)	(1.90)	(4.61)*	(1.72)
Wednesday	0.0017	0.0005	-0.0028	0.0006	0.0002	-0.0001	-0.0000
	(1.24)	(1.51)	(6.47)*	(2.58)*	(0.24)	(0.44)	(0.20)
Thursday	0.0026	-0.0001	-0.0020	0.0004	-0.0006	-0.0003	0.0001
	(1.91)	(0.25)	(4.65)*	(1.69)	(0.83)	(1.30)	(0.70)
Holiday	-0.0034	-0.0001	0.0035	-0.0000	0.0001	0.0002	-0.0002
	(1.79)	(0.28)	(5.81)*	(0.06)	(0.09)	(0.49)	(1.23)
Short Rate	0.0669	-0.0029	-0.0197	-0.0058	-0.0267	-0.0100	-0.0018
	(3.89)*	(0.69)	(3.62)*	(2.15)*	(2.91)*	(2.98)*	(1.28)
Term Spread	0.0073	0.0009	-0.0036	-0.0007	-0.0023	-0.0014	-0.0002
	(2.09)*	(1.00)	(3.27)*	(1.20)	(1.24)	(1.99)*	(0.78)
Quality Spread	-0.0195	0.0019	0.0057	0.0010	0.0079	0.0024	0.0006
	(4.14)*	(1.66)	(3.79)*	(1.33)	(3.16)*	(2.62)*	(1.55)
GDP(1-2)	0.0007	-0.0008	0.0001	-0.0001	-0.0002	0.0002	0.0000
	(0.51)	(2.22)*	(0.25)	(0.31)	(0.30)	(0.81)	(0.09)
GDP (0)	0.0050	-0.0009	-0.0004	-0.0006	-0.0021	-0.0010	-0.0000
	(2.63)*	(1.93)	(0.74)	(1.91)	(2.07)*	(2.61)*	(0.12)
UNP (1-2)	-0.0036	0.0004	0.0016	0.0000	0.0014	-0.0000	0.0001
	(1.75)	(0.85)	(2.42)*	(0.13)	(1.33)	(0.00)	(0.62)
UNP (0)	-0.0013	-0.0001	-0.0010	0.0004	0.0019	0.0000	0.0001
	(0.64)	(0.20)	(1.47)	(1.22)	(1.73)	(0.10)	(0.31)
CPI (1-2)	-0.0007	0.0002	0.0006	0.0001	0.0002	-0.0004	0.0000
	(0.39)	(0.35)	(1.05)	(0.39)	(0.18)	(1.02)	(0.16)
CPI (0)	-0.0003	0.0003	-0.0007	0.0005	0.0001	-0.0001	0.0000
	(0.16)	(0.73)	(1.11)	(1.67)	(0.11)	(0.16)	(0.50)
Adj. R^2	0.1126	0.0475	0.1601	0.0290	0.0499	0.0426	0.0134

* Statistically Significant at the 5% level.

Note: This tables shows the daily change in the percentage of trades on each exchange regressed against the CRSP equally weighted daily returns, and dummy variables for each day of the week (Wednesday is omitted), a dummy variable for holidays, changes in various key interest rates and dummy variables indicating macroeconomic news announcements.

In table 4 the dependent variable is the change in the in the percentage of trades on each exchange. We report the regression for the NYSE and each of the six regional exchanges. Because we are examining the change in percentage of trades across the exchanges, the coefficient estimates for each variable should sum to zero across the seven regression models. This allows us to see where net gains in percentage trades are offset by net losses.

Some striking results are evident. The coefficient on MKTUP is negative and significant for the NYSE but positive and significant on all the other exchanges. Conversely for MKTDN, the coefficient is positive for the NYSE but negative for the other exchanges. These results suggest that when the market moves up trades move from the NYSE to the regionals, but in a down market the trades move back to the NYSE. In a down market, immediacy of execution may be of greater priority to traders, and this evidence suggests that the NYSE is better able to meet that need.

For MA5MKTUP, which measures a five day run up, there is a weak positively significant effect for the NYSE, however for MA5MKTDN, there is a significant negative coefficient for the NYSE and a positive and significant coefficient for Chicago, although all the other exchanges have positive signs. The pattern emerging here is that when there is a negative market shock, at the margin, trades move to the NYSE, but if the negative market shock is sustained, trades return to the regionals.

Looking at the days of the week, we find that for the NYSE, Monday is negative and significant, while several of the regionals are positive and significant. This result is consistent with a larger volume of retail trades being executed on Monday (after retail investors do their analysis over the weekend). Such trades are usually routed through preferencing arrangements to regional exchanges. On Tuesday, the coefficient is positive and significant indicating a correction to a more normal distribution of trades for the rest of the week.

Changes in interest rates also impact the percentage of trades on the NYSE. An increase in the Short Rate (the Fed Funds rate) has a positive impact on the percentage of trades on the NYSE while having a negative impact for Chicago, Cincinnati, NASDAQ and Pacific. Given that increases in the Fed Funds rate are usually greeted negatively this result is related to the MKTDN result which also finds a percentage shift in trades to the NYSE in down markets. An increase in the term spread is also related to a move to the NYSE while a decline in the quality spread results in a move from the NYSE to the regionals (specifically Chicago, NASDAQ and Pacific).

The remaining coefficients in the regressions in table 4 measure the impact of GDP and unemployment announcements. GDP(0) is positive and significant for the NYSE but negative and significant for NASDAQ and Pacific. The rest of the macroeconomic variables are largely insignificant.

In table 5 we re-run the regressions in table 4 using the change in the percentage of volume for each exchange. Again we find a negative relation for MKTUP for the NYSE, and significant positive coefficients for all exchanges except NASDAQ and Philadelphia. The MKTDN variable is also negative but weakly significant for NYSE and positive and significant with a coefficient of about the same size for NASDAQ. This result is somewhat puzzling compared to the table 4 regressions which finds trades move back to the NYSE in down markets.

Table 5. Change in Percentage Volume of Trades

	NYSE	Boston	Chicago	Cincinnati	NASDAQ	Pacific	Philadelphia
Intercept	0.0020	-0.0001	-0.0002	-0.0001	-0.0015	0.0001	-0.0002
	(2.54)*	(0.38)	(0.81)	(1.03)	(3.08)*	(1.06)	(2.56)*
MKT +	-0.1488	0.0466	0.0626	0.0285	-0.0063	0.0216	-0.0042
	(2.33)*	(4.01)*	(2.55)*	(3.65)*	(0.16)	(2.23)*	(0.56)
MKT –	-0.1121	-0.0076	0.0097	-0.0137	0.1119	-0.0010	0.0128
	(1.90)	(0.71)	(0.43)	(1.90)	(3.07)*	(0.11)	(1.87)
MA5MKT+	0.0342	-0.0065	-0.0094	-0.0015	-0.0104	-0.0041	-0.0022
	(1.36)	(1.42)	(0.98)	(0.49)	(0.67)	(1.08)	(0.77)
MA5MKT-	0.0010	0.0044	0.0074	0.0007	-0.0169	0.0024	0.0011
	(0.03)	(0.86)	(0.68)	(0.20)	(0.97)	(0.55)	(0.34)
MA5|MKT|	0.0337	-0.0075	-0.0798	-0.0188	0.0209	-0.0152	0.0067
	(0.35)	(0.43)	(0.53)	(1.59)	(0.35)	(1.03)	(0.60)
Monday	-0.0147	0.0011	0.0022	0.0012	0.0077	0.0015	0.0009
	(15.26)*	(6.35)*	(6.03)*	(10.17)*	(13.04)*	(10.18)*	(8.29)*
Tuesday	0.0041	-0.0009	-0.0007	-0.0007	-0.0007	-0.0012	0.0001
	(4.46)*	(5.24)*	(2.08)*	(5.96)*	(1.25)	(8.69)*	(0.85)
Wednesday	0.0001	0.0000	-0.0003	0.0001	0.0003	-0.0004	0.0002
	(0.12)	(0.04)	(0.85)	(0.61)	(0.49)	(2.79)*	(2.09)*
Thursday	-0.0010	-0.0000	0.0001	-0.0001	0.0009	-0.0002	0.0003
	(1.11)	(0.23)	(0.29)	(1.18)	(1.72)	(1.23)	(2.66)*
Holiday	-0.0042	0.0006	0.0010	0.0005	0.0015	0.0006	0.0000
	(3.50)*	(2.60)*	(2.08)*	(3.46)*	(2.05)*	(3.49)*	(0.11)
Short Rate	0.0495	-0.0032	-0.0125	-0.0034	-0.0250	-0.0041	-0.0013
	(4.57)*	(1.64)	(3.01)*	(2.54)*	(3.75)*	(2.50)*	(1.03)
Term Spread	0.0041	0.0000	-0.0008	-0.0002	-0.0025	-0.0004	-0.0001
	(1.84)	(0.03)	(0.96)	(0.91)	(1.82)	(1.19)	(0.56)
Quality	-0.0047	0.0004	0.0012	0.0003	0.0018	0.0008	0.0002
Spread	(1.57)	(0.69)	(1.06)	(0.86)	(0.98)	(1.72)	(0.59)
	-0.0011	-0.0001	0.0005	-0.0000	0.0007	0.0000	-0.0000
GDP(1-2)	(1.22)	(0.71)	(1.47)	(0.37)	(1.30)	(0.24)	(0.06)
	0.0004	-0.00001	0.0005	-0.0000	-0.0005	-0.0002	-0.0001
GDP (0)	(0.33)	(0.49)	(0.99)	(0.22)	(0.62)	(1.01)	(0.50)
	0.0013	-0.0001	-0.0004	-0.0004	-0.0002	-0.0001	-0.0001
UNP (1-2)	(1.02)	(0.33)	(0.79)	(2.62)*	(0.26)	(0.57)	(0.80)
	-0.0026	-0.0000	-0.0002	0.0002	0.0020	0.0003	0.0003
UNP (0)	(1.99)*	(0.02)	(0.41)	(1.32)	(2.50)*	(1.52)	(1.90)
	-0.0008	0.0004	0.0004	-0.0002	0.0004	-0.0000	-0.0001
CPI (1-2)	(0.67)	(1.84)	(0.81)	(1.30)	(0.50)	(0.24)	(0.73)
	0.0011	0.0001	-0.0005	0.0003	-0.0007	-0.0001	-0.0002
CPI (0)	(0.92)	(0.46)	(1.06)	(1.85)	(0.95)	(0.51)	(1.40)
Adj. R^2	0.2014	0.0675	0.0439	0.1174	0.1373	0.1657	0.0402

* Statistically Significant at the 5% level.

Note: This tables shows the daily change in the percentage of volume on each exchange regressed against the CRSP equally weighted daily returns, and dummy variables for each day of the week (Wednesday is omitted), a dummy variable for holidays, changes in various key interest rates and dummy variables indicating macroeconomic news announcements.

We find the same result as in table 4 when we look at the effect of Mondays on the change in percentage volume – again there is a significant movement of volume away from the NYSE. The trading day that follows a holiday is also associated with movement of volume away from the NYSE. We find a positive coefficient on the change in the short rate variable for the NYSE, which is consistent with trades moving to the NYSE when interest rates increase, which is generally greeted with a negative market reaction. This variable may be picking up some of the effect that we saw in table 4 on the MKTDN variable.

Chordia, Roll and Subrahmanyam's (2001) study takes place in a bull market and they question whether their results would hold in a bear market. Tables 6 and 7 replicate tables 4 and 5, but using the time frame of March 11th, 2000[3] through December 2002. Table 6 presents the change in percentage trades regressions for the bear market. The results are broadly in line with those reported in table 4. Notably, the coefficient on the MKTDN variable is significantly negative and larger than in table 4 – perhaps indicating that the importance of trading on the NYSE on bad market days is more significant in a bear market than in a bull market. The Monday effect is no longer manifested in the trade regression during this time period, possibly in part due to the significant decline in retail order flow that followed the collapse of the technology bubble. Table 7 reports the results for the change in percentage volume regressions. In these regressions none of the market variables seem to impact the volume on the NYSE. We cannot rule out that this result is due to the lower power of our tests due to the smaller sample size. Counter to table 6, Mondays are negative and significant, and the short rate variable is positive and significant for the NYSE.

Overall the results from tables 4 through 7 indicate that market conditions, in particular, result in significant trade and volume movements to and from the NYSE and regional exchanges. The impact of retail order flow also has some impact on the volume of the exchanges, particularly on Mondays.

The Impact of Tick Size Reductions

Two tick size changes occur during our analysis period– from \$1/8 to \$1/16 and from \$1/16 to decimals. Numerous studies examine the impact of these changes but largely ignore the regional exchanges. In this section, we examine the impact of tick size changes on the share of volume between the exchanges. Such changes may have significant impacts on the trades and volume of different exchanges. In particular, if the NYSE has an cost advantage over the regionals, the reduction in tick size may result in the NYSE being able to more cost effectively execute trades. Furthermore, if regional exchanges obtain much of their order flow through preferencing arrangements, their ability to pay for such order flow will be reduced following tick size reductions.

[3] March 11th 2000 was the peak of the NASDAQ index, hence we use this point as the beginning of the bear market.

Table 6. Change in Percentage Number of Trades– Bear Market (March 11th 2000 forward)

	NYSE	Boston	Chicago	Cincinnati	NASDAQ	Pacific	Philadelphia
Intercept	0.0012	0.0001	0.0010	-0.0001	-0.0014	-0.0004	-0.0004
	(0.41)	(0.07)	(1.28)	(0.27)	(0.97)	(1.53)	(2.65)*
MKT +	-1.2269	0.2616	0.3099	0.0982	0.4894	0.0368	0.0310
	(7.74)*	(5.44)*	(7.65)*	(5.03)*	(6.23)*	(2.97)*	(4.18)*
MKT –	1.2374	-0.3007	-0.2771	-0.1407	-0.4445	-0.0505	-0.0238
	(7.95)*	(6.37)*	(6.97)*	(7.35)*	(5.77)*	(4.16)*	(3.27)*
MA5MKT+	0.0799	-0.0209	-0.0255	-0.0025	-0.0222	-0.0030	-0.0058
	(1.24)	(1.07)	(1.55)	(0.32)	(0.70)	(0.59)	(1.93)
MA5MKT-	-0.1374	0.0371	0.0477	0.0065	0.0344	0.0047	0.0069
	(2.06)*	(1.83)	(2.79)*	(0.80)	(1.04)	(0.90)	(2.22)*
MA5|MKT|	0.8898	-0.1967	-0.1954	-0.0889	-0.3788	-0.0166	-0.0134
	(3.52)*	(2.57)*	(3.02)*	(2.86)*	(3.02)*	(0.84)	(1.13)
Monday	-0.0017	0.0007	0.0011	-0.0004	-0.0003	0.0003	0.0004
	(0.52)	(0.68)	(1.34)	(0.98)	(0.21)	(1.12)	(2.28)*
Tuesday	0.0028	-0.0016	-0.0041	-0.0003	0.0022	0.0004	0.0005
	(0.85)	(1.58)	(4.93)*	(0.65)	(1.35)	(1.68)	(3.52)*
Wednesday	-0.0051	0.0017	-0.0018	0.0005	0.0037	0.0005	0.0005
	(1.71)	(1.89)	(2.31)*	(1.38)	(2.47)*	(2.28)*	(3.33)*
Thursday	-0.0012	0.0006	-0.0012	0.0001	0.0012	0.0001	0.0005
	(0.39)	(0.69)	(1.51)	(0.17)	(0.76)	(0.31)	(3.29)*
Holiday	0.0010	-0.0013	0.0024	-0.0005	-0.0008	-0.0004	-0.0004
	(0.24)	(1.06)	(2.33)*	(0.91)	(0.40)	(1.35)	(2.11)*
Short Rate	0.0313	-0.0091	-0.0130	-0.0035	-0.0062	0.0001	0.0005
	(1.04)	(1.00)	(1.71)	(0.94)	(0.42)	(0.03)	(0.33)
Term Spread	-0.0149	0.0038	-0.0014	0.0024	0.0078	0.0014	0.0009
	(1.80)	(1.53)	(0.64)	(2.36)*	(1.90)	(2.12)*	(2.23)*
Quality	0.0048	-0.0013	0.0031	-0.0022	-0.0032	-0.0006	-0.0006
Spread	(0.53)	(0.47)	(1.34)	(1.94)	(0.72)	(0.88)	(1.51)
	0.0058	-0.0024	-0.0006	-0.0004	-0.0020	-0.0004	-0.0001
GDP(1-2)	(1.88)	(2.53)*	(0.77)	(1.01)	(1.29)	(1.49)	(0.88)
	0.0046	-0.0014	-0.0004	-0.0003	-0.0022	-0.0003	-0.0000
GDP (0)	(1.12)	(1.09)	(0.40)	(0.65)	(1.09)	(0.86)	(0.09)
	-0.0010	0.0008	-0.0002	-0.0001	0.0005	-0.0001	0.0002
UNP (1-2)	(0.23)	(0.56)	(0.21)	(0.17)	(0.23)	(0.26)	(0.80)
	-0.0035	-0.0006	0.0011	0.0004	0.0024	-0.0000	0.0002
UNP (0)	(0.76)	(0.46)	(0.91)	(0.79)	(1.05)	(0.01)	(1.09)
	0.0009	-0.0001	-0.0002	0.0004	-0.0003	-0.0008	0.0001
CPI (1-2)	(0.22)	(0.08)	(0.22)	(0.74)	(0.16)	(2.40)*	(0.69)
	0.0038	-0.0009	-0.0009	-0.0002	-0.0012	-0.0004	-0.0002
CPI (0)	(0.93)	(0.71)	(0.86)	(0.50)	(0.59)	(1.26)	(0.89)
Adj. R^2	0.1713	0.1214	0.1797	0.1254	0.1217	0.0596	0.0767

* Statistically Significant at the 5% level.

Note: This tables shows the daily change in the percentage of trades on each exchange regressed against the CRSP equally weighted daily returns, and dummy variables for each day of the week (Wednesday is omitted), a dummy variable for holidays, changes in various key interest rates and dummy variables indicating macroeconomic news announcements.

Table 7. Change in Percentage Volume– Bear Market (March 11th 2000 Forward)

	NYSE	Boston	Chicago	Cincinnati	NASDAQ	Pacific	Philadelphia
Intercept	0.0033	-0.0001	0.0000	-0.0001	-0.0029	-0.0000	-0.0002
	(1.99)*	(0.37)	(0.03)	(0.51)	(2.74)*	(0.34)	(1.34)
MKT +	-0.0536	0.0586	0.0496	0.0145	-0.0721	0.0000	0.0031
	(0.62)	(2.97)*	(1.56)	(1.81)	(1.31)	(0.00)	(0.47)
MKT –	0.0726	-0.0501	-0.0181	-0.0271	0.0247	-0.0050	0.0031
	(0.85)	(2.59)*	(0.58)	(3.45)*	(0.46)	(0.93)	(0.48)
MA5MKT+	-0.0105	-0.0094	0.0018	-0.0008	0.0216	-0.0005	-0.0023
	(0.30)	(1.17)	(0.14)	(0.23)	(0.96)	(0.20)	(0.87)
MA5MKT-	0.0182	0.0100	0.0046	-0.0012	-0.0319	-0.0010	0.0014
	(0.50)	(1.21)	(0.34)	(0.35)	(1.37)	(0.44)	(0.48)
MA5|MKT|	0.1033	-0.0352	-0.0480	-0.0210	-0.0034	0.0027	0.0016
	(0.75)	(1.12)	(0.95)	(1.64)	(0.04)	(0.31)	(0.15)
Monday	-0.0147	0.0019	0.0027	0.0009	0.0084	0.0004	0.0005
	(8.15)*	(4.67)*	(4.05)*	(5.19)*	(7.26)*	(3.86)*	(3.38)*
Tuesday	0.0005	-0.0013	-0.0007	-0.0006	0.0021	-0.0002	0.0002
	(0.26)	(3.29)*	(1.02)	(3.63)*	(1.88)	(1.43)	(1.25)
Wednesday	-0.0001	0.0006	-0.0012	-0.0001	0.0008	-0.0002	0.0002
	(0.05)	(1.47)	(2.02)*	(0.41)	(0.76)	(1.60)	(1.44)
Thursday	-0.0030	0.0003	-0.0003	-0.0000	0.0029	-0.0002	0.0002
	(1.77)	(0.85)	(0.42)	(0.12)	(2.71)*	(1.55)	(1.43)
Holiday	-0.0040	0.0010	0.0011	0.0006	0.0012	0.0001	-0.0001
	(1.79)	(1.95)	(1.36)	(3.06)*	(0.84)	(0.92)	(0.36)
Short Rate	0.0572	-0.0075	-0.0189	-0.0042	-0.0239	-0.0009	-0.0017
	(3.50)*	(2.01)*	(3.16)*	(2.77)*	(2.30)*	(0.89)	(1.39)
Term Spread	-0.0061	0.0010	-0.0004	0.0008	0.0037	0.0006	0.0005
	(1.36)	(0.96)	(0.25)	(1.96)*	(1.28)	(2.12)*	(1.33)
Quality Spread	0.0055	-0.0005	0.0009	-0.0007	-0.0043	-0.0005	-0.0006
	(1.13)	(0.43)	(0.51)	(1.57)	(1.35)	(1.48)	(1.49)
GDP(1-2)	0.0003	-0.0006	0.0002	-0.0001	0.0004	-0.0001	-0.0001
	(0.20)	(1.58)	(0.34)	(0.83)	(0.36)	(0.69)	(1.03)
GDP (0)	0.0002	-0.0003	0.0004	0.0004	-0.0009	0.0000	0.0001
	(0.11)	(0.51)	(0.43)	(1.96)*	(0.64)	(0.17)	(0.85)
UNP (1-2)	0.0044	-0.0003	-0.0015	-0.0003	-0.0022	-0.0001	0.0000
	(1.82)	(0.50)	(1.71)	(1.42)	(1.41)	(0.83)	(0.00)
UNP (0)	-0.0030	0.0000	0.0010	0.0004	0.0016	-0.0000	0.0001
	(1.21)	(0.06)	(1.04)	(1.53)	(1.00)	(0.08)	(0.51)
CPI (1-2)	-0.0016	0.0009	0.0002	0.0003	0.0001	-0.0001	0.0001
	(0.73)	(1.85)	(0.30)	(1.28)	(0.06)	(0.37)	(0.81)
CPI (0)	0.0031	-0.0003	-0.0009	-0.0001	-0.0015	-0.0002	-0.0000
	(1.40)	(0.63)	(1.08)	(0.64)	(1.08)	(1.75)	(0.05)
Adj. R^2	0.1727	0.1209	0.0785	0.1573	0.1134	0.0744	0.0158

* Statistically Significant at the 5% level.

Note: This tables shows the daily change in the percentage of volume on each exchange regressed against the CRSP equally weighted daily returns, and dummy variables for each day of the week (Wednesday is omitted), a dummy variable for holidays, changes in various key interest rates and dummy variables indicating macroeconomic news announcements.

Table 8 examines changes in trading (panel A), volume (panel B), and trade size (panel C) surrounding the minimum tick size changes from \$1/8 to \$1/16 and from \$1/16 to decimals. We find consistent results for the 30 trading days before and after the two minimum tick size changes for the percentage of trading activity (panel A of table 8). The percentage of trades executed by the NYSE significantly increases, while the other exchanges that trade NYSE-listed securities show significant declines in the percentage of trades (two exceptions are: the Pacific Stock Exchange for the change to 16ths, and the Boston Stock Exchange in the change to decimals).

Table 8. The Impact of Tick Size Reductions on Trading Activity Between Exchanges

	16ths				Decimals			
	Before	**After**	**Diff**	**T-Stat**	**Before**	**After**	**Diff**	**T-Stat**
Panel A: % of the Total Number of Trades								
NYSE	60.07	61.87	0.18	3.41†	64.58	71.39	6.81	8.42†
Boston	3.29	3.14	-0.15	2.74†	4.52	4.20	-0.32	1.27
Chicago	6.92	6.75	-0.17	1.75*	7.49	6.58	-0.91	4.98†
Cincinnati	4.14	3.61	-0.53	5.67†	3.60	2.88	-0.72	6.70†
NASDAQ	16.80	16.08	-0.72	2.69†	15.92	12.06	-3.86	10.81†
Pacific	6.03	5.97	-0.06	0.64	2.30	1.55	-0.75	8.57†
Philadelphia	2.74	2.59	-0.15	3.69†	1.59	1.34	-0.25	6.16†
Panel B: % of Volume								
NYSE	84.07	84.44	0.37	1.35	83.93	85.91	1.98	4.57†
Boston	1.08	1.08	0.00	0.10	1.44	1.42	-0.02	0.24
Chicago	2.99	3.12	0.13	1.63	3.80	3.64	-016	1.45
Cincinnati	1.23	1.17	-0.06	2.51†	1.24	1.05	-019	3.51†
NASDAQ	7.76	7.37	-0.39	2.46†	8.25	6.92	-1.33	5.80†
Pacific	1.89	1.96	0.07	1.41	0.74	0.51	-0.23	6.42†
Philadelphia	0.95	0.88	-0.07	2.40†	0.60	0.54	-0.06	2.60†
Panel C: Average Trade Size								
NYSE	1933.42	1779.39	-154.03	4.68†	1674.98	1370.10	-304.88	11.60†
Boston	759.08	752.33	-6.75	0.32	812.53	755.23	-57.30	0.99
Chicago	936.15	941.91	5.76	0.23	1053.27	1032.39	-20.88	0.51
Cincinnati	676.35	789.55	113.20	2.59†	756.01	738.36	-17.65	0.48
NASDAQ	1358.10	1257.45	-100.65	2.19*	1432.86	1459.20	26.34	0.44
Pacific	608.82	599.59	-9.23	0.69	718.57	663.97	-54.60	2.21*
Philadelphia	770.16	731.20	-38.96	1.17	1022.52	1022.77	0.25	0.00

* Statistically significant at the 5% level.

† Statistically significant at the 1% level

Note: The minimum tick size was reduced to \$1/16 in 1997 and to 1¢ in early 2001. Each panel reports the means, differences and test statistics for changes from 8ths to 16ths and 16ths to decimals. Means are computed 30 days before and 30 days after each change.

We find statistically significant declines in the percentage of volume accompanying the change to \$1/16 for the Cincinnati, NASDAQ and Philadelphia Stock Exchanges (panel B of table 8). The NYSE shows a significant increase in volume with the change to decimals and all other exchanges show a decline in the percentage of volume (Note that the Boston and Cincinnati Stock Exchanges' declines are not statistically significant).

Changes in the average size of trades accompanying the minimum tick size changes show mixed results (panel C of table 8). For both minimum tick size changes, the NYSE shows a statistically significant decline in the average trade size. But, the Cincinnati Stock Exchange shows a statistically significant increase in the average trade size following the change to \$1/16. Other changes in trade size following the two minimum tick size changes are either as expected (decreases) or are not statistically significant. The impact of tick size reductions appears to primarily benefit the NYSE at the expense of the regional exchanges as is evidenced by a consistent movement of volume and trades from the regionals to the NYSE.

CONCLUSIONS

We provide a comparison of NYSE and regional trading activity for NYSE-listed stocks over a ten year time period (1993-2002). We find that NYSE's percentage of volume is reasonably constant over the ten-year time period, but the percentage of trades executed on the NYSE is increasing. We find that three of the regional exchanges (the Cincinnati, Pacific and Philadelphia Stock Exchange) show declines in the percentage of volume of the NYSE-listed stocks over the ten-year time period, while NASDAQ registers an increase in its percentage of volume.

Up and down markets play an important role in determining the proportion of trades and volume that is executed on the NYSE relative to the other exchanges. In particular, we find that trades move to the NYSE in down markets. Mondays are characterized by a movement in trading activity away from the NYSE. We hypothesize that this is related to increased regional-based retail order flow that follows the weekend.

We find that the NYSE increases its percentage of trades and volume from 30 days before to 30 days following the change in minimum tick size to decimals. Most of the regional stock exchanges show declines in percentage of trades and volume following the change in minimum tick size to \$1/16 and to decimals. Overall, the NYSE appears to benefit at the expense of the regionals following tick size reductions.

APPENDIX 1: SUMMARY STATISTICS OF ABSOLUTE VALUES

Exchange	1993	1994	1995	1996	1997	1998	1999	2000	2001	2002
Panel A: Number of Trades										
NYSE	25,671,426	27,109,407	30,731,430	37,964,090	54,056,917	71,815,422	86,906,114	107,655,315	154,869,853	224,797,532
Boston	1,545,440	1,490,218	1,936,588	1,684,710	2,654,842	4,735,763	7,078,281	8,813,942	9,036,901	13,257,077
Chicago	3,810,972	3,636,224	3,960,037	4,045,029	5,832,094	9,216,976	12,855,468	15,839,010	13,526,923	14,177,339
Cincinnati	1,678,539	2,136,070	3,201,313	3,276,805	3,194,216	2,905,900	3,822,609	6,142,765	4,145,726	2,251,936
NASDAQ	5,805,004	5,851,226	8,362,913	10,326,737	13,652,929	18,270,315	25,649,967	29,796,035	27,020,174	37,099,817
Pacific	3,373,555	3,155,236	3,842,674	4,193,766	4,957,632	5,761,908	7,386,642	6,224,207	1,600,167	1,297,030
Philadelphia	1,687,393	1,526,661	1,593,563	1,812,797	2,115,507	2,126,311	2,384,686	2,922,683	2,209,682	1,857,263
Panel B: Volume (divided by 1,000,000)										
NYSE	60,846.11	67,480.70	79,756.84	95,396.54	123,137.79	156,053.83	186,688.13	240,971.57	274,975.59	316,147.04
Boston	932.10	945.54	1,203.47	1,232.42	1,525.99	2,619.91	3,737.54	4,529.27	5,321.26	9,081.49
Chicago	2,715.00	2,697.47	3,073.56	3,236.50	4,412.09	6,724.78	8,765.07	11,515.02	12,389.43	14,162.76
Cincinnati	945.42	1,268.44	1,723.24	1,690.14	1,691.48	1,561.45	1,984.26	3,370.87	2,608.43	1,851.08
NASDAQ	4,651.78	5,284.17	7,161.01	8,734.96	10,477.62	14,042.47	18,671.90	22,629.60	25,784.45	35,944.83
Pacific	1,762.21	1,630.76	1,935.41	2,226.99	2,630.07	3,065.36	3,829.52	3,195.31	928.55	773.87
Philadelphia	884.41	896.43	995.31	1,102.74	1,242.84	1,194.43	1,294.37	1,677.70	1,513.83	1,539.19
Panel C: Number of Firms Trading on Each Exchange										
1 Exchange	20	6	5	3	6	3	6	1	2	20
2 Exchanges	103	92	74	81	70	77	91	99	143	169
3 Exchanges	221	227	227	229	272	301	369	384	458	396
4 Exchanges	354	414	408	370	422	461	456	446	438	553
5 Exchanges	404	485	511	427	503	612	611	551	464	499
6 Exchanges	629	725	815	1130	1117	1068	794	624	557	502
All 7 Exchanges	632	614	646	602	645	570	719	826	693	606
Total # of Firms	2363	2563	2686	2842	3035	3092	3046	2931	2755	2745

Note: This table shows the number of firms and average price for each year (1993 through 2001) for the sample of NYSE listed stocks (panel A). Panel B the percentage of the number of trades that occurs on each of the exchanges that trade NYSE listed stocks (NYSE, Boston, Chicago, Cincinnati, NASDAQ, Pacific, and the Philadelphia Stock Exchanges). Panel C shows the percentage of volume that each exchange receives for each of the nine years in the sample. Panel D shows the average size of a trade that occurs on each of the exchanges that trade NYSE listed stocks from 1993 through 2001.

REFERENCES

Arnold, Tom, Philip Hersch, J. Harold Mulherin, and Jeffry Netter, 1999, Merging markets, *The Journal of Finance* 54, 1083-1107.

Bacidore, J.M., R. H. Battalio, and R.H. Jennings, 2001b, *Changes in order characteristics, displayed liquidity, and execution quality on the New York Stock Exchange around the switch to decimal pricing*, working paper, Indiana University.

Barclay, Michael, William Christie, Jeffrey Harris, Eugene Kandel, and Paul Schultz, 1999,, Effects of market reform on the trading costs and depths of NASDAQ stocks, *The Journal of Finance* 54, 1-34.

Bessembinder, H., 1999. Trade execution costs on NASDAQ and the NYSE: a post-reform comparison. *Journal of Financial and Quantitative Analysis* 34, 387-408.

Bessembinder, Hendrik, 2002, Quote-based competition and trade execution costs in NYSE-listed stocks, forthcoming *Journal of Financial Economics*.

Blume, Marshall, and Michael Goldstein, 1997, Quotes, order flow, and price discovery, *The Journal of Finance* 52, 221-244.

Chakravarty, Sugato, Robert Wood, and Robert Van Ness, 2002, *Decimals and liquidity: A study of the NYSE*, working paper University of Mississippi.

Chorida, Tarun, Richard Roll, and Avanidhar Subrahmanyam, 2001, Market liquidity and trading activity, *The Journal of Finance* 56, 501-530.

Lee, Charles, 1993, Market integration and price execution for NYSE-listed securities, *The Journal of Finance* 48, 1009-1038.

ACKNOWLEDGEMENTS

We would like to thank Michael Goldstein for helpful discussions and suggestions. Robert Van Ness acknowledges support from a Hearin Foundation Grant, School of Business Administration, University of Mississippi.

In: Stock Exchanges, IPO's and Mutual Funds
Editor: E. Klein, pp. 21-53
ISBN 1-59454-173-6

Chapter 2

COMPETITION AND REFORMS ON STOCK EXCHANGES

Sofia B. Ramos*
CEMAF/ISCTE

ABSTRACT

The landscape of stock exchanges has undergone changes in the recent times. Most of the exchanges are currently for-profit organizations with diversified activities. The authors start by analyzing what functions a stock exchange in this new setting has. Next, they characterize the key factors of competition for order flow and for listing such as liquidity, transaction costs, listing fees, price discovery, regulation and accounting standards. The most interesting feature of trade is that two contrary forces seem to co-exist simultaneously: Consolidation fostered by economies of scale and network externalities, and fragmentation, a consequence of informational frictions, heterogeneity of investors and informational advantages.

INTRODUCTION

Competition is an incentive to reform. In the last two decades drastic changes have affected exchanges. Exchanges moved from an era of monopolies to a new era marked by competition. In this study we analyze the relation between reforms and competition. We describe recent stock exchange reforms, emphasizing aspects such as electronic trading systems, mergers, corporate governance issues and the creation of new markets.

---

* Address correspondence should be send to: Department of Finance and Accounting, ISCTE-Business School, Av. Forças Armadas, 1649, Lisbon, Portugal Tel.++351217958607/Fax ++351217958605, sofia.ramos@iscte.pt. JEL classification: G15, G29. *Keywords:* Stock Exchanges, Reforms, ECNs, Mergers, Demutualization, Cross-Listing.

In most countries, the history of exchanges can be briefly described as a monopoly enhanced by regulation. Now that barriers to competition are being removed, it is necessary to have a better understanding of the forces driving competition like consolidation and fragmentation, and the critical factors that investors and firms look for.

In the new competitive framework, listing and trading are separate activities and there is evidence to suggest that physical location is no longer an indispensable factor. The consolidation of trade is due to economies of scale and scope, and positive network externalities. But competition acts as a disaggregated force, since investor's preferences differ, leading to segmentation. While greater concentration of trading in dominant market centers can be foreseen, fragmentation will be induced by the intensification of competition, segmentation and the political intervention of authorities to protect domestic markets.

In the 80s, the London Stock Exchange (LSE) was the first European exchange to initiate a transformation, the effects of which still have a major influence in Europe today. The LSE opened dealership to competition by banks and other financial institutions, liberalized commission charges, introduced extensive use of computerized systems in price quoting and order placement procedures, and reduced the stamp duty, which implied a gain on competitiveness by a decrease in costs (Tonk and Webbs, 1989).

While advances in communications have brought new opportunities, they also present a threat. Market geography has been modified in such a way as to potentially create an international base of investors through terminals in other countries. The flip side is that the traditional base of investors of an exchange has access to more opportunities than merely on the domestic market.

Competition was also fostered by the progressive liberalization of economies and the waves of privatization have reanimated stock exchanges and established new ones. As this paper illustrates, the business of exchange was very dynamic in the last decade. Clayton, Jorgansen and Kavajecz (1999) report that sixty new financial exchanges have been created since 1990. They identify the likely factors they consider as having been critical for the establishment of these new exchanges: economic freedom in taxes, regulation and banking, and the existence of larger economies. In contrast, technology shocks that increase communication links reduce the likelihood of new exchanges being established.

More recently, the emergence of Electronic Communication Networks (ECNs) animated the debate on competition again and on the relevance of transaction costs.

Reforms in exchanges, fostered by competition, lead to improvements in various domains such as trading systems and the decrease of transactions costs, which in turn have intensify competition.

CHARACTERIZATION OF STOCK EXCHANGE COMPETITION

The landscape of exchanges has undergone changes in the recent times. Most of the exchanges are currently for-profit organizations with diversified activities. We start by analyzing what functions a stock exchange in this new setting has. Next, we characterize the key factors of competition for order flow and for listing such as liquidity, transaction costs, listing fees, price discovery, regulation and accounting standards. The most interesting feature of trade is that two contrary forces seem to co-exist simultaneously: Consolidation fostered by economies of scale and network externalities, and fragmentation, a consequence of informational frictions, heterogeneity of investors and informational advantages.

Characterization of a Stock Exchange

A stock exchange can be defined as an entity that provides a centralized forum for stock trade (Macey and Kanda, 1990). The World Federation of Exchanges (WFE) refers that an exchange should "establish asset values through efficient price discovery, enabling the public to know how much companies are worth according to the latest news and economic outlook". As a market, an exchange aims to satisfy actual and potential traders by minimizing transaction costs, establishing market prices that accurately reflect the equilibrium values, and offering liquidity.

Exchanges have wide-ranging functions such as organizing trade and the dissemination of market information. They are also responsible for regulatory functions such as writing rules for market trade, for the admission and competition of intermediaries, and for the listing of securities. In addition, exchanges supervise trade of intermediaries, the disclosure of corporate and market information.

Stock exchanges have long been seen as philanthropic institutions organized to act in the public interest. This view has drastically changed with the appearance of private markets and the demutualization of most of the exchanges. A recent survey of World Federation of Exchanges[1] shows that 63% of its members are for-profit organizations. Currently, exchanges see themselves more as market-oriented firms, having major implications in the way the business is conducted.

The exchanges' new commercial approach has lead many to developing new business areas like outsourcing technology,[2] price-information services, clearing and settlement, besides listing firms and trading securities, the traditional business areas.

A recent survey (WFE, 2003) analyzed stock exchanges' sources of revenues. Trading and services are the key sources of revenues of all members and the importance of these sources of income increased in the recent years (Table 1). Services comprise clearing and settlement activities, depository and computer services, membership fees and dissemination of market data and information. Clearing, settlement and depository activities were a key source of service income, particularly for listed exchanges. Transaction fees were the most important component of trading revenues while dissemination of market data and information was the largest component of services revenues.

Table 1. Sources of Revenues of Stock Exchanges

	1996 (%)	1998(%)	2000(%)	2002(%)	Variation 1996- 2002(%)
Listing Revenues	18.59	17.89	11.59	10.87	14.61
Trading Revenues	36.86	38.63	42.80	44.55	136.85
Services Revenues	31.05	29.50	29.78	28.81	81.83

1 Cost Survey 2002, World Federation of Exchanges (2003).

2 Many exchanges have supplied technology solutions for other exchanges. Paris Euronext technology has sold its trading platform technology to at least fifteen countries, while that XETRA, the trading system of the Frankfurt stock exchange, has been commercialized for instance to Ireland and Austria.

Other revenues	13.49	13.98	15.83	15.77	129.17

Source: World Federation of Exchanges (2003).

The variation in the revenue items is presented in the last column of Table 1, and is computed with the absolute values. There has been a large growth in trading revenues and other revenues in the period under analysis, mainly due to a diversification of traded assets. Exchanges have tried to be less dependent on trading revenues, which is very sensitive to market downturns as we have seen recently. Listing revenue has been the component with the smallest growth; this can be attributed to a decrease of initial public offerings and new listings and is also a consequence of the recent events in stock markets.

Exchanges used to be easily identifiable. However, today, technological improvements have facilitated the creation of new types of market, ironically known under the acronym "MONSTERs" (a Market-Oriented New System for Terrifying Exchanges and Regulators) (Lee, 1998), like ECNs,[3] which are presented as alternative trading structures. Listing seems to be the main difference in the kind of services offered by "organized exchanges" and the new entrants, since electronic exchanges are essentially markets for trading.

Characterizing the Key Factors of Competition

Competition between exchanges has increased in recent years for many reasons "*such as the provision of immediacy, price discovery, low price volatility, liquidity, transparency and transaction costs*" (Ferrarrini, 1998). Factors like reputation and quality have also contributed to making many regulators and/or exchanges reform their governance structure, trading systems and surveillance rules (Di Noia, 1998).

In this subsection, we attempt to identify what investors and firms look for in the trading and listing decision, respectively. These factors are extremely important since they define the attributes that exchanges can exploit to increase business.

Competition for Order Flow

Transaction costs indicate the explicit costs that are paid in brokerage commissions and taxes for carrying out a transaction, plus the implicit costs of the time required for its settlement (Pagano and Roell, 1990). Investors obviously look for markets with smaller transaction costs, thus transaction costs are normally also associated with higher liquidity. With the stiffening of competition, transaction costs have declined almost throughout the world.

A second important factor is liquidity. Higher liquidity increases the satisfaction of market participants. Traders want to trade in the same market as all other traders and where they can find the best terms for their trades, minimizing effort and time. Liquidity can be viewed in two dimensions: immediacy, the market's ability to supply immediate execution for an incoming market order; and market depth, the ability to complete market orders without entailing major changes in the market price. Liquidity is inversely related with the level of transaction costs, as mentioned above, and positively related with the accessibility of markets.

---

[3] See section Electronic Trading Venues.

Price discovery is the way a market attempts to find transaction prices that are in suitable alignment with theoretical equilibrium. Investors prefer markets with a greater flow of information, thus, where price risk is smaller. Larger markets are therefore preferred as they have a greater flow of information as well as a bigger pool for investors which accurates price discovery and increases liquidity.

Easy access to markets is also a key factor. The accessibility of markets has improved in recent times with the deregulation of markets as well as the progress in technology. Computerization of trading systems enabled cross-border trade, making exchanges within the reach of a greater number of investors.

Fair access means all traders have equal access to the market, that is, no traders have a special advantage over other traders. Investors also take into account that all market participants operate under similar conditions, where no one has a persistent advantage over another.

Overall, it is difficult for the trading system to fulfill all those features. Given that investors have different preferences, Schwartz (1995) has the opinion that it is not possible to achieve "*transparency, liquidity and immediacy*" simultaneously, thus there is scope for segmentation.

Competition for Listing

Next, we analyze the factors considered by companies in the listing decision. Firms' decision variables do not differ from those of investors: the costs for firms are listing fees. However, firms also regard trading costs, which is certainly linked to the fact that firms can raise capital cheaply in more liquid markets, with more investors and intermediaries. Pagano et al. (2001) studying cross-listing preferences, find that companies are more likely to cross-list in more liquid and larger markets, and in markets where several companies from their industry already cross-list.

Listing can be unbundled into several components according to Macey and Kanda (1990). When exchanges provide listing, they are also providing other valuable services: liquidity, monitoring of trading, publicity and a signaling function to inform investors that the issuing companies' stocks are of high quality. Therefore, it is natural that firms look for list in larger markets where they can gain more visibility, such as analyst coverage,[4] and increased reputation.

In the listing decision, firms also have to consider regulation and accounting standards. Coffee (2001) defends that strong legal standards tend to attract rather than repel listing. The idea is supported with evidence that exchanges with strong protection for minority shareholders have received comparatively higher listing. Jain (2001) finds that better shareholder protection rights and enforcement of insider trading laws is related with lower spreads. Pagano, Roell and Zechner (2002) found that European companies in their sample appear more likely to cross-list in countries with better investor protection and more efficient courts and bureaucracy, and with language and institutions similar to their home country. However, cross-listing decisions were negatively correlated with differences between accounting standards of the destination and home country.

---

[4] However, this is not confirmed by empirical evidence. Pagano et al. (2001) found that the decision to cross-list is not correlated with the difference in analyst coverage between exchanges.

Consolidation versus Fragmentation of Trade

Large markets have several features that please investors, but as already referred, the trading system cannot satisfy all the preferences. Therefore, an interesting feature of the stock exchange industry is that contrary forces seem to co-exist. On the one hand, markets tend to segment due to competition, but on the other hand, strong agglomerating forces cause them to consolidate.

Why does Trade Tend to Consolidate?

Several reasons lead trade to concentrate in one market place as economies. Exchanges attempt to exploit scope and scale economies by matching more investors and firms. The higher the trading volume, the smaller the average operating costs of exchanges and the bid-ask spreads. This attracts new investors that in turn make trade increase, creating a virtuous cycle. Also, there are benefits from trading multiple assets in the same trading structure. An example of the exploitation of economies of scope can be seen through the mergers between derivative and spot markets.

The initial models of competition between stock exchanges followed work in industrial organizations by focusing on economies of scale, transportation costs, and liquidity. Early work states that trading of a particular security tends to cluster in a single location (Stigler 1961, 1964). Doede (1967) and Demsetz (1968) elaborate on the economies of scale present in securities markets. Other theories predict that trading occurs in a single market due to liquidity effects (Telser and Higinbotham, 1977; Telser 1981; Pagano, 1989a; Chowdry and Nanda, 1991 and Glosten, 1994).

Recent research focuses on transportation costs and economies of scope. Gehrig (1998) suggests a framework for modeling competition between market places that endogenously differentiates the interests of firms within a market place from the interests of outside firms. The model presents competition in two dimensions: one dimension can be interpreted as geographic distance; the other dimension is the characteristic of the product. Agglomeration economies arise endogenously due to savings in transportation costs for consumers. The author argues that the wave of deregulation in financial markets may be understood as an equilibrium reaction to a significant decline in transportation costs. Pirrong (1999a) focuses on economies of scope and the organization of financial exchanges markets. According to the author, the creation of a single exchange with multiple membership classes with restricted trading rights has lower fixed costs than multiple single-product exchanges due to economies of scope.

Empirical research has tried to find evidence of economies of scale in exchanges. Malkamaki (1999) studied the existence of economies of scale in stock exchanges. According to the study, trading clearly entails economies of scale. The functions related to the listing procedure and to other activities involving company-specific information have fewer returns to scale, except for the larger stock exchanges. Hasam and Malkamaki (2000) could not find economies of scale in all the exchanges. Exchanges in North America and Europe report substantially larger economies of scale than those in the Asia-Pacific regions.

Exchanges can be considered as networks in which the greater the number of customers, the higher the utility is for all participants (Economides, 1993, 1995). Based on that reasoning, exchanges benefit from positive network externalities. The attractiveness of the market grows with the number of traders in it. Businesses characterized by networks effects start with very low value, but grow exponentially after reaching a critical mass (Arthur, 1989 and Hagel III-Armstrong, 1997). Consequently, networks are self-reinforcing by nature (Economides, 1993). A financial network, like any other network, needs to reach a critical mass to experience positive externalities. Pagano (1993) specifically emphasizes critical mass as the reason for the disparity in the development level of stock exchanges: countries with an equal level of economic development still have stock exchanges with varying degrees of development.

Liquidity is the main externality that appears in a financial network. But consumers also prefer larger markets because they are more likely to find their preferred item (Gehrig, 2000). In addition, a large number of investors leads to more accurate price information which, in turn, attracts more investors.

In the absence of frictions, volume tends to consolidate in one marketplace, in both space and time due to the network nature of business. The spatial network externality is matched by a similar temporal network externality: traders have incentives to send their orders to a trading system all at the same time, thereby increasing the likelihood that orders will be executed.

According to network externality literature, only one exchange survives when there is no cooperation between exchanges (Di Noia, 2001). The results can be seen as a good stimulus for exchanges to cooperate in the form of implicit mergers and remote membership, since more than one exchange can survive and specialize.

Listing also concentrates on a single exchange in the absence of information frictions (Gehrig, Stahl, and Vives, 1996). If there are barriers to information, firms prefer to list on more than one exchange, since investors have more precise information on the domestic exchange.

The recent wave of mergers and alliances suggests that exchanges are attempting to gain scale advantages and liquidity. But empirical evidence, still scarce in this area, seems to support the idea that economies of scale are only important for large exchanges and that network effects are important only after reaching a critical mass (Cybo-Ottone, Di Noia, Murgia, 2000).

Why Trade Fragments?

A large market is undoubtedly attractive for investors, but competition operates as a fragmentation force. Fragmentation arises because of the heterogeneity of investors creating market segments. It is difficult to have a trading system that satisfies all the requirements of the trading orders. Hence, exchanges try to segment according to investor's preferences, such as speed execution and anonymity. ECNs are striking examples of how new exchanges try to take advantage of gaps in "regulated markets".

Gehrig (2000) argues that there is geographical dispersion of financial activity because financial markets are not frictionless. The author divides the factors underlying the development of financial markets into centripetal and centrifugal groups. Centrifugal forces arise from market access costs and localization of information, while centripetal forces are economies of scale, informational spillovers, market liquidity and thick market externalities. The author argues that centrifugal forces should be particularly relevant in markets for assets priced on the basis of complex local information, like stocks and derivatives.

Other justifications are offered for the persistence of different marketplaces: First, handling complex information may require face-to-face contacts and hence motivate the existence of multiple market places for securities. Moreover, information collection takes a lot of time and money. Investors and intermediaries may prefer to concentrate on small and familiar markets where it is easy to manage information. Thus, it may be optimal to keep company- specific information and related functions close to the source of original information[5] i.e. in the local exchange (Malkamaki, 1999). In addition, differences in language and culture also reduce the quality of communication if trading activities are centralized in one market place. Local proximity is connected with informational advantages and this translates into profit differences (Hau, 2001a).

Foucault and Parlour (2004) also found that competition for listing induces exchanges to differentiate themselves through a choice of trading system or listing requirements. Exchanges with different trading costs, listing requirements and listing fees can co-exist, because entrepreneurs with different characteristics choose to list on different exchanges.

Madhavan (1995) also advocates that securities markets do not have always to consolidate. The author shows that large traders who pace multiple trades can benefit from the absence of trade disclosure in a fragmented market, as can dealers who face less price competition in a unified market. This leads to order flow fragmentation unless trade disclosure is mandatory even if there are informational economies.

Impact on Competition of Stock Exchanges Reforms

In this section a summary is given of the major events that affected stock exchanges and their impact on competition.

European Union Reforms

One of the goals of the European Union (EU) is to stimulate the overall level of economic activity by increasing integration in financial markets. The study of London Economics (2002) estimates that integrated equity and corporate bond markets could reduce trading costs and thereby boost overall EU GDP by 1.1% and employment by 0.5%. Moreover, it estimates a reduction in the cost of capital by 50 basis points and in the cost of market debt by 40 basis points.

European market integration is responsible for encouraging a set of reforms in the exchanges scenario. A first step aimed at market integration was taken by the Euro. The launch of a single currency is responsible for fostering competition between European exchanges as it increases comparability between them. The home currency effect, sometimes responsible for competitive advantage, disappears causing more direct competition between exchanges. In addition, it simplifies international transactions and increases market liquidity by eliminating conversion costs and the exchange rate risk.

[5] Gaspar and Glaeser (1996) model cities as a means of reducing the fixed-cost involved in face-to face interactions. Since complex information and instructions can easily be misunderstood, face-to-face communication is required.

The Investment Service Directive (ISD) is the legislative centerpiece of the single European market program for the securities domain and has been effective since January 1996. It defines a unified regulatory framework for the securities industry in the European Union with the aim of providing equal opportunities for its members.

The ISD was intended to remove barriers on the securities and derivatives business within the European Union. The directive gives investment firms a "passport" to establishing branches and conducting cross-border business in other member states, free from additional local licensing requirements but subject to the local business norms. Member states that implement the ISD can therefore guarantee their investment firms freedom to provide services in other EU states. In the same vein, each recognized exchange is automatically accepted in other EU countries. Indirectly, the ISD promotes remote membership and authorizes the creation of new exchanges and OTC trading. Competition increases with the access of foreign members, who change the traditional equilibrium of decisions between members, favoring less corporative reforms, and the creation of several new European stock exchanges.

In practical terms, the implementation of the ISD was slow (Wymeersh, 1998) and reflected "political compromises that invariably allow a considerable degree of protectionism to persist" (Steil, 1996, p.137).[6] In practice, investment firms also found that it is an unnecessary burden to have to comply with two or more sets of rules for business conduct: the rules of the home country which are automatically enforced and those of the destination country which generally opt to impose their rules on incoming investment services.

Currently, the ISD is under revision. The upgrading of the ISD aims to make the single passport for investment firms work better and to adapt new trading formats like alternative trading systems and e-brokerage.

In July 2000, the Committee of the Wise Men was formed, chaired by Alexandre Lamfalussy; it had instructions to recommend changes to EU securities market regulations. The proposed reforms should aim at a more homogeneous regulatory environment in EU securities markets in order to achieve market integration and to better the process of rule-making, supervision and enforcement of common securities provisions.

The first part of the "Lamfalussy Report" (LR)[7] identified several barriers to the development of a single financial market.

- A slow European legislative system. Legislation takes time to follow the rapid development of markets. For instance, in December 2002, the European Commission issued a proposal to upgrade the ISD "*after an intensive two-year consultation process*" (European Commission Press Release IP/02/1785).
- Slow implementation of directives by members. Many delays occurred in the transposition and implementation of EU directives by member states, as happened with the ISD.
- Many of the directives in the financial services field failed to distinguish between core principles and the detailed provision to implement those principles. Moreover, there is an absence of EU-wide regulation in a large number of areas.
- Market integration is blocked by differences in legal and tax systems, in cultural and political approaches, and protectionism.

---

6 The ISD Article 15.5 allows countries to prohibit the creation of new markets in their territory.

7 See The Committee of the Wise Men (2000), Initial Report on the Regulation of European Securities Markets.

- The efficiency of a regulatory system is deterred by the existence of many regulatory authorities, more than forty, all concerned with the regulation of the securities markets.

Following the diagnostic, the LR makes recommendations for a regulatory reform and changes to the current regulatory structure. It suggests a new framework to consolidate infrastructure using a four level approach ("The Lamfalussy Process"). The levels are briefly as follows:

Level I consists of framework principles for the regulation of securities markets as European directives and regulation. The Commission adopts them after a co-decision process.

Level II refers to the implementation of principles. It comprises technical measures necessary to make Level I directives operational and keep them updated.

Level III is therefore dedicated to ensuring cooperation among regulators and supervisors. It aims to ensure consistent, timely and uniform implementation of Level I and II in member states, via enhanced cooperation and networking among EU securities regulators.

Finally, Level IV ensures enforcement of the EU law. The Commission checks member states compliance with EU legislation.

The Lamfalussy Process was subsequently ratified and adopted by all the key EU institutions. Hertig and Lee (2003) show some skepticism on its effects, as it does not address, in their opinion, the causes of problems: national protectionism and bureaucratic inertia.

The Financial Services Action Plan (FSAP) is a program of the Commission adopted in 1999 to improve the single market in financial services. It contains several legislative measures to be implemented by 2005 in retail markets, and wholesale markets as prudential rules and supervision as well as other aspects necessary for an optimal single market for financial services.

The FSAP has several objectives:

- To reinforce financial stability and market integrity. This includes the establishment of a policy of market abuse, disclosure of financial information and comparable information throughout the EU.
- To promote European regulatory cooperation, which includes implementation and enforcement of common EU financial legislation.
- To create a stable framework for the smooth financial integration of the new members.

Member states have agreed on certain proposals, such as the Directive on Market Abuse or the Directive on Pensions Fund but most of them are still under negotiation. The Directives planned to be adopted by the first quarter of 2004 include the Prospectuses Directive, Directive on Taxation of Savings Income, Take Over Bids, Transparency Directive and the revision of the ISD.

Reforms will continue to foster European financial markets toward a single financial market; however, the process has been historically slow. Meanwhile, the harmonization of regulation and legislation will gradually eliminate differences between exchanges and increase comparability, which creates incentives to reforms toward efficiency on trading venues. Also, as regulation becomes similar, barriers to consolidation and cooperation of markets fall. At the moment, some alliances between markets are already visible, and it is likely that exchanges will extend their networks.

Implementation of Electronic Trading Systems

One of the major reforms was the computerization of trading. In 1977, Toronto was the first exchange to computerize its trade. Since then, a growing number of exchanges have opted for electronic trading, while floor trading is progressively being abandoned. Electronic order matching systems essentially operate as order-driven markets. A recent survey by O'Hara (2003) reports that floor systems are only used in 5% of a sample of 52 exchanges, while electronic systems are used by 79% and 17% use a mixed system.

The systems are fully computerized in the sense that the information system, order routing, queuing and execution systems are automated. Auctions markets are centralized systems and, as such, are more suitable for automation of trading than dealer markets are, which are set up as separated networks.

Harris (2000)[8] makes a comparison between floor and automated systems and advocates that automated systems are more transparent since trading rules are uniformly applied; they are also more flexible and cheaper since they allow traders to trade from desks in their offices rather than on an exchange; in addition, they are more scaleable than oral order matching technologies, operating with equal efficiency at small and large scale.

Globally, automated systems are fast and generally cheap to operate, becoming attractive for active markets and markets that serve small trades. The inconvenience is that exchanges must make substantial investment into redundant hardware and software systems to build a reliable trading system.

Floor markets may be less transparent because floor traders have advantage over off-floor traders as they observe all the information on the floor. Floor-based trading systems are, nevertheless, better at facilitating the exchange of non-price information. Floor-based systems have somewhat lower creation costs, depending on the price of real estate,[9] but are often quite costly to operate.

The adoption of these new systems is intimately related with progress in technology. But the massive adoption would not be so fast if exchanges, under competition, were not pressured to lower transaction costs and improve efficiency. Automated systems with lower operational costs allow for smaller transaction costs. Domowitz (2001) states that all things equal average total trading costs are lower by 33 to 46 basis points in markets that are largely automated. A second advantage is that electronic trading promotes cross-border trading. Exchanges can install local access points or direct computer connections, thus expanding their business. Indirectly, technology creates more liquidity[10] in markets causing more financial transactions to take place through securities markets (Pirrong, 1995 and Mahoney, 2002).

---

[8] For a comparison of the advantages and disadvantages of systems see also Sarkar and Tozzi (1998).

[9] Estimates exchange setup costs of Domowitz (2001) suggest that development of the trading floor is from two to forty times more expensive than in electronic marketplaces due to real estate prices.

[10] The impact of trading systems on liquidity and volume of share trading has also been studied in Domowitz and Steil (1999), Domowitz et al. (2001a), Domowitz (2001) and Jain (2001).

Although some studies indicate that exchanges have an incentive to choose different trading technologies in order to relax competition for listing (Foucault and Parlour, 2004), in Europe, trade and execution systems are becoming very similar (Pagano, 1998 and Demarchi and Foulcault, 2000).[11] Pagano (1998) states that European exchanges are converging towards a dualistic structure, or "hybrid," formed by an automated auction system specializing in small- and medium-sized trades and a market-making segment devoted to large trades.

While electronic systems were widely adopted in Europe, markets in the US are not making transition to full automation. For the most part, the computer there has been used for order routing and information dissemination rather than for trade execution.

Decrease of Trading Costs

One of the most visible effects of competition between stock exchanges was in trading costs. In the mid 80s, the LSE was the first European exchange to initiate a process of liberalization, but soon was followed by other continental European exchanges. The main catalyzing event is the so-called Big Bang, a set of reforms that liberalized the London stock market in 1986, and with a major impact on commissions and spreads. Pagano and Roell (1990) refer a fall of 1/3 on large transaction costs after the Big Bang. Progressively, the same reforms were applied all over the world. Recent evidence refers that transaction costs still exhibited sharp declines over the period 1996-1998, with the exception of Eastern Europe, ranging from 10% in the Latin America to 53% in North America (Domowitz, Glenn and Madhavan, 2001a). Despite the decrease, empirical evidence shows that there is still a large discrepancy between transaction costs in stock markets. Evidence on equity trading costs for the third quarter of 2000 shows a range from 22 basis points in the Netherlands to 184 points in Venezuela (Domowitz, Glen and Madhavan, 2001b).

Transaction costs play an important role for stock exchanges to the extent that they are directly related with trading revenues and liquidity. Estimates of Domowitz and Steil (2002) report that every 10% decline in trading costs results in a 1.5% decline in the cost of capital of blue-chip listed companies. Also each 10% decline in trading costs yields an 8% increase in trading volume. Moreover, listing and cross-listing also depends on transaction costs since firms tend to look for places with smaller costs to cross-list their securities (Pagano, Roell and Zechner, 2002); further, they are also noted as having a negative impact on price discovery and volatility (Steil, 1996).

The adoption of automated trading systems made the decrease of transaction costs possible, but profound factors such as stock market integration and stock exchange competition are at the root of the decrease of transaction costs (Ramos and von Thadden, 2003).

The decrease of transaction costs seems threatened with the recent wave of mergers of stock exchanges. In 2003, the German exchange, Deutsche Börse, increased fees by 20% justifying a more efficient clearing system. Big customers of the three largest European exchanges, Paris, Deutsche Börse and LSE fear they use their monopoly power to increase tariffs unfairly, and threaten to report to the European competition authorities (Financial Times, 20 November 2003).

[11] See Pagano and Roell (1990) and Pagano and Steil (1996) for previous literature on trading systems in Europe.

Mergers, Alliances and Cooperation

Exchanges are reorganizing their business and their operations toward a more integrated trading and settlement infrastructure via mergers, alliances, links or agreements. This has been visible in Europe where were reported around 100 deals between European exchanges (Table 2) Cybo-Ottone, Di Noia and Murgia (2000).

Table 1. Types of Deal between European Exchanges

	Domestic		Cross-Border			
	Mergers	Others	Mixed integration	Mergers	Others	Total
96-97	9	2	6	1	8	26
97-99	11	1	29	2	20	63

Source: adapted from Cybo-Ottone, Di Noia and Murgia (2000).

"Mergers and acquisitions are a response to new technologies or market conditions which require a strategic change in a company's direction or use of resources" (Michael C. Jensen in Ross, Westerfield, and Jaffe, 2005).

The belief that technological shocks cause merger waves is based on the evidence of a positive relationship between both variables. Angel (1998) studying the story of US exchanges refers that as technology gradually evolved, regional exchanges became extinct. Nevertheless, niches for smaller markets survived due to communication barriers, time zones and regulatory measures. Arnold et al. (1998) studied mergers as a specific method of competition for order flow by US regional exchanges.[12] The authors report that, in 1940, there were 18 regional stock exchanges registered in Securities Exchange Commission (SEC), whereas there were only seven in 1980. They found that mergers proved to be an effective mean of competition as they were successful in attracting market share, at least by comparison with the regional exchanges that did not merge, and narrowing bid-ask spreads of merging exchanges.

The reasons for mergers in exchanges are strongly related to the factors that are the core of consolidation. In theory, a merger happens if there are sources of synergy to promote revenue enhancement (like network effects or reputation effects), cost reductions (like economies of scale, economies of vertical integration, complementary resources) or elimination of inefficient management.

Economies of scale are the natural goal of horizontal mergers. They come from sharing central services such as office management, optimizing the use of a fixed-cost network, and sharing common facilities. They can consequently cut costs and enhance service levels. Malkamaki (1999) addresses the relevance of the size of economies of scale in stock exchanges. The study shows that economies of scale in stock exchanges are an increasing function of size, thus mergers between large exchanges save more costs.

[12] Research has historically pointed out that the regional exchanges shifted from their traditional role of trading local securities and began to serve as auxiliary markets for New York Stock Exchange. This was due to a reduction in communications in costs in the 1920s and 30s, and to changes in securities regulation, following the great crash.

Vertical integration arises because listing, trading, clearing, settlement and central custody are different parts of the same value chain, creating economies of scope. An example of vertical integration between the exchanges, clearing house and depository was achieved in the Deutsche Börse.

The agreements have taken different forms, where mergers were only implemented within borders,[13] suggesting difficulties in bypassing country and regulatory factors. Exchanges have thus looked for other forms of cooperation. Many deals were in the form of implicit mergers:[14] "*an agreement between two exchanges such that the securities listed in one exchange are listed by the other and remote access is offered to the traders of each exchange, with reciprocity and without further requirements*" (Di Noia, 2001). In this kind of merger, entities can opt for a common trading platform, or a different trading platform, while offering remote membership. They consequently merge their activities without merging as entities, thereby avoiding possible "political" implications.

Again it is the potential advantages of the technology that produce these new forms of cooperation. Electronic systems and other communication devices enable connection between geographically distant markets. Indeed, the differences in integration usually lie in the type of access to the trading platform: a single access to a common platform, a common access to different platforms or remote membership.

Cooperation tries to take advantage of mergers without some of the inconveniences. For instance, small exchanges find it difficult to prosper alone due to the lack of critical mass. By cooperating, they can take advantage of economies of scale maintaining their presence in the market at the same time. Pirrong (2000) supports the idea that when assets of exchanges become closer substitutes, consolidation reduces fixed costs without substantially increasing competition between members of the previously separated exchanges.

Hasan and Schmiedel (2003)[15] investigate the impact of the adoption of network strategies. They find that it is significantly associated with higher growth and efficiency among the sample markets. Also it helps markets in lowering transaction costs as well as operational costs for exchanges.

Although there are several barriers to the complete integration of stock markets in Europe, several mergers and strategic alliances have been undertaken, such as NOREX and Euronext, to create pan-European stock exchanges.

Changes in Corporate Governance

Traditionally, exchanges have been seen either as public entities, like continental European exchanges, or as private structures, deeply regulated by public rules like the Anglo-Saxon exchanges. In all cases, they were closed-membership organizations with high barriers to entry.

---

13 The existence of mergers with a complete union of both entities has been limited to two areas: between stock and derivatives exchanges in the same country and between regional exchanges of the same country.

14 The term is accredited to Domowitz (1995) which applied to derivative exchanges: "*consist of a set of derivative products, offered by at least two existing exchanges and sharing a common membership for the purpose of trading via direct access to the market*".

15 See also Di Noia (2001) and Shy and Tarkka (2001) for a discussion on the effects of networks.

More recently, many exchanges, mostly European, have undergone a process of demutualization[16] i.e. they have become for-profit corporations. In a 2002 survey, 63% of the WFE members were for-profit structures, while in the mid 90's this number was around 10%. In addition, a growing number of exchanges have introduced shares of their companies on the stock market they operate, emphasizing at the same time the for-profit and public nature of the activity.

Currently, the WFE separate the legal structures in five categories:

- Member-owned limited companies: exchanges registered as private companies where intermediaries are almost the sole owners of the exchange. This has been the case of the Anglo-Saxon countries: in the US, markets have historically been private entities and member-owned exchanges. They represent 18% of members while market capitalization is 42% of the total; this difference is due to the fact that this category includes the New York Stock Exchange (NYSE), the biggest stock exchange in the world.
- Private, limited companies: exchanges that have demutualized but which not are listed. The ownership is slightly more open, for instance, it can include institutional investors. They represent 30% of the total exchanges while market capitalization is 24% of the total.
- Publicly listed exchanges. The exchange shares are listed on their own exchange and they are freely negotiable among investors. This category represents 20% of the members of the WFE and 26% of its market capitalization.
- Associations, or mutual structures. These member cooperatives generally have no share capital, and access to membership is restricted. They represent 20% of members while market capitalization represents 6%.
- Finally, we have other legal status such as government and semi-government agencies. They represent 12% of the WFE members and only 2% of capitalization.

Table 3 shows some of the world stock exchanges by the corresponding category.

Steil (2002a) relates the change of the governance structure with the progress of technology. According to the author, the mutual exchange is a product of the pre-techno era, and as markets become fully electronic " the traditional concept of membership becomes untenable". That would explain why NYSE, still a floor market with strong presence of members, is a mutual association.

Supporters of demutualization see it as a trigger for the restructuring of stock exchanges, as the passage to market-oriented organizations seems to respond better to stiff competition. The diversification of the exchange's shareholder base modifies corporate governance, allowing a separation of owner and trading rights, causing members to lose influence and privileges.

The cause of the problem seems to lie in the fact that mutual exchanges are ultimately focused on maintaining their members' interests. Intermediaries in trying to maximize their own profits from trade intermediation can act to impair the ability of exchanges to serve firms and investors efficiently. For instance, automation of trading and remote membership are often refused as they are seen as having major implications on the profitability of brokerage

[16] See a detailed list of demutualization of exchanges in Domowitz and Steil (1999).

and dealer firms, commonly exchange members. The same motive leads members to block the consolidation and the integration process or the direct access of institutional investors to exchanges.

Table 2. WFE Exchanges by Legal Form (December 2002)

Member-owned limited companies	Private, limited companies not listed	Publicly listed exchanges	Associations, or mutual structures.	Other legal status
Luxembourg Stock Exchange	American Stock Exchange	Athens Stock Exchange	Swiss Exchange	Istanbul Stock Exchange
Chicago Board Option Exchange	NASD	German Stock Exchange	Shanghai Stock Exchange	Malta Stock Exchange
Chicago Stock Exchange	Italian Exchange	Euronext	Sao Paulo Stock Exchange	Warsaw Stock Exchange
Irish Exchange	Copenhagen Stock Exchange	London Stock Exchange	Buenos Aires Stock Exchange	Korea Stock Exchange
New York Stock Exchange	Montreal Stock Exchange	Australian Stock Exchange	Lima Stock Exchange	Thailand Stock Exchange
	Tokyo Stock Exchange	Toronto Stock Exchange	South Africa Stock Exchange	
	Oslo Stock Exchange	Stockholm Stock Exchange		

Source: World Federation of Exchanges (2003).

Theoretical studies also address the influence of members in competition. Hart and Moore (1996) argue that cooperative exchanges members may be reluctant to accept changes that would affect their own businesses, even if this is not in their own interest in the long run. They analyze the efficiency of an exchange run as a member cooperative relative to that of a for-profit exchange with a single outside owner. The growing inter-exchange competition should have the effect of increasing the prevalence of for-profit exchanges. Pirrong (2000) demonstrates that when exchanges are not perfect substitutes, they may adopt inefficient rules that benefit members at the expense of customers and third parties. The argument is that many stock exchanges are owned or controlled by financial intermediaries who are also the major buyers of the exchanges services.

Steil (2002b) points out two reasons that lead exchanges to demutualize. First, a high level of direct competition between exchanges makes it difficult for members to block reforms and protect their intermediation rights, becoming more open to governance reforms and outside ownership. Secondly, the internationalization of membership reduces the weight and the influence of domestic intermediaries. Large international banks, members of numerous exchanges, have much less motivation to defend mutualization than local intermediaries.

In a demutualized exchange, the commercial interest of exchanges and brokers diverge. For-profit exchanges have the incentive to minimize trading costs that do not accrue to them as revenue, such as brokerage commissions. The new commercial strategy leads to a restructuring of stock exchanges such as automation, the development of cross-border exchange linkages and international alliances, opening the access to other intermediaries.

Empirically, there starts to be evidence of a relation between governance and the profitability of exchanges. Results indicate that demutualized exchanges are more profitable, in particular, listed exchanges. For instance, in the year 2002 trading revenues increased by 20%, an increase mainly driven by listed exchanges as they diversified their trading assets. Listed bourses generated the highest revenues among the various legal groups in 2002 comprising 44% of the WFE total (WFE, 2003).

Listed exchanges are the most profitable bourses. Their return on capital, 20%, was significantly above the average of other legal categories 12%. Interestingly, stock exchanges with other status had a return on capital of 17%. Below the average, were limited exchanges with 10%, demutualized exchanges and associations, both with a return on capital of 8%.

European exchanges were the most profitable stock exchanges with an average return on capital of 17%. The second most profitable group was Asia/Pacific bourses with an average return on capital of 8%. Stock exchanges in America had a small average return on capital of 6%, mainly driven by the NASDAQ stock market. A notable exception was the Toronto Stock Exchange, a publicly listed exchange, with a return on capital of 22%.

The process of demutualization has however been criticized since many exchanges are still controlled by intermediaries despite demutualization (Steil, 2002a). For the author, for successful demutualization, it is essential that non-members are free to buy equity stakes in the exchange from current owners.

Lee (2002) does not see demutualization as necessary or sufficient for the prosperity or even survival of exchanges. Detractors of demutualization give the counter example of the largest stock exchange in the world, the NYSE, which is still mutual despite rumors[17] that it also plans to become a for-profit company and even self-list.

There is a widespread belief among regulators that mutual structures are more consistent with self-regulation than demutualized exchanges. One of the arguments is that the assurance of regulatory services, such as market surveillance, fair and equitable treatment of customers or listing requirements, is not entirely compatible with a for-profit environment. Therefore, the new commercial approach would make it more difficult to ensure that exchanges perform their public duties equitably.

One of the main fears is that listing standards are set too low in order to increase trading volume. However, the evidence indicates the opposite. Stock exchanges have upgrade disclosure requirements. For instance, the Deutsche Börse established that in the Prime Standard segment, the firms will offer quarterly reports, international accounting standards such as IAS or US-GAAP, a corporate calendar, at least one analyst's meeting per year as well as ad-hoc disclosers also in English (FESE, 2002a). Also, theoretical research analyzing competition for trading volume found that exchanges do not look for excessive low standards (Santos and Scheinkman, 2000), they even engage in a "race to the top" regarding disclosure requirements (Huddart, Hughes and Brunnermeier, 1998).

Another fear is that the diversification of activities of stock exchanges can create conflicts with listed firms. For instance, several stock exchanges developed the technological solutions branch. It is not impossible that commercial conflicts arise with rival companies in the same area of business.

---

17 It came out in The Wall Street Journal (29 July 1999), that the NYSE, a two-hundred year old institution, was planning to issue capital. See also the NYSE Chairman Richard A. Grasso's Letter to Members Concerning "Demutualization" of September 2, 1999 in http://www.nyse.com/press/1044027444806.html.

Steil (2002a) refers that most conflicts between the interest of members and investors are in the fair treatment of investors, and recalls that a mutualized exchange exists to serve the interest of its members, while a demutualized exchange aims to satisfy the clients. He concludes that in a demutualized exchange the scope for conflict should be less.

Cross-listing

Firms have intensified their listing in foreign markets in the last years, which has brought profits for both parts. Exchanges benefit from listing fees and trading volume, and firms expand their base of investors and strengthen their public image.

Cochrane, Shapiro and Tobin (1995) refer that firms are looking for equity as a source of finance more now than in the past, and domestic markets are often too small for firms to expand. This is the case of some firms like Nokia and Ericsson[18] who are listed in several European and US exchanges.

At the same time, investors are more receptive to invest in foreign equity, but trading cross-borders still involves higher brokerage commissions and bypassing regulatory barriers.

The US market has been the main beneficiary of these two trends, acting as an intermediary between the increasing demand and supply. For instance, in 1995, NYSE had 252 non-US companies listed from 40 countries against 472 in 2002 (Table 4). Pagano, Roell and Zechner (2002) studied the geographic pattern of foreign listing from 1986-1997. They concluded that while European companies are more outward oriented, European stock exchanges are not, bringing about a great loss for the exchanges from 1991 to 1997. European companies have gone abroad, particularly to US exchanges, while US companies have reduced cross-listing. The decline of foreign listings on European exchanges appears to be part of a more general decline in the ability of exchanges to attract new listings. Most of them have not attracted many new domestic listings, as is clear in Table 4, despite tremendous reforms of their trading platforms following the London Big Bang. The opposite is true of US exchanges, where both domestic and foreign listings have increased over the sample period. According to the authors, trading costs are the indicator that appears to have the closest correlation with normalized net change of cross-listings.

Participation of foreign issues in the US market could be higher if it was not for the obstacle of the US regulatory requirement, whereby non-US companies have to reconcile their home financial accounting documents to US-Generally Accepted Accounting Principles (GAAP). Nevertheless, US exchanges and regulators have made a concerted effort to reduce regulatory costs and facilitate foreign listings (Pagano et al., 2001). The American Depository Receipts programs include several levels of compliance with US GAAP standards. To trade on an exchange, they just need to partially comply with US GAAP. Only when firms want to issue new capital on US exchanges, they have to comply with US GAAP.

Table 4 shows that the growth in the number of listed firms in the domestic segment was interrupted in the year 2002. Foreign firms have a reduced presence in European exchanges

[18] Nokia is listed in the Helsinki Stock Exchange (HEX), the Frankfurt and Paris Stock Exchanges within the euro zone, New York Stock Exchange (NYSE), and Stockholm Stock Exchange, and de-listed from London Stock Exchange at the end of 2003. Ericsson is traded on the Stockholm Stock Exchange, Nasdaq and the London Stock Exchange and de-listed from Euronext (Paris), the German Stock Exchanges (Düsseldorf, Frankfurt and Hamburg) and the Swiss Exchange.

except for London, Luxembourg and German exchanges, but they still all register a decrease of presences in 2002. Both markets in the US register a considerable presence of foreign firms, where the majority, 65%, were European (FIBV, 1999).

Table 3. Number of Companies with Listed Shares

Market	1994		1998		2000		2002	
	Domestic Cies	Foreign Cies	Domestic Cies	Foreign Cies	Domestic Cies	Foreign Cies	Domestic Cies	Foreign Cies
Amsterdam	317	215	255	146	234	158	-	-
Athens	165	0	229	0	309	1	313	1
Brussels	155	141	146	122	161	104	-	-
Copenhagen	243	10	242	12	225	10	193	8
Irish	56	9	79	21	76	20	62	14
Deutsche Börse	423	227	452	210	744	245	715	219
Helsinki	65	0	129	2	154	4	147	2
Lisbon	83	0	135	0	109	1	-	-
London	1747	462	1957	466	2428	501	1,890	382
Luxembourg	55	217	53	223	54	216	48	197
Madrid/Spanish Exchanges	375	4	479	5	1020	16	2,986	29
Paris	459	195	914	183	1021	164	-	-
Stockholm	106	8	258	18	293	19	278	19
Vienna	94	41	96	32	97	14	109	20
Euronext	1014	551	1450	451	1525	427	1,114	NA
NYSE	1689	216	2278	392	-	-	1,894	472
NASDAQ	4577	325	4627	441	-	-	3,268	381
Tokyo	1651	110	1838	52	-	-	2,119	34

Source: FIBV and Steil (1996).

Cross-listing in the US is mainly sought for firms that have relatively high growth, are high tech and strongly outward-oriented, while recently privatized European companies are more likely to hunt for a second listing within Europe (Pagano et al. 2001).

Cross-listing presents two kinds of costs. Administrative costs, as it is necessary to comply with listing requirements of both markets and it may be necessary to produce accounts under two different sets of accounting rules. Therefore, it obliges extra costs on accountants and lawyers, to produce Depository Receipts. The second cost is fragmentation in the domestic market. Foucault and Gehrig (2002) show that the entrepreneur decides to cross-list when the benefit of more efficient investment decisions is large enough to compensate the liquidity cost of market fragmentation. Hargis and Ramanlal (1998) found an overall positive impact of international cross-listing on domestic market liquidity and volume traded.

New Markets

Growth in markets is achieved through the acquisition of another company and by developing new products, markets and processes. As already pointed out, the former means of acquisition is already being used, but exchanges have not excluded the latter, creating markets, for instance, for companies with great potential growth.

With the exception of US, capital markets are not known for normally supplying capital to new firms. For instance, there is evidence that listing in European stock markets come from large and well-established firms that operate in a mature sector, and go public for motives other than raising new capital for investment.[19] The secondary status of stock markets for small- and medium-sized firms in Europe has made firms frown upon raising funds from exchanges.

Today, the perspective is different; new markets are launched based more on an alternative market view. The creation of these markets is in line with economic and political goals[20] and aims to finance high-tech and economy enterprises, which are believed to be instrumental in creating economic growth, technological innovation and jobs. To bypass some prejudices against these firms, firm's listings on new markets must conform to tighter disclosure procedures, including the use of international accounting standards. Kukies (2002) find a positive relation between the number and characteristics of initial public offers (IPOs) with strict disclosure rules of new markets.

The creation of the new markets reports to the late 90's. Table 5 shows the evolution in the number of listed firms in the new markets. In Europe, the Neuer Market from Deutsche Börse, the New Market from Euronext, the AIM , and the O_list from the Stockholm exchange were the most dynamic markets, while in America it was the TSE Venture and in Asia the Hong Kong and Singapore new market.

Table 4. Total Number of Listed Companies

Exchange	Name of the Market	2002	2001	2000	1999
TSX Toronto Stock Exchange	TSX Venture	2,504	2688	-	-
Deutsche Börse	Neuer Markt	240	326	339	201
Euronext (1)	New Market	158	174	189	137
Helsinki	(2)	44	47	51	48
Irish Exchange	(3)	17	20	20	16
Italian Exchange	Nuovo Mercato	45	45	40	6
London	AIM	704	629	524	347
Spanish Exchanges (BME)	Nuevo Mercado	14	13	-	-
Stockholm	O-List	235	235	228	204
Swiss Exchange	SWX New Market	9	15	17	6
Hong Kong	Growth Enterprise Market	166	111	54	7
Kuala Lumpur	Mesdaq	12	4	-	-
New Zealand	New Capital Market	7	10	10	-
Osaka	New Market Section	4	4	6	2
Singapore	Sesdaq	117	107	92	81
Tokyo	Mothers	43	36	29	2

Source: FIBV. (1)The years of 2000 and 1999 correspond to the sum of Euro-NM Amsterdam, Euro-NM Belgium, Nouveau Marche; (2) Helsinki corresponds to I List (Investors' List), NM List (New

[19] See Rydqvist and Hogholm (1995), Pagano, Panetta and Zingales (1998) and Pagano, Roell and Zechner (2002).

[20] This trend corresponds to a political goal of the EU. Europe needs to set up a market for shares of innovative high growth companies, generally small and medium size enterprises, which are key components of European economies, but often with difficulties in raising capital.

Market) and Prelist. (3) Irish corresponds to the sum of Exploration Securities Market, Developing Companies Market, and ITEQ.

Bottazzi and Da Rin (2002) study the features of 538 non-financial firms that list on the new European markets between 1996-2001. Listing firms are small, growing fast and investing extensively in research and development. They are highly leveraged and unable to further expand their bank credit, consistent with a situation of credit rationing. After the IPO, companies experience a dramatic change, rebalancing their capital structure, increasing their debt, accelerating growth and becoming less profitable. An interesting result is that they find that the adoption of international accounting standards substantially increases the firm's ability to raise capital. More specifically, firms that conform to the US GAAP standard raise more capital per unit of assets.

The new markets opened during a period of high and rising valuation of technology stocks worldwide that was followed by a dramatic fall since mid 2000. The market capitalization of new markets (Table 6) shows a severe decline related to the post dot-com bubble. Some have experienced low liquidity and turnover and failed to attract investors and listing companies since the beginning, others seemed very successful, but then closed. The Neuer Market, for instance, which suffered from the collapse in technology stocks and some corporate scandals and bad publicity, closed in 2003. Other new markets that closed were EASDAQ from NASDAQ, NASDAQ Japan and the Parallel Market of Athens.

Table 5. Market Capitalization of Firms (000.000 USD)

Exchange	Name of the Market	2002	2001	2000	1999
TSX Toronto Stock Exchange	TSX Venture	7 098	6 633	-	-
Deutsche Börse	Neuer Markt	10 342	44 460	113 597	110 011
Euronext (1)	New Market	7 244	13 604	24 016	16 562
Helsinki (2)		725	833	-	-
Irish (3)		936	1 876	3 934	840
Italian Exchange	Nuovo Mercato	6 706	11 120	20 811	6 997
London	AIM	16 433	16 893	22 311	21 706
Spanish Exchanges (BME)	Nuevo Mercado	9 759	14 710	-	-
Stockholm	O-List	47 443	50 144	55 641	73 183
Swiss Exchange	SWX New Market	662	2 240	7 497	-
Hong Kong	Growth Enterprise Market	6 696	7 818	8 627	931
Kuala Lumpur	Mesdaq	203	47	-	-
New Zealand	New Capital Market	6	13	6	-
Osaka	New Market Section	28	20	83	33
Singapore	Sesdaq	1 747	1 650	2 299	5 056
Tokyo	Mothers	4 128	5 312	5 565	7 950

Source: FIBV. (1)The years of 2000 and 1999 correspond to the sum of Euro-NM Amsterdam, Euro-NM Belgium, Nouveau Marche ; (2) Helsinki corresponds to I List (Investors' List), NM List (New Market) and Prelist ; (3) Irish corresponds to the sum of Exploration Securities Market, Developing Companies Market, ITEQ.

Strategic Challenges for Exchanges

Increased Market Participation versus Home Bias

In the past years, capital markets have registered an explosive growth. Table 7 shows the change of the ratio of market capitalization over the GDP indicating the level of maturity of a financial market. In countries like Finland or Greece the ratio grew 800%, even though the year 2001 reveals a slight inversion of the importance of capital markets due to the post-bubble effect.

Table 6. Market Capitalization/GDP (%)

Countries	1987	1994	1996	1998	2001
Austria	-	14.74	14.9	16.8	13.4
Belgium	26.4	37.09	48.4	97.7	-
Denmark	17.5	31.89	42.3	56.8	52.8
Finland	19.6	43.38	52.6	121.6	157.6
France	17.1	34.2	37.4	67.8	-
Germany	17	23.3	29.9	50.9	58.1
Greece	8.5	18.45	21.8	66.4	69.5
Ireland	-	37.87	53.5	67.4	72.9
Italy	14	17.73	24.1	48.33	48.5
Luxembourg	-	208.47	180.66	218.2	125.4
Netherlands	35.4	68.1	103.3	158.7	-
Spain	21.7	32.26	36.6	72.3	-
Sweden	41.8	61.14	96.5	123.1	112.7
United Kingdom	87	112.72	145.7	171	152.2
USA	49.2	75.8	116.6	148.6	137.1

Source: Pagano (1993), Steil (1996), Dermine and Hillion (1999), FIBV.

The development of markets was encouraged by increasing stock market participation (Guiso, Haliassos and Jaipelli, 2002). European investors traditionally looked for safe and liquid assets to invest their wealth, and were considered as not having an "equity culture". In the late 80 and 90's, individual investors' direct participation in stock markets developed due to the wave of privatization and through collective investment, such as mutual funds. Overall, the importance of shareholders as shareowners increased. Table 8 shows the percentage of domestic stocks held by individual investors individually and in the form of collective investment at the end of 2002.

Changes in demographics are also responsible for the growth in financial markets. The decrease of young workers, the main contributors of the social security system, made households rely more on pension funds. The difference of the importance of public pension schemes in Europe and Anglo-Saxon countries explains the difference of the importance of financial markets in the economy, as Table 7 clearly demonstrates. The growing involvement of institutional investors in direct trading, jointly with their large share in the market, pressured exchanges for more efficient and cost-effective trading structures.

Table 7. Share Ownership Structure of Listed Companies in Europe

Exchange	Year	Individual Investors	Foreign Investors	Total Households Includes collective investment
Italy	2000	25%	15%	38%
Helsinki	2000	7%	74%	-
Portugal	1999	4%	25%	12%
London	2000	16%	32%	63%
Madrid	2000	30%	36%	37%
Stockholm	2000	13%	40%	-
Athens	May 2001	31%	22%	-
Deutsche Börse	2000	16%	20%	26%
Norway	2000	8%	34%	25%
Paris	2000	8%	36%	28%
Copenhagen stock exchanges	2000	16%	26%	29%

Source: FESE (2002b).

Given the restructuring of social security systems around the world, markets are expected to grow significantly in the coming years. Reforms are likely to continue, as is the pressure for cutting trading costs. The increasing influence of institutional investors is expected to cause a greater corporate disclosure, as they are more demanding in terms of the disclosure of information and they are more actively involved in monitoring.

Despite the integration market and an increasing accessibility to international markets, empirical evidence shows the existence of home bias[21] in equity portfolios: stock market investors maintain a puzzling preference for home assets. This was initially explained in terms of barriers to international investment, such as government restrictions on foreign and domestic capital flows, taxes, tariffs and fees. However, empirical evidence has not provided a clear support of these hypotheses.[22] Dissatisfaction with institutional explanations has led some authors to consider explanations based on investor behavior. French and Poterba (1991) suggest that investors may simply be relatively more optimistic about their domestic markets. Strong and Xu (2003) found evidence that fund managers are comparatively biased in their outlooks towards their domestic market.

The more consensual explanation relies on local informational advantages. Gehrig (1993) states that, until the early 1990s, the home bias could be explained by informational problems facing domestic investors when valuing foreign securities. This view is supported by the work of Tesar and Werner (1995), and Hau (2001b), who explicitly introduce variables such as geographical distance and language barriers in order to proxy informational frictions. Hau (2001b) finds that local proximity is positively correlated with intra-day profits, indicating local informational advantages.

The problem could be bypassed by cross-listing. As discussed above, the strength of home equity bias lies in behavioral components and on informational factors, like linguistic and cultural barriers. Thus, if exchanges notice that investors are more prone to investing in

21 See Lewis (1999) for survey on home bias literature.

22 Tesar and Werner (1995) state that transaction costs cannot explain the equity home bias. Cooper and Kaplanis (1994) explain the motive as hedging domestic inflation, but that implies levels of investor risk aversion below those conventionally assumed.

the domestic listing, a good solution is to expand the set of investments. Furthermore, if firm visibility increases, as reported by Baker, Nofsinger and Weaver (2002), capturing the attention of analysts, then the informational barriers are broken and the bias is expected to decrease. Interestingly, the share of foreign firms publicly listed in domestic markets captures the attention of investors and influences the bias in foreign stock ownership (Ahearne, Griever, and Warnock, 2001).

Home bias limits the business of exchanges since they become restricted to domestic investors. This is penalizing for the case of small exchanges that need to achieve critical mass but it might also be a problem for some companies since they are restricted in their capital basis. More international firms are then obliged to cross-list, which creates the problem of the fragmentation of trade. Evidence shows that foreign investors tend to hold those securities that are more familiar to them. Foreign ownership of stocks tends to underweigh small, high levered firms and less exported oriented firms, in Japan, (Kang and Stulz, 1997), and overweigh (Swedish) firms with an important presence in international markets (Dalquist and Robertson, 2001).

In Europe, the effects of the single currency are contradictory. In a first phase, EU investment in securities can be concentrated in countries adopting the single currency since information costs of European cross-border investment will be reduced (Danthine, Giavazzi and von Thadden (2000)). However, European investors will also diversify outside EU borders, since European equity markets will be more correlated, offering lower diversification benefits. That will force European investors to look more at non-EU markets in order to diversify. "*One can therefore anticipate an enormous growth in the size of capital markets in Europe and in cross-border trading*" (Dermine, 1999).

In the last decade the interest in financial markets has promoted the exchange business. A class of international investors has emerged with a more active and intervenient profile in trading. Demand for foreign equity is expected to increase due to the decrease in restrictions to cross-borders investments, the growth of pension funds, the reduction of informational and agency costs, and the computerization and interconnection of trading centers. The interest in financial markets will also be high due to demographic imbalances. The number of ageing investors relying on private pensions will create more demand for financial assets and the perspectives are that market capitalization will continue to increase in exchanges around the world.

Electronic Trading Venues

The growing number of electronic trading systems that automatically match buy and sell orders, known as Electronic Communication Networks (ECNs), is a main source of competition for exchanges. By providing an alternative trading structure without the need for human broker dealers they compete with stock exchanges offering lower transaction costs.

The ECNs commercial strategy tries to take advantage of the weak points of exchanges. Competition is mainly based on lower costs. Domowitz and Steil (1999, 2002) found that total trading costs savings achieved through non-intermediated electronic trading systems were 32.5% on NASDAQ trades, and 28.2% on trades of the NYSE listed stocks. For commissions, they found that automated execution fees were on average 70% less than those levied by institutional brokers in the sample.[23]

Opportunities to trade increase due to after-hour trading capacities. In response, some exchanges, like Deutsche Börse or NASDAQ, also implemented after-hour trading. However, only 4% of NASDAQ trading volume occurs after hours. After-hours trading generates significant price discovery, but because prices are noisier, price discovery is less efficient (Barclay and Hendershott, 2003).

Studies addressing the competition between NASDAQ and ECNs find that trades are more likely to occur in ECNs when information asymmetry is greater and when trading volume and volatility is high (Barclay, Hendershott and McCormic, 2003). The higher frequency of ECNs trades during periods of high trading volume and high stock volatility also suggests that ECNs attract a higher fraction of informed trades than market makers trades.

ECNs have US roots. Because of their increasingly important role, the US congress provided the SEC in 1996 with greater flexibility to regulate the new trading systems. Since 1997, the Securities Exchange Commission (SEC) has given ECNs a special statute. The Reform of 1997 have it made possible for ECNs to offer information dissemination, price quotation and order matching mechanisms for NASDAQ securities. In addition, it enables public access to superior prices posted by market makers in ECNs.

Including ECNs quotes in the NASDAQ system caused an overall decline in average trading cost. Round trip costs fell on average by 30% (Barclay et al., 1999). After the implementation in 1997 of order handling rules and tick sizes changes, the cost advantage of trading in ECNs apparently decreased.

Another step was given by the Regulation on Alternative Trading Systems in 1999. It establishes a regulatory framework to integrate alternative trading systems more fully into the national market system. It created an intermediate market participant category between brokers and exchanges. The new rules set out a comprehensive framework that allows ECNs to choose whether to register as an exchange or to be licensed as a broker-dealer. If it chooses to register as an exchange it must satisfy all the requirements that apply to national securities exchanges. If it chooses to register as a broker-dealer it should also comply with specific requirements. The SEC ruling allowed ECNs to quickly gain substantial market share in NASDAQ. Figures from June 2000 report that ECNs had captured 30% of the volume in NASDAQ stocks and 3% of share in NYSE stocks.

ECNs appear in Europe later. In November 2000, OM, the Swedish exchange group with Morgan Stanley Dean Witter, launched JIWAY a cross-border trading system for retail brokers. Jiway was a pan-European platform for retail investors to trade and settle equities listed in the US or European markets. Virt-X is a joint venture of Tradepoint, a UK exchange, and the Swiss stock exchange, that has offered trading in all fully listed U.K. common stocks and in continental European blue-chip stocks since 2001. The commercial strategy of European ECNs targeted the high cross border settlement costs, since in terms of efficiency and operations, the European systems were in good standing.[24]

---

23 Conrad, Wahal and Jonhson (2003) also confirm that realized execution costs are generally lower on crossing systems and ECNs. See also Bias, Bisiere and Spatt (2002) and Simaan, Weaver and Whitcom (2003).

24 Cross-border trades tend to have much higher clearance and settlement costs than domestic transactions. The major problem seems to be clearing and settlement infrastructure, which has failed to follow the wave of consolidation sweeping in the various exchanges in Europe. The Giovannini Report (2001) reports 11 times higher costs on international securities depositories than domestic but this value is overestimated according to

Attempts to launch ECNs have been unsuccessful. Jiway closed at the end of 2002, and while in the US they represent 37% of NASDAQ, European ECNs have gained only 1% of European markets (JP Morgan/McKinsey, 2002). Even though they are not important, the European Union approved rules in 2002 about Alternative Trading Systems, in particular about the information and the operation of markets, transparency, communication duties and prevention of fraud. Benhamou and Serval (2000) emphasize the importance of the critical mass in the exchange business. The logic of liquidity makes flow migration from large incumbent unlikely.

The presence of ECNs is obviously not peaceful. Market participants defend that established exchanges mechanisms provide liquidity and buffering , mainly trough the presence of specialists and market makers, which are absent from ECNs. Others cite risks such as opacity in after-hour trading, lack of fraud control, lack of transparency and enforcement and "price piracy".

One of the strongest impacts of ECNs is fragmentation, which merits criticism for its effect on market liquidity and price formation. The free-riding of information weakens the exchange where price is discovered and the validity of market price. Piracy causes exchanges not to reveal the equilibrium price accurately, damaging the transparency in financial markets. On the other hand, some state that fragmentation is a natural phenomenon of free markets, given the different specificities of clients (Blume, 2002). Forced consolidation of order flow prevents competition between market centers that offer different trading systems. Following this reasoning, Schwartz (1995) defends that order flow fragmentation must be allowed. The benefits of consolidation can be obtained in a fragmented market when information freely flows between market segments and when all traders do not have to trade in only one segment. The question is open "*fragmentation deriving from market architecture is desirable; fragmentation deriving from free-riding on price discovery is not*" (Steil, 1996, p.61).

Huang (2002) finds that the proliferation of ECNs may promote quote quality rather fragmenting markets. The most liquid ECNs contribute to price discovery and ECNs quoted spreads are smaller than dealer quoted spreads.

Consolidation of Markets

The logic of consolidation has raised the debate on the possible convergence for a single exchange, mainly within EU borders. Davis (1990) argues that economies of scale in financial services may lead to the emergence of a single global center in Europe, with smaller centers in each country. A pan-European exchange would lead to some important gains such as economies of scale, elimination of redundant investment in trading platforms, increase of market liquidity and reduction of market fragmentation (McAndrews and Stefanadis, 2002).

Although the goal of a single market is pursued, the existence of multiple regulators, multiple legal systems and the difficulty in harmonizing national legislation make it difficult to have only one stock trading market.

Political factors such as nationalisms are the main barrier to cross-border mergers in Europe. Till now mergers in Europe have been strictly within borders. For cross-border deals,

the JP Morgan/McKinsey (2002) estimates. A cross-border trade costs 1.3 times the cost of a domestic wholesale trade.

exchanges have then to go for less radical agreements like implicit mergers, with less political implications. Members, who are also the intermediaries, tend to prefer the latter solution to protect their business.

The future of small exchanges does not seem therefore to be in danger for the moment (Cybo-Ottone, Di Noia and Murgia, 2000). Political factors are a significant contributor to exchange survival. Also, governments still enjoy some freedom in setting economic policy, like fiscal policy, which may give incentives to trade in local exchanges.

Local exchanges can represent small niches for trading local stocks. Many investors might prefer to trade with domestic intermediaries[25] and since brokers have a tendency to act in their domestic countries, consequently they also draw investors. A possible equilibrium is the concentration of trading of a set of securities in one exchange and concentration of trading of another set of securities in another exchange (Pagano, 1989b). That is viable if share ownership tends to be concentrated in one market. Also home equity bias can lead investors and exchange members to show a strong attachment to their domestic products due to informational advantages for national firms.

For now in Europe some exchanges are already aggregating others. A multi-polar market model is emerging in Europe with Euronext and Deustche Börse already extending their influence to other exchanges. The other important players are the LSE and Scandinavian exchanges. But also in the US, there have been deals between exchanges, after the merger of AMEX and NASDAQ and there are occasionally rumors about a merger between the main markets NYSE and NASDAQ.

There is also the intention to extend the integration between USA and European markets, forming a single transatlantic market. Steil (2002b) addresses this possibility. Expanding the electronic access of exchanges to US brokers and institutional investors, those could buy cheaply than in US, as it is already happening in some derivative exchanges. The author defends that this type integration does not imply a need for prior harmonization of rules, standards, and institutions.

CONCLUSIONS

Competition has made exchanges change their commercial approach. Most of the exchanges are now for-profit organizations, with diversified activities where trading and services are the most important sources of revenues. Liquidity, transaction costs, listing fees, price discovery, regulation and accounting standards are key factors of competition.

Competition between financial markets is marked by the co-existence of two contrary forces. Consolidation is fostered by economies of scale and network externalities, and fragmentation is pushed by informational frictions, heterogeneity of markets and informational advantages. These two features are driving the evolution of markets. At the same time, markets dissolve by merging and new markets appear.

Technology has had a severe impact on competition causing several types of agreements between exchanges, changes in corporate governance and automation of trade. The latter allows trading costs to be smaller, increasing liquidity and rivalry between markets.

---

[25] Dermine (1999) identifies sources of the competitive advantage of domestic intermediaries: customer relationship, better assessment of credit risk that provides control of underwriting, and secondary trading.

European stock markets are expected to constitute a single financial market, although with some geographically dispersed markets. The deregulation of markets has caused a more direct race between stock exchanges.

Financial markets have registered an explosive growth in the last years due to investors being more familiar with markets as well as to the emergence of private pension funds. A new class of active and sophisticated investors has gained importance and they have pressured exchanges for reforms in costs, efficiency and the disclosure of information.

Investors' preferences are however still biased towards domestic assets due to information barriers. Some exchanges have followed the strategy of becoming international centers, capturing international firms, which in turn attract international investors. Small and less international firms are then restricted to being traded by domestic investors, enhancing domestic markets.

ECNs compete with exchanges and traders, members of exchanges by offering low cost and after-hour trading capacity, attracting mainly informed and active investors. Detractors of ECNs cite their lack of transparency, enforcement, prevention of fraud as well as fragmentation of trade as potential problems. Despite detractors' criticisms, there has already been a positive impact on transaction costs due to competition, and empirical evidence does not indicate that ECNs have a negative impact on fragmentation. ECNs services are better tailored to specific user group needs, like active institutional traders, as they offer crossing and direct access to exchanges. European and American supervision authorities have already started to regulate ECNs, although attempts to copy the American model of ECN in Europe were not successful.

Market-driven fragmentation and the diversity of trading mechanisms are seen as desirable by academics, but clearly confront the interests of organized exchanges.

The existence of small markets seems to be jeopardized by the logic of consolidation. Other authors see consolidation very improbable due to the existence of strong barriers to consolidation. A standard comparison is with telephone services, a very similar business to that of exchanges: a worldwide telephone company is not observed.

Home equity bias reduction is anticipated. Investors face fewer constraints and are expected to invest more in foreign markets, thus increasing cross-border trade. This gives an edge to exchanges while endangering local monopolies, since exchanges lose their natural base of investors because the latter are free to seek more attractive markets.

A first glance at the recent developments reveals that the increase of competition has been beneficial for investors and firms. Competition between exchanges has led to improvements in market architecture and efforts to trim down costs. Specifically, in Europe structural reforms have contributed to increasing the role and efficiency of securities markets. Nevertheless, competition is still blocked by institutional rigidities and the vested interests of various sell-side participants.

References

Ahearne, A.G., W.L. Griever, and F.E. Warnock, 2004, Information costs, and home bias: An analysis of US holdings of foreign equities, *Journal of International Economics* 62, 313-336.

Angel, James J., 1998, Consolidation in the global equity market: An historical perspective, Working Paper, Georgetown University.

Arnold, Tom, Philip Hersh, J. Harold Mulherin and Jeffrey Netter, 1998, Merging markets, *Journal of Finance* 54, 1083-1107.

Arthur, W. B., 1989, Competing technologies, increasing returns, and lock-in by Historical events, *The Economic Journal* 99,116-131.

Baker, H.K., J.R. Nofsinger, and D.G. Weaver, 2002, International cross-listing and visibility, *Journal of Financial and Quantitative Analysis* 37 (3), 495–521.

Barclay, Michael J., Terrence Hendershott and D. Timothy McCormik, 2003, Competition among trading venues: Information and trading on electronic communication networks, *Journal of Finance* 58, 2639-2667.

Barclay, Michael J., William G. Christie, Jeffrey H. Harris, Eugene Kandel and Paul Schultz, 1999, The effects of market reform on the trading costs of Nasdaq stocks, *Journal of Finance* 54, 1-34.

Barclay, Michael, and Terence Hendershott, 2003, Price discovery and trading after hours, *Review of Financial Studies* 16, 1041-1073.

Benhamou, E. and Thomas Serval, 2000, On the competition between ECNs, stock markets and market makers, Financial Markets Group Discussion Paper, London School Economics.

Bias, Bruno, Christophe Bisiére and Chestter Spatt, 2002, Imperfect competition in financial markets, Working Paper, Carnegie Mellon University.

Blume, Marshall E., 2002, The structure of the US market, Wharton Working Paper 02-16.

Chowdry, Bhagwan and Vikram Nanda, 1991, Multi-Market trading and market liquidity, *Review of Financial Studies* 3, 483-511

Clayton, M., Bjorn Jorgansen and Kenneth Kavajecz, 1999, On the formation and structure of international exchanges, Working Paper Wharton R. White Center for Financial Research 99-22.

Cochrane, James L., James E. Shapiro and Jean Tobin, 1995, Foreign equities and US investors: Breaking down the barriers separating demand and supply, Working Paper NYSE.

Coffee Jr., Jonh C., 2001, The coming competition among securities markets: What strategies will dominate? Working Paper 192, Columbia University School of Law.

Conrad Jennifer, Johnson Kevin M. and Wahal Sunil, 2003, Institutional trading and alternative trading systems, *Journal of Financial Economics* 70 (1), 99-134.

Cooper, Ian and Evi Kaplanis, 1994, Home bias in equity portfolios, inflation hedging and international capital market equilibrium, *Review of Financial Studies* 7, 45-60.

Cybo-Ottone, A., Carmine Di Noia and Maurizio Murgia, 2000, The consolidation of securities exchanges, Brooking-Wharton Papers on Financial Services.

Dahlquist, M.L. and G. Robertson, 2001, Direct foreign ownership, institutional investors and firm characteristics, *Journal of Financial Economics* 59 (3), 423-441.

Danthine, Jean Pierre, Francesco Giavazzi and Ernst-Ludwig von Thadden, 2000, European Financial Markets after EMU: A First Assessment, CEPR Paper 2413.

Davis, E.P., 1990, International Financial Centers- An Industrial Analysis, Bank of England Paper 51.

Demarchi, Marianne and Thierry Foucault, 2000, Equity trading systems in Europe: A survey of recent changes, *Annales d'Economie et Statistiques*, Octobre/Décembre.

Demset, Harold, 1968, The cost of transacting, *Quarterly Journal of Economics* 82, 33-53.

Dermine, Jean and Pierre Hillion (Ed.), 1999, European Markets with a Single Currency, Oxford, University Press.

Dermine, Jean, 1999, European Capital Markets: Does the Euro matter?, in European Markets with a Single Currency, edited by Jean Dermine and Pierre Hillion, Oxford, University Press.

Di Noia, Carmine, 1998, Costumer-controlled firms: The case of stock exchanges, Working Paper Wharton R. White Center for Financial Research.

_____ , 2001, Competition and integration among stock exchanges in Europe: Network effects, implicit mergers and remote access, *European Financial Management* 7, 39-72.

Doede, Robert W., 1967, The monopoly power of New York Stock Exchange, Unpublished Ph.D. Dissertation, University of Chicago.

Domowitz, Ian and Benn Steil, 1999, Automation, trading costs and the structure of the securities trading industry, Brookings-Wharton Papers on Financial Services.

_____ , 2002, Securities trading, Chapter 12 of Steil, B., Victor D. and Nelson, R. (Ed), Technological Innovation and Economic Performance, Princeton University Press.

Domowitz, Ian, 1995, Electronic derivatives exchanges: Implicit mergers, network externalities and standardization, *Quarterly Review of Economics and Finance* 35 (2), 163-175.

Domowitz, Ian, 2001, Liquidity, transaction costs and reintermediation in electronic markets, eBusiness Research Center Working Paper.

Domowitz, Ian, Jack D. Glen and Ananth Madhavan, 2001a, Liquidity, volatility and equity trading costs across countries and over time, *International Finance* 4, 221-255.

_____ , 2001b, Global Equity trading costs, http://www.itginc.com/research/whitepapers/domowitz/globaleqcost.pdf.

Economides, Nicholas, 1993, Network economics with application to finance, *Financial, Markets Institutions & Instruments* 2 (5), December, 89-97.

_____ , 1995, How to enhance market liquidity, in Global Equity Markets: Technological, Competitive, and Regulatory Exchanges, R. Schwartz (Ed.), Irwin Professional, New York.

Ferrarrini, G. (Ed.), 1998, European Securities Markets: The Investment Service Directive and Beyond, Kluwer Law International.

FESE (2002a), Newsletter October 2002.

_____ , (2002b), Share Ownership in Europe 2002, http://www.fese.be/statistics/share_ownership/share_ownership.pdf.

FIBV News Letters July 1999.

Foucault, Thierry and Christine Parlour, 2004, Competition for listing, *RAND Journal*, forthcoming.

Foucault, Thierry and Thomas Gehrig, 2002, Cross-listing and the geography of firms ownership, Working paper.

French, K.R. and J. M. Poterba, 1991, Investor diversification and international equity markets, *American Economic Review* 81, 222-226.

Gaspar, J. and E.L. Glaeser, 1996, Information technology and the future of the cities, NBER Working Paper 5562.

Gehrig, Thomas, 1993, An information based explanation of the domestic bias in international equity investment, *The Scandinavian Journal of Economics* 21, 97-109.

Gehrig, Thomas, 1998, Competing markets, *European Economic Review* 42, 227-310.

_____ , 2000, Cities and the geography of financial centers, in Jacques Thisse, J.M. Huriot (ed.): The Economics of Cities, Cambridge University Press, 2000, 415-445.

Gehrig, Thomas, K. Stahl and X. Vives, 1996, Competing exchanges: Do large markets drive out small?, CEPR- Conference Paper.

Giovannini Report , 2001, Cross-border clearing and settlement arrangements in the European Union, http://europa.eu.int/comm/economy_finance/giovannini/clearing_settlement_en.htm

Glosten, L.R., 1994. Is the electronic open limit order book inevitable?, *Journal of Finance* 49 (4), 1127-1162.

Guiso, Luigi, Michael Haliassos and Tullio Jappelli, 2002, Household stockholding in Europe: Where do we stand and where do we go?, Centre for Studies in Economics and Finance Working Papers 88, University of Salerno.

Hagel, J. III and A. G., Armstrong, 1997, Net Gain, Harvard Business School Press.

Hargis, K. and P. Ramanlal, 1998, When does internationalization enhance the development of domestic stock markets, *Journal of Financial Intermediation* 7, 263-292.

Harris, Lawrence E., 2000, Floor versus Automated Trading Systems: A Survey of the issues, prepared for the Financial Markets Group Conference "The future of exchanges: Strategic choices ahead".

Hart, Oliver and Jonh Moore 1996, The governance of exchanges: members' cooperatives versus outside ownership, *Oxford Review Economic Policy* 12, 53-69.

Hasam, Iftekhar and Markku Malkamaki, 2000, Are expansions cost effective for stock exchanges? A global perspective, Bank of Finland Discussion Paper 20/2000.

Hasan, I. and H. Schmiedel , 2003, Do networks in the stock exchange industry pay-off? European Evidence, Bank of Finland Working Paper 2/2003.

Hau, Harald, 2001a, Location matters: An examination of trading profits, *Journal of Finance* 56 (5), 1959-1983.

_____ , 2001b, Geographic patterns of trading profitability in Xetra, *European Economic Review* 45, 757-769.

Hertig, Gérad and Ruben Lee, 2003, Four Predictions about the future of EU Securities Regulation, Forthcoming in *Journal of Comparative Law Studies.*

Huang, Roger, 2002, The quality of ECN and NASDAQ market-makers quotes, *Journal of Finance* 57, 1285-1319

Huddart, Steven and John S. Hughes and Markus Brunnermeier, 1998, Disclosure requirements and stock exchange listing choice, *Journal of Accounting and Economics* 26, 237-269.

J.P. Morgan and McKinsey, 2002, The Future of Equity Trading in Europe: Balancing Scale, Scope and Segmentation.

Jain, Panjak, 2001, Institutional design and liquidity on stock exchanges, Working Paper Indiana University.

Kang, Jun-Koo and Rene Stulz, 1997, Why there is a home bias? An analysis of foreign portfolio equity in Japan, *Journal of Financial Economics* 46, 3-28.

Kukies, Jorg, 2002, The effects of introducing a new stock exchange in the IPOs process, Working Paper, University of Chicago.

Laura Bottazzi and Marco Da Rin, 2002, Europe's 'New' stock markets, CEPR Discussion Papers 3521.

Lee, R., 1998, What is an Exchange, Oxford University Press.

Lewis, K. K., 1999, Trying to explain the home bias in equities and consumption, *Journal of Economic Literature* 37(2) , 571-608.

London Economics, 2002 Quantification of the Macro-Economic Impact of Integration of EU Financial Markets. Final Report to European Commission

Macey, Jonathan and Hideki Kanda, 1990, The stock exchange as a firm: The emergence of close substitutes for the New York and Tokyo stock exchange, *Cornell Law Journal* 1007.

Madhavan, Ananth, 1995, Consolidation, fragmentation, and the disclosure of trading information, *Review of Financial Studies* 8, 579-603.

Mahoney, Paul G., 2002, Information Technology and the Organization of Securities Markets, Wharton Working Paper 02-17.

Malkamaki, Markku, 1999, Are there economies of scale in stock exchange activities?, Bank of Finland Discussion Papers 4/99.

McAndrews, James and Chris Stefanadis 2002, The consolidation of European Stock Exchanges, *Current Issues in Economics and Fina*nce 8, Number 6, Federal Reserve of Bank of New York.

O'Hara, Maureen, 2003, World Federation Trading Survey 2003.

Pagano, Marco and Ailsa Roell, 1990, Trading systems in European stock markets: Current performance and policy options, *Economic Policy*, 10.

Pagano, Marco and Benn Steil, 1996, Equity Trading I: the Evolution of European Trading Systems, chapter 1 in The European Equity Markets, edited by B. Steil, The Royal Institute of International Affairs, London, 1996

Pagano, Marco, 1989a, Endogenous market thinness and stock price volatility, *Review of Economic Studies* 56, 269-287.

_____ , 1989b, Trading Volume and Asset Liquidity, *Quarterly Journal of Economics*, May, 255-274.

_____ , 1993, The flotation of companies on the stock market, *European Economic Review* 37, 1101-1125.

_____ , 1998, The Changing Microstructure of European Equity Markets, in European Securities Markets – The Investment Services Directive and Beyond by Guido Ferrarrini (Ed.), Kluwer Law International

Pagano, Marco, Ailsa A. Röell and Josef Zechner, 2002, The geography of equity listing: Why do companies list abroad?, *Journal of Finance* 57(6), 2651-2694.

Pagano, Marco, Otto Randl, Ailsa A. Roell and Josef Zechner, 2001, What makes stock exchanges succeed? Evidence from cross-listing decisions, *European Economic Review* 45, 110-782.

Pagano, Marco, F. Panetta and L. Zingales ,1998, Why do companies go public? An empirical analysis, *Journal of Finance* 53, 27-64.

Pirrong, Craig, 1995, The self-regulation of commodity exchanges: the case of market manipulation, *The Journal of Law and Economics* 38, April, 141-206.

_____ , 1999, The organization of financial exchanges markets: Theory and evidence, *Journal of Financial Markets* 2, 329-357.

_____ , 2000, A positive theory of financial exchange organization, Journal of Law and Economics 2, 437-71.

Ramos, Sofia B. and Ernst-Ludwig von Thadden, 2003, Stock exchanges competition in a simple model of capital market equilibrium, FAME Working Paper No 109.

Ross, Stephen A., Randolph W. Esterfield, Jeffrey Jaffe, 2005, Corporate Finance, Seventh Edition, Irwin.

Rubin Lee, 2002, The Future of Securities Exchanges, The fifth annual conference of the Brookings-Wharton Papers on Financial Services.

Rydqvist, R. and K. Hogholm, 1995, Going Public in the 1980s: Evidence from Sweden, *European Financial Management* 1 (3), 287-351.

Santos, Tano and José Scheinkman, 2000, Competition among exchanges, CRSP Working paper 514.

Sarkar, Asani and Michelle Tozzi, 1998, Electronic trading in future exchanges, *Current Issues in Economics and Finance* 4(1).

Schwartz, R., 1995, in Global Equity Markets: Technological, Competitive, and Regulatory Exchanges, Robert Schwartz (Ed.), Irwin.

Shy, Oz and Juha Tarkka, 2001, Stock exchanges alliances, access fees and competition, Bank of Finland Discussion Paper 22/2001.

Simaan, Yusif, Daniel G. Weaver and David K.Whitcomb, 2003, The quotation behavior of ECNs and Nasdaq market makers, *Journal of Finance* Vol. 58, no. 3, 2003, 1247-1267.

Steil, Benn (Ed.), 1996, The European Capital Markets: The state of the Union and an Agenda for the Millennium, The Royal Institute of International Affairs, London.

Steil, Benn, 2002a, Changes in the ownership and governance of securities exchanges: Causes and consequences, Brooking-Wharton Papers on Financial Services, http://www.fese.be/initiatives/other_reports/brookings_wharton_2002.pdf

_____ , 2002b, Building a transatlantic securities market, http://www.fese.be/ initiatives/other_reports/steil_2002.pdf

Stigler, George, 1961, The economics of information, *Journal of Political Economy* 49, 213-225.

Stigler, George, 1964, Public regulation of securities markets, *Journal of Business* 37, 117-142.

Strong, Norman and Xinzhonh Xu, 2003, Understanding the equity home bias: Evidence from survey data, on *Review of Economics and Statistics* 85 (2), 307-312.

Telser, Lester and Harlow Higinbotham, 1977, Organized futures exchanges: Costs and benefits, Journal of Political Economy 85, 969-1000.

Telser, Lester, 1981, Why there are organized future markets?, *Journal of Law and Economics* 24, 1-22.

Tesar, Linda and Ingrid Werner, 1995, Home Bias and High Turnover, *Journal of International Money and Finance* 14, 467-92.

The Committee of the Wise Men, 2000, Initial Report on the Regulation of European Securities Markets.

The Wall Street Journal, 29 July 1999.

Tonk, Ian and D. Webbs, 1989, The reorganization of the London Stock Market: The causes and the consequences of the Big Bang, London School of Economics, Financial Markets Group Special Paper 20.

World Federation of Exchanges, 2003, Cost & Revenues Survey 2002.

In: Stock Exchanges, IPO's and Mutual Funds
Editor: E. Klein, pp. 55-63
ISBN 1-59454-173-6

Chapter 3

Alteration of Systematic Risk Due to Derivatives Markets

James Ang
Florida State University, Tallahassee, FL
Carol Marie Boyer
William Patterson University, Wayne, NJ
Mark Popiela
Florida State University, Tallahassee, FL

Abstract

Widespread use of derivatives can cause the relationship of market fundamentals to price of a stock to be distorted. When the index was only an indicator of general price movement, there was no trading of the underlying securities. Then, came the advent of S&P500 Mutual Funds. With the ability to invest in indexes, demand for shares can be unrelated to the changes in the fundamentals. Therefore, demand became a function of fundamentals and index related demand. Moreover, the influence of the index related demand will depend on the relative volume of the index related trades to all trades. This can be defined as Index Derivative Related Demand. Demand for indexes depends upon, in turn depends demand for index derivatives.

Introduction

This paper will show that the introduction and widespread use of derivatives involving a security can cause the market fundamentals of a stock to be distorted. Specifically, we show that due to the introduction of markets to trade in portfolio of index, such as the S&P 500, or its derivatives options or futures that investors are able to make market neutral bets in the stock market. We also show that greater acceptance by the market investors of these products, as well as finding more usage for them from hedging, such as with portfolio insurance, to speculating by using the index to eliminate the market risk on a portfolio, thus, enable the investors to make so called market neutral, but firm specific risks. Or, simply allow investors to bet on the market index. These strategies would now involve real trades in the securities included in the index.

In comparison, when the index was only an indicator of general price movement, there was no trading of the underlying securities. Thus, demand for shares that are unrelated to the change in the fundamentals of the firm are created. Prices of these securities are now not only a function of its own demand, but also a function of the demand for the index portfolio. The price of the securities in the index will now be determined by both demand: fundamental and index related. The influence of the index related demand will depend on the relative volume of the index related trades to all trades. Which, in turn depends on factors affecting the volume of index trades, such as availability of market to trade, introduction of index derivatives, acceptance by investors, and also, the way index is constructed, equal versus value weighted, in the former case of equal weighing, smaller market capitalization firm will be affected more.

The topic can be shown to be of importance, as it affects some of the most fundamental questions in Finance: from an explanation of the declining role of market fundamentals and the adverse effect of derivatives introduction on the market in general.

Various studies have documented a stock price effect after the announcement of inclusion in or removal from the S&P 500 [4] [5] [6] [13]. Specifically, when a stock is added to the index, its price exhibits an approximately 3% increase and when a stock is removed from the index, its price exhibits an approximately 1.5% decrease [4] [5].

Price movement can be described as sympathetic as changes in price of a share due to changes in the demand for the portfolio index in which the security is a part of. Since the securities in the same portfolio index move in synchrony with each other, thus the term 'sympathetic' price movement seems appropriate. It is to be differentiated from 'fundamental' price changes that are the result of the changes in the fundamentals of the company, such as expected earnings.

Since sympathetic price movements is not related to the security's fundamental, prices are distorted, and consequently, the statistical properties of prices, many of which are also the market fundamentals of the security are also distorted.

Specifically, we have the following empirically testable hypotheses:

1. Systematic risks of all securities in the index, measured with respect to the index, will converge to one, and away from their fundamental value betas, which could be either above or below one previously.
2. The probability distribution of betas of the securities in the index will exhibit the following properties:
   a) first moment, mean is 1.0 by definition of index. No change.
   b) Standard deviation, will be reduced as each security's beta approaches one.
   c) Skewness will also be reduced.
   d) It will be more leptokurtic, as there will be greater concentration of masses around the mean, or one.

And if so, there is also no guarantee that there be arbitrage opportunity from exploiting the distortion, for instance, in the more extreme case of a security's volume dominated by index related trades. Here, prices may not ever have a chance to get back to their fundamentals.

There are two related empirical designs. The first involves additions and deletions of securities into or out of the index. It can be hypothesized that for such security that its beta converges to one, either from above or below. All predictions are for additions, the opposite is for deleted stocks. Thus, when a stock is deleted from S&P 500, its beta goes back to being driven by its fundamentals.

The second involves all the securities in the index. It makes similar predictions as in above, but is common to all shares in the index, around (before and after) changes in the market practices and institutions, affecting the use of index, from new markets, to new products, to new uses, or increased acceptance.

METHODOLOGY

Several tests are used to evaluate whether there are significant differences between Pre-S&P 500 Index Futures Beta and Post-S&P 500 Index Futures Beta. First a variance ratio test where:

$$\text{Variance Ratio} = \frac{\text{Variance before S\&P 500 Addition or Removal}}{\text{Variance after S\&P 500 Addition or Removal}} \quad (1)$$

The average ratio, $\overline{Y}$, is computed to test the null: $H_0 : \overline{Y} - 1 = 0$, where $\overline{Y} = (1/N)\sum_{1}^{N} Y_i$, Y_i, is the variance ratio for stock i and N is the number of stocks in the sample. The t-statistic is calculated:

$$\sqrt{N}\,\frac{\overline{Y} - 1}{\sigma(Y_i)} \approx N(0,1), \quad (2)$$

where $\sigma(Y_i)$ is the cross-sectional standard deviation of the variance ratios, and the test statistic is distributed asymptotically normal with mean zero and variance one. It is assumed that variance ratio estimates of different stocks in the sample are independent. Similar methodology for testing variance changes is used other studies [2] [9] [11].

Data on S&P 500 Index inclusions (stocks added to S&P 500) and exclusions (stocks removed from the S&P 500) are obtained from the Standard and Poor's *Statistical Service Security Price Index Record* and the *Wall Street Journal*.

A comparison of the pre and post-variances is made. An F-statistic, which is calculated as $F = s_1^2 / s_2^2$, where s_1^2 is the larger variance, tests the null: $H_0 : \sigma_1^2 = \sigma_2^2$. The percentage increase in firms that have higher post-listing variances is also reported.

A non-parametric test of the median tests the null: the binomial proportion is $p = .5$. This tests whether the number of firms with variance increases is significantly different from 50%. The null hypothesis $H_0 : \mu_d = 0$, where μ_d equals the mean of the difference values for the pre- and post-samples. The t-statistic is calculated:

$$t = \frac{\bar{d} - u_d}{s_d / \sqrt{n}}, \tag{4}$$

where $\bar{d}$ is the average of the mean differences, s_d is the standard deviation of the difference values, and n is the sample size. Similar methodology is used in other studies [1] [3] [8] [10].

Results

We examine the properties and probability distribution of betas of the securities in the index, by documenting the mean, variance, skewness and kurtosis. For stocks included on the S&P 500 Index, when comparing the Pre-S&P 500 Index Futures Beta to the Post-S&P 500 Index Futures Beta, the variance increases from 0.301 to 0.409. However, the skewness and kurtosis both decrease in the Post-S&P 500 Index Futures period. This implies that derivatives have lead to more volatility in the underlying securities. These results can be seen in table 1.

In terms of raw volatility, for stocks included on the S&P 500 Index Futures, the beginning raw volatility was compared with ending raw volatility. Ending volatility is higher than the beginning volatility. The variance increases from 0.000000105 to 0.000000162. In addition, the skewness increases from 2.20 to 2.75, and the kurtosis increases from 6.701 to 12.58. These figures can be seen in table 2.

Table 1.

Pre S&P 500 Index Futures Beta Moments			
N	119	Sum Wgts	119
Mean	1.412001	Sum	168.0281
Std Dev	0.549254	Variance	0.301679
Skewness	0.66471	Kurtosis	1.150507
CV	38.89896	Std Mean	0.05035
T:Mean=0	28.04371	Pr>|T	0.0001
Num ^= 0	119	Num > 0	119
M(Sign)	59.5	Pr>=|M|	0.0001
Sgn Rank	3570	Pr>=|S|	0.0001
Post S&P 500 Index Futures Beta Moments			
N	120	Sum Wgts	120
Mean	1.543219	Sum	185.1862
Std Dev	0.639988	Variance	0.409585
Skewness	0.597339	Kurtosis	0.999426
CV	41.471	Std Mean	0.058423
T:Mean=0	26.41473	Pr>|T|	0.0001
Num ^= 0	120	Num > 0	120
M(Sign)	60	Pr>=|M|	0.0001
Sgn Rank	3630	Pr>=|S|	0.0001

Table 2

Beginning Raw Volatility Moments			
N	120	Sum Wgts	120
Mean	0.000462	Sum	0.05541
Std Dev	0.000324	Variance	1.05E-7
Skewness	2.202476	Kurtosis	6.701547
CV	70.17286	Std Mean	0.00003
T:Mean=0	15.61067	Pr>|T|	0.0001
Num ^= 0	120	Num > 0	120
M(Sign)	60	Pr>=|M|	0.0001
Sgn Rank	3630	Pr>=|S|	0.0001
Ending Raw Volatility Moments			
N	120	Sum Wgts	120
Mean	0.000534	Sum	0.06408
Std Dev	0.000403	Variance	1.621E-7
Skewness	2.759798	Kurtosis	12.58064
CV	75.38692	Std Mean	0.000037
T:Mean=0	14.53097	Pr>|T|	0.0001
Num ^= 0	120	Num > 0	120
M(Sign)	60	Pr>=|M|	0.0001
Sgn Rank	3630	Pr>=|S|	0.0001

There is no guarantee that there be arbitrage opportunity from exploiting the distortion, for instance, in the more extreme case of a security's volume dominated by index related trades. Here, prices may not ever have a chance to get back to their fundamentals.

Next, we determine whether the systematic risks of all securities in the index, measured with respect to the index, will converge to one, and away from their fundamental value betas, which could be either above or below one previously.

The first test involves additions of securities into the index. It can be hypothesized that for such security that its beta converges to one, either from above or below (all predictions are for additions, the opposite is for deleted stocks). The results of this test found that of those stocks with betas greater than one, 42 had betas that moved closer to 1 and of those stocks which had betas less than one, 17 had betas that moved closer to 1. Therefore, 59 out of 120 showed a sympathetic movement, as shown in table 3. But, note that this is only additions and deletions.

Table 3. Additions of Securities into the Index

	Betas moved closer to one	Betas moved further from one
Stocks with betas greater than one	42	18
Stocks with betas less than one	17	43

The second test involved all the securities in the index. This test makes similar predictions as in above (convergence to 1), but is common to all shares in the index, around (before and after) changes in the market practices and institutions, affecting the use of index, from new markets, to new products, to new uses, or increased acceptance.

Here, we determine whether the systematic risks of all securities in the index, measured with respect to the index, will converge to one, and away from their fundamental value betas, which could be either above or below one previously. The results show that out of 132 stocks, 106 showed a sympathetic movement with the index, as shown in table 4. In other words, if the stock included on the S&P 500 Index showed an increase in variance, the S&P 500 Index showed an increase in variance, and vice versa. This is roughly an 80% sympathetic movement. So stocks which happen to be on the S&P 500, but have a life of their own, start to move with the index.

Table 4. All Securities in the Index

Stocks which showed Sympathetic Movement	Stocks which did not Show Sympathetic Movement
106	26

Next, we examine variance before and after a stock is included on the S&P 500 Index to see whether there is convergence in variance. For the inclusions variance increasing sample of stocks shown in table 5, both the mean and median show convergence towards the variance of the S&P 500 after a stock is included onto the Index. Our results indicate that higher variance stocks exhibited a decrease in variance. The mean increases from 0.000319 to 0.000538 and the median also moves closer to one, from 0.000250 to 0.000441. It was also found that lower variance stocks exhibited an increase in variance. The mean decreased from 0.000413 before being added to the index to 0.000284 after being added to the index. The majority of stocks (94 out of 162) had variance increases when added to the S&P500, as shown in table 5.

Table 5. Pre S&P 500 Future Index Return Volatility: Inclusions

	Pre	Post	Change	VR test	F-test	% Inc	z-stat	t-test
Inclusions (162)								
Mean	0.000358	0.000431	0.000073	0.73	2.52	58.02%	2.04	2.12
Median	0.000293	0.000304	-0.000011					
Variance Increasing (94)								
Mean	0.000319	0.000538	0.000219		3.82			5.95
Median	0.000250	0.000441	0.000191					
Variance Decreasing (68)								
Mean	0.000413	0.000284	-0.000129		2.10			8.03
Median	0.000354	0.000244	-0.000110					

Note: Return variances are estimated using 500 days of returns before and after listing. The change is the cross-sectional average of changes in return variances. Variance ratio test: the t-statistic is computed on the variance ratio; Variance ratio = Variance before listing / Variance after listing. In an average variance ratio test, Y, is used to test the null: Ho: Y - 1 = 0, Where: Y = (I / N) $\sum$ Yi , Yi, is the variance ratio for stock i, N is the number of securities in the sample. The test statistic is distributed asymptotically N (0, 1). Mean difference t-test: the t-test tests the difference between the means of the pre- and post-listing samples. The null hypothesis Ho: μd = 0, where μd equals the mean of the difference values for the pre and post-listing samples. The F-test compares the pre- and post-listing variances. % Inc is the percentage of firms with higher post-listing variances than pre-listing variances. Z-stat tests if the percentage of post-listing firms is significantly different from 50%. An equally weighted NYSE/AMEX/NASDAQ index is used as the market index.

Similar convergence results are found for the Post S&P 500 Futures Index sample which is shown in table 6. For the variance increasing sample, variance increased from 0.000322 to 0.000558. For the variance decreasing sample, the variance decreased from 0.000430 to 0.00029. Thus, after introduction of index futures, we see more variance increasing than variance decreasing.

Table 6. Post S&P 500 Future Index Return Volatility: Inclusions

	Pre	Post	Change	VR test	F-test	% Inc	z-stat	t-test
Inclusions (129)								
Mean	0.000371	0.000438	0.000067	1.25	2.48	55.04%	1.14	1.61
Median	0.000304	0.000330	0.000026					
Variance Increasing (71)								
Mean	0.000322	0.000558	0.000236		4.03			5.03
Median	0.000251	0.000466	0.000215					
Variance Decreasing (58)								
Mean	0.000430	0.000290	-0.000140		2.14			7.67
Median	0.000364	0.000251	-0.000113					

Note: Return variances are estimated using 500 days of returns before and after listing. The change is the cross-sectional average of changes in return variances. Variance ratio test: the t-statistic is computed on the variance ratio; Variance ratio = Variance before listing / Variance after listing. In an average variance ratio test, Y, is used to test the null: H_0: Y - 1 = 0, Where: Y = (I */ N)* $\sum$ Yi , Yi, is the variance ratio for stock i, N is the number of securities in the sample. The test statistic is distributed asymptotically N (0, 1). Mean difference t-test: the t-test tests the difference between the means of the pre- and post-listing samples. The null hypothesis Ho: μ_d = 0, where μ_d equals the mean of the difference values for the pre and post-listing samples. The F-test compares the pre- and post-listing variances. % Inc is the percentage of firms with higher post-listing variances than pre-listing variances. Z-stat tests if the percentage of post-listing firms is significantly different from 50%. An equally weighted NYSE/AMEX/NASDAQ index is used as the market index.

For the sample of stocks deleted from the S&P 500 sample, divergence in variance is expected. For both the Pre-S&P 500 Futures Index sub-sample and the Post-S&P 500 Futures Index sub-sample, it is predicted that high variance stocks will exhibit increases in variance and low variance stocks will exhibit decreases in variance. Divergence in variance is found for those stocks removed from the S&P 500 Index. For the variance increasing sample, we find that higher variance stocks exhibit increases in variance, as shown in table 7. The mean increases from 0.002285 in the inclusion period to 0.005046. We find divergence for the variance decreasing stocks with variance decreasing from 0.000549 to 0.000202.

Table 7. Pre S&P 500 Future Index Return Volatility: Exclusions

	Pre	Post	Change	VR test	F-test	% Inc	z-stat	t-test
Inclusions (49)								
Mean	0.001506	0.002871	0.001365	3.95	1.84	55.10%	0.74	2.41
Median	0.000588	0.00408	-0.000180					
Variance Increasing (27)								
Mean	0.002285	0.005046	0.001365		3.54			3.15
Median	0.000948	0.001563	0.000615					
Variance Decreasing (22)								
Mean	0.000549	0.000202	-0.000347		2.22			4.92
Median	0.000553	0.000160	-0.000393					

Similar results are found for the Post-S&P 500 Futures Index subsample. For the variance increasing subsample, the variance converges closer to one, moving from 0.00253 to 0.00561. For the variance decreasing subsample, the variance diverges further from one, moving from 0.000608 to 0.000216, as seen in table 8.

Table 8. Post S&P 500 Future Index Return Volatility: Exclusions

	Pre	Post	Change	VR test	F-test	% Inc	z-stat	t-test
Inclusions (42)								
Mean	0.001702	0.003298	0.001596	3.93	1.85	57.14%	0.93	2.41
Median	0.000647	0.000461	-0.000186					
Variance Increasing (24)								
Mean	0.002523	0.005610	0.003087		3.46			3.20
Median	0.001466	0.002905	0.001439					
Variance Decreasing (18)								
Mean	0.000608	0.000216	-0.000392		1.67			4.95
Median	0.000585	0.000189	-0.000396					

CONCLUSION

This paper shows that the introduction and widespread use of derivatives involving a security can cause the market fundamentals of a stock to be distorted. Specifically, we show that due to the introduction of markets to trade in portfolio of S&P 500 index , or its derivatives options or futures. We also show that greater acceptance by the market investors of these products, as well as finding more usage for them from hedging, such as by using portfolio insurance, to speculating with the use index to eliminate the market risk on a portfolio, thus, enable the investors to make so called market neutral, but firm specific risks, bet. Or, investors could simply to bet on the market index while eliminating market risk.

REFERENCES

[1] Ajinkya, B., and Jain, P. The behavior of daily stock market volume. *Journal of Accounting and Economics.* 1989, 11, 331-359.

[2] Amihud, Y. and H. Mendelson. Trading Mechanisms and Stock Returns: An Empirical Investigation, *Journal of Finance*, 1987, 42, 533-553.

[3] Copeland, T. and D. Mayers, The Value Line Enigma (1965-1978): A Case Study of Price Adjustment. *Journal of Financial Economics*, 1982, Nov., 289-321.

[4] Jain, Prem C., The Effect on Stock Price of Inclusion in or Exclusion from the S&P 500, *Financial Analysts Journal*, 1987, Jan.-Feb., 58-65.

[5] Lynch, Anthony W. and Richard R. Mendenhall,. New Evidence on Stock Price Effects Associated with Changes in the S&P 500 Index, *Journal of Business*, 1997, 70, 351-383.

[6] Murray, Scott, *Wall Street Journal*, 1989, Sept. 6, C1, col.2.

[7] Ohlson, J., On Financial Disclosures and the Behavior of Security Prices, *Journal of Accounting and Economics*, 1979, Dec., 211-232.

[8] Roll, R. A Simple Implicit Measure of the Bid-Ask Spread in an Efficient Market, *Journal of Finance*, 1984, 39, 1127-1139.

[9] Ronen, T. Tests and Properties of Variance Ratios in Microstructure Studies, *Journal of Financial and Quantitative Analysis*, 1997, 32 (2), 183-203.

[10] Scholes, M., The Market For Securities: Substitution Versus Price Pressure and Effects of Information on Share Prices, *Journal of Business*, 1972, 179-211.

[11] Stickel, S. E., The Effect of Value Line Investment Survey Rank Changes on Common Stock Prices, *Journal of Financial Economics*, 1985, March, 121-143.

[12] *Standard and Poor's Statistical Service Security Price Index Record.* 1992, 319-337.

[13] *Wall Street Journal.* Studies Suggest Price Effect If In S&P 500, 1987, Nov.12, p.41, C3.

[14] *Wall Street Journal Index.* 1992-1977.

In: Stock Exchanges, IPO's and Mutual Funds
Editor: E. Klein, pp. 64-78

ISBN 1-59454-173-6

Chapter 4

THE GOVERNANCE ROLE OF SECONDARY MARKETS

Solomon Tadesse [*]
University of South Carolina, Columbia, SC

ABSTRACT

The importance of equity markets as a vehicle for capital formation is well recognized. However, the role of secondary equity markets in providing economically valuable governance services is equally significant. Secondary equity markets serve as a monitoring and control conduit — through facilitating value-enhancing control activities, enabling implementation of incentive-based management contracts, and aggregating information that guide management decisions. The ability of secondary equity markets to deliver governance is related to those markets' liquidity. A liquid market provides better price discovery, and allows active shareholders and outside bidders to build positions in a company's stock so as to influence corporate policies. Furthermore, secondary equity market liquidity is found to have a positive relationship to real firm performance. Thus, the governance services of secondary equity markets have real economic value. Public policy can have a positive impact on the effectiveness of secondary equity markets in delivering monitoring and control services through enhancing market liquidity.

The paper examines the impact on market liquidity of two significant U.S. Securities and Exchange Commission (SEC) regulatory reforms applied to The Nasdaq Stock Market: SEC's 'trade reporting' rules of 1992, and SEC's "order handling" reforms of 1997. The paper concludes that public policies that increase market transparency and efficiency — such as "trade reporting" requirements and better "order handling" rules — promote the effectiveness of the secondary equity markets in delivering corporate governance through increased market liquidity.

---

[*] Moore School of Business, University of South Carolina, Columbia SC 29208; Phone: (803) 777-4917; E-mail: tadesse@sc.edu. I would like to thank Mark Schultz, Ana Carrion-Sague, and Chas Cadwell for helpful comments. Funding from the Nasdaq research foundation is gratefully acknowledged.

INTRODUCTION

At different stages of their growth, firms face various options in financing their investment and credit needs. These include, but are not limited to, venture capital, bank loans, public-debt issues, private placement, and public offerings of equity. As small and emerging firms mature and grow, the need for larger investment outlays naturally leads to a search for capital. The primary motive for "going public" has been to search for more capital than otherwise could be obtained by the entrepreneur. This paper takes a different focus. There are other equally-important considerations to take into account when electing to raise capital in equity markets — namely, trading in secondary equity markets[1] allows these companies to benefit from more effective corporate governance.

While access to capital is an essential service provided by equity markets, an equally important, but often neglected, role of secondary equity markets is their service as a conduit for effective monitoring and control. We start with the premise that capital markets play two critical roles in an economy — allocation of capital through risk-pooling and risk-sharing, and promotion of responsible corporate governance through a variety of monitoring and control mechanisms aimed at internal decisionmaking. The latter is primarily performed through secondary equity markets.

In its capital-mobilization function, the secondary equity market helps transfer resources from individual savers to "agents" with management and entrepreneurial talents, and helps provide firms and investors with risk-pooling and risk-sharing facilities. In their governance function, secondary equity markets provide monitoring and information-production services that help mitigate various "agency" problems, thus resulting in better corporate decisionmaking even in the absence of the need for new capital.

Previous research indicates that the governance services provided through secondary equity markets have significant economic value, in that such services induce real economic efficiency at a firm level (see, e.g., Levine and Zervos (1998)). This paper illustrates the importance of secondary equity market-driven governance services for small and emerging firms. Based on a large sample of Nasdaq firms, this paper looks at the possible link between the governance services of the supporting secondary equity market and the firm's real economic performance. By arguing that the core feature of secondary equity markets from a governance perspective lies in the market's liquidity, the paper attempts to identify the structural characteristics of the secondary equity market's effectiveness in delivering governance services.

Specifically, it examines the impact on market liquidity of two significant U.S. Securities and Exchange Commission (SEC) regulatory reforms applied to Nasdaq. The first is the SEC's requirement of June 15, 1992, which subjects Nasdaq's "regular" or "small cap" firms to "trade reporting" rules. The second involves the implementation of the SEC's "order handling" reforms, effective January 20, 1997, which requires Nasdaq to display "public limit orders," thus imposing a traditional "auction market feature" to a purely "dealer trading venue."

The paper provides evidence that public policies that increase market transparency and efficiency — such as new "trade reporting" requirements and "order handling" rules —

[1] Secondary equity markets are equity trading venues, in which already existing securities are traded among investors, while primary equity markets are where new issues of securities are offered to the public.

promote the effectiveness of the secondary equity market in delivering governance through increased market liquidity.

Section II discusses the importance of good governance. Section III establishes the link between market liquidity and market-based governance. Section IV provides empirical evidence of the economic value of market-based governance, and identifies some structural characteristics of secondary equity markets that contribute to their effectiveness in providing corporate governance. Section V provides the paper's conclusions.

Governance Services and the Role of the Secondary Equity Market

When company management has different objectives than its outside investors, "agency" and "information" problems may result. For example, management may exert less than optimal effort, may pursue goals that simply enhance its own power and control, or may squander or divert company resources.

In addition, to the extent that management is better informed than outside investors about the company's financial situation, this creates an informational asymmetry. This, in turn, may result in management being unable to convince its outside investors of the true value of the company as well as of management's intentions. As a consequence, management also may find that it is not able to raise as much capital as it wants or needs to finance new projects, or that management may have to surrender too much of the value of the firm to raise the capital it wants or needs.

"Governance" refers to the various mechanisms that exist to mitigate these agency and information problems. These mechanisms are numerous, some involving capital markets (e.g., facilitation of corporate control via takeover) while others do not, at least not directly (e.g., the role of the board of directors as a monitoring device).

These major mechanisms will be discussed in detail below.

We use the term "market-based governance" to refer to the role of capital markets in alleviating the agency and information problems, by functioning as an effective conduit for monitoring and controlling management's sub-optimal behavior.

Market-based governance may take different forms. However, generally speaking, such governance takes the form of facilitating the monitoring of management by outsiders, and aggregating information — in the form of equilibrium prices (or price discovery) — to help guide management decisions within the firm.

Monitoring and Control

As noted, secondary equity markets serve as a conduit for monitoring and controlling management by outsiders. First, markets generate information that help outside investors evaluate the quality of past management decisions. Second, the threat of a takeover may mitigate management inefficiencies. Third, information on stock-market prices provides for effective incentives for management. And fourth, the rich menu of contracts provided in the market allow private work-outs of financial distress, easing the transfer of control.

For purposes of our analysis below, we have divided monitoring into two categories — market-based and non market-based.

Information Production

Markets serve to aggregate the diverse opinions held by investors regarding the financial prospects of a company, thereby providing management with an important guide when it comes to its investment decisions. This price-discovery role of secondary equity markets is well recognized. Prices aggregate the diverse opinions and convey that collective wisdom to management. This flow of information from the market to the firm might be especially relevant in today's economy, since consensus on the optimal management actions is so difficult to achieve due to rapid technological change and constantly-changing market conditions.

- *Market-based Monitoring*
  - *Active shareholders.* The secondary equity market can facilitate effective monitoring by providing the ability to build positions so as to influence management decisions in situations where a change in corporate policies could increase a firm's value.
  - *The market for corporate control.* The threat of a corporate takeover by outside investors could serve as a deterrent to mismanagement. Secondary equity markets provide the means for launching a credible takeover threat, which could influence actions by management.
  - *Facilitation of incentive-based compensation.* Management could be aligned with its outside shareholders through a proper structuring of incentive-based compensation. Management's equity ownership and stock options provide management with additional incentives to act in the interest of outside shareholders.
  - *Certification by investment banks.* When issuing securities to the public, management is monitored by the underwriting investment bankers. When certifying a firm that hires them to sell its securities, these investment bankers place their own reputations and capital at stake.
- *Non market-based monitoring*
  - *Board of directors.* A board of directors is the primary method of non market-based monitoring. Management reports directly to the board, and the board has a fiduciary obligation to stay informed of management's major activities. The board has the power to terminate management that does not act in the best interests of the company's shareholders. The key to a board's being an effective monitoring mechanism is its independence. In this regard, the composition of the board, especially the presence of outside board members, is critical to its effectiveness as a monitor.
  - *Financial intermediaries as delegated monitors.* Banks closely monitor their business borrowers, and collect information and scrutinize major investment and

financing decisions. In doing so, they can threaten to withhold financing should management act in a manner contrary to the banks' interests.

- *Monitoring via business groups.* In some countries, such as Japan and Korea, corporate actions are coordinated within a family of interrelated firms, with a main bank at the center. Firms in the group are interconnected through intricate vertical and horizontal business relationships and cross-ownership. Members of the business group, with the lead participation of the main bank, closely monitor the actions of a member firm's management.
- *The legal system.* The legal system governs both the rights of management and the rights of investors. The legal system also specifies the recourse available to investors. Recent research indicates that countries vary in the level of protection afforded to minority shareholders (La Porta et al (1996)). Generally, countries with common-law traditions afford the highest protection, while civil-law countries, particularly the French civil-law systems, provide the least amount of protection.

For purposes of this paper, the main focus and emphasis are on market-based governance services.

Market Liquidity and Market-Based Governance

This section examines how market-based governance impacts a company's value, and what determines the market's effectiveness in delivering governance services. Such an assessment is difficult due to problems with direct measurement. However, one can establish a link between market-based governance and a measurable aspect of the secondary equity market — market liquidity — using the latter as an indirect proxy for or measurement of market-based governance.

Market liquidity impacts market-based governance in several ways. First, greater market liquidity implies more and better information — prices reflect information about the firm and its investment prospects more accurately. Also, increased market activity promotes more information-gathering, which, in turn, increases the information content of stock prices (Holmstrom and Tirole (1993)). The more shares of stock actively being traded and the more liquid the market, the easier it becomes for an informed party to make a good return on investment. The resultant increased information flow into the market improves the information content of stock prices.

Second, greater liquidity makes it easier for active shareholders to build positions so as to effect changes in corporate policies. Bhide (1993) argues that more liquidity implies less monitoring, since shareholders can dispose easily of positions if they disagree with management's policies. On the other hand, Maug (1997) argues that the benefits to shareholders from building positions and effecting good governance is so significant, that the impact of greater market liquidity on effective monitoring is unambiguously positive.

Third, the effective use of the secondary equity market for corporate-control activities requires that the market be liquid. Takeovers require a liquid capital market — a market where bidders can access a vast amount of capital on *short* notice. Therefore, with liquid markets, investors who want to acquire a firm can do so.

Finally, better-informed stock prices in liquid markets facilitate the monitoring of management, as well as the implementation of incentive-based compensation designed to align management's interests with those of outside shareholders.

While market liquidity could be influenced by a host of factors not related to governance, one would expect, however, a positive relationship between the extent of governance-related services and market liquidity. For example, a public-policy change that requires fuller and higher standard of corporate disclosure would be expected to increase market governance, since that greater disclosure makes it less costly to monitor and reduces information asymmetry. With the increased public confidence this would engender, one would expect a rise in market liquidity. Therefore, market liquidity could be used as a proxy for or measurement of market-based governance.

EVIDENCE OF THE ECONOMIC VALUE OF MARKET-BASED GOVERNANCE

There is much empirical evidence of the likely impacts of various governance mechanisms on a company's value. Shleifer and Vishney (1997) provide an extensive survey while recent studies in the finanance-growth literature investigate governance-provision as one of the channels through which capital markets may positively affect company's real economic performance.

One such study that focused on the relations between the development of stock markets as a whole and economic performance is Levine and Zervos (1998). In the study, the authors measure stock market development by the degree of its liquidity and examined to see if differences in stock market turnover explain cross-country differences in economic performance such as growth rates in real per capita GDP, per capita capital stock and national productivity. The results, shown in Table 1, are striking. Controlling for other common determinants of cross-country growth such as human capital, initial level of development etc., stock market turnover has a robust positive impact on economic performance.

Table 1. Market Liquidity of Secondary Equity Markets and Real Economic Performance: Country Level International Evidence

Independent Variable	Dependent Variables		
	Growth in Real Per Capita GDP	Growth in Real Capital Stock	Growth in National Productivity
Turnover Ratio	0.0269*	0.0222*	0.0201*

* Indicates that the corresponding values are statistically significant at 1%.

Note: Turnover ratio is defined as annual dollar trading volume divided by total market capitalization at the end of the year. The dependent variables are the annual growth rates in real per capita GDP, per capita capital stock, and national productivity for 47 countries over the period of 1976-1993.

Source: Levine and Zervos (1998)

To extend this evidence to the micro level, we examine, in this paper, the relation between market liquidity as a proxy for market-delivered governance and various measures of real economic performance at industry level. The data consists of performance measures of ten manufacturing industries in 38 countries over the period of 1980 to 1995, obtained from the United Nations' Industrial Development Yearbook. The paper uses the secondary equity market's turnover ratio — defined as the total annual dollar value of trading volume divided by total market capitalization by the end of the year — as a proxy for market-based governance. The dependent variables are the annual growth rates in real output, real value-added, and total factor productivity. Because industry-level performance can also be affected by a multitude of country related, industry-specific and period-related factors, we use a random-effects specification to control for country, industry, and time-related variations in economic performance.

Table 2. Market Liquidity of Secondary Equity Markets and Real Economic Performance: Industry-Level International Evidence

Independent Variable	Dependent Variables		
	Growth in Real Output	Growth in Real Value-Added	Growth in Productivity
Turnover Ratio	0.0358*	0.057*	0.0389*

* Indicates that the corresponding values are statistically significant at 1%.

Note: Turnover ratio is defined as annual dollar trading volume divided by total market capitalization at the end of the year. The dependent variables are the annual compound growth rate in the real value-added, the annual compound growth rate in the real gross output, and the annual productivity growth for each of the ten industries in 38 countries for the period of 1980-1995. Value-added is gross output less value of intermediate inputs. Other variables, not reported in the respective regressions, are average GDP per capita, as well as country, industry, and time effects.

The results are consistent with Levine and Zervos (1998). There is a strong statistically-significant positive relation between market liquidity and real economic performance,[2] after controlling for country, industry, and time-related sources of variation in market liquidity. The results also indicate that the relationship between market liquidity and performance is economically meaningful. For example, an industry, operating in a country with a stock market one standard deviation above the average of our measure of market liquidity, would have a growth rate of 1.05% per annum in real output more than that of the average industry. Over the sample period of 15 years, real output for such an industry would have been about 17% higher in 1995, the end of the study period. To the extent that market liquidity reflects the governance services rendered possible via the secondary equity markets, these results can be interpreted as evidence of the economic value of market-based governance.

---

[2] The correlation between liquidity and performance is positive and strong when we use exogenous determinants of liquidity as instruments, implying that the relationship could be causal.

Market Liquidity and SEC Regulatory Reforms vis-à-vis NASDAQ

To the extent that market liquidity is partly a function of the regulatory regime that governs the conduct of market participants, the link between market liquidity and a firm's economic performance provides a means for looking at the role of public policy in promoting good governance via secondary equity markets.

This paper addresses the questions of what characterizes effective market-based governance, and how public policy impacts this effectiveness. For the most part, the effectiveness of market-based governance has to do with the quantity and quality of information, and the speed and accuracy with which that information is reflected in stock prices (informational efficiency).

This, in part, could be determined by the characteristics of the secondary equity market, much of which reflects its current regulatory environment. The information environment of the market could be a function of market regulations that are meant to promote transparency of market transactions, fairness, and market efficiency. Such regulations include insider-trading rules, trade-reporting requirements, and the accounting-disclosure rules governing financial reporting. It also may be a function of the microstructure of the market (e.g., level of transaction costs, margin requirements, and the degree of human involvement in the execution of a trade).[3]

For the purposes of this paper, we examined two major regulatory changes that occurred during the period of 1990 to 1998.

In June of 1992, the SEC introduced a "trade reporting" rule that required dealers in Nasdaq "regular" or "small cap" stocks to report sales within 90 seconds of execution, thereby elevating the level of reporting to that of "large cap" firms. In January of 1997, Nasdaq began implementing the SEC's new "order handling" rules which, among other things, requires dealers to display customer "public limit orders" in "large cap" securities.

We collected data on the market and financial performance of firms that traded in The Nasdaq Stock Market over the period of 1990 to 1998. Monthly market data, such as prices, returns, and trading volume, were obtained from the database maintained by the Center for Research in Security Prices (CRSP). Data on financial performance, such as annual sales and earnings, was collected from COMPUSTAT.

We started with all Nasdaq-traded securities trading in the "large caps" as well as Nasdaq "regular" or "small cap" securities. We excluded all securities issued by financial institutions. Of the remaining, we retained all securities with market data and financial performance data available for all the years between January 1, 1990, and December 31, 1998. The final sample contained a total of 938 firms, of which 206 were classified as "small cap" as of June 1992, and the balance belonging to "large caps."

---

[3] For example, it has been suggested that price discovery could be better enhanced in markets with a higher degree of human involvement (see Handa, Puneet, Schwartz and Tiwari (1998)).

Market Liquidity and the SEC "Trade Reporting" Requirement

Effective June 15, 1992, the SEC began to subject Nasdaq "regular" or "small cap" firms to the same "trade reporting" rules that existed for "large cap" securities. According to the new rule, Nasdaq members were required to report both broker-to-broker and internalized transactions in "small cap" securities within 90 seconds of execution. According to the SEC, among other things, transaction reporting was intended "to increase transparency of information for investors and issuers, permit immediate collection and scrutiny of trading information for regulatory purposes and facilitate best execution...." At the same time, the rule placed Nasdaq "small cap" securities on equal footing with the Nasdaq "large cap" securities and other exchange-traded securities with respect to information availability for customers and brokers/dealers. Because the rule affects only one segment of the market ("small caps"), this regulatory reform provides a unique opportunity to examine the likely impact of disclosure and market transparency on our proxy (market liquidity) for market-based governance.

Table 3 shows a comparison meant only to *suggest* the likely impact of the "trade reporting" rules on market liquidity. Table 3 provides a statistical comparison of market liquidity — our proxy for market-based governance services — before and after the introduction of the SEC's "trade reporting" requirements. The table shows a comparison of average turnover ratios — defined as total dollar value of shares traded during a month, divided by total market capitalization at the end of the month — before and after the rule change for all the firms in the sample, which included "large caps" and "small caps."

Table 3. Market Liquidity After Introduction of SEC's "Trade Reporting" Rule for NASDAQ "Regular" or "Small Cap" Securities

Variables	01/90 to 06/92	07/92 to 12/98	T-test of Difference in Means
Turnover Ratio			
All Stocks	0.083	0.136	-27.0*
Stocks in The Nasdaq Stock Market (Large Cap Stocks)	0.106	0.144	-11.7*
Nasdaq "Regular" Stocks(Small Cap Stocks)	0.050	0.120	-37.8*
Small Cap LESS Large Cap	-0.055	-0.024	-17.5*

* Indicates that the values in the corresponding row are statistically different from each other at the 1% level.

Note: Turnover ratio is defined as monthly dollar trading volume divided by market capitalization at the end of the month. Numbers in the Table represent monthly average turnover ratios for the category of stocks specified. The second column shows monthly averages of turnover ratios over the sample period prior to the introduction in June of 1992 of the SEC's last-sale "trade reporting" requirement for the Nasdaq "small cap" stocks. The third column reports monthly averages of turnover ratios for the sample period after the implementation of the requirement. Small Cap LESS Large Cap represents cross-sectional averages of excess turnover of "small cap" stocks over the monthly average of "large cap" stocks.

Naturally, the "large caps" have higher market liquidity than the "small caps" in both periods. However, of statistical significance, the average market liquidity for all firms after the rule was promulgated was much larger than before the rule was promulgated. More importantly, the average market liquidity of "small caps" increased dramatically after the implementation of the "trade reporting" requirement.

To isolate further the impact of the SEC rule change on market liquidity of small firms, while controlling for other possible contributors to increased market liquidity, we computed the excess of "small cap" turnover ratios over the monthly averages of "large cap" turnover ratios, and compared the average of this excess turnover before and after the introduction of the rule change. Evaluation of the excess liquidity of 'small cap' over 'large cap' also measures the effect of the rule more accurately because the length of period before and after the introduction of the rule varies. The focus on the excess eliminates the influences of other factors on liquidity related to the periods because such factors would most likely affect both 'small cap' and 'large cap' alike. Table 3 shows that the gap between the market liquidity of "small caps" and "large caps" narrowed after the introduction of the SEC regulation. Figure 1 and Figure 2 show that, while turnover for both "large caps" and "small caps" increased over time, the gap between the average turnover ratios for large "caps" compared to "small caps" declined markedly after mid-1992.

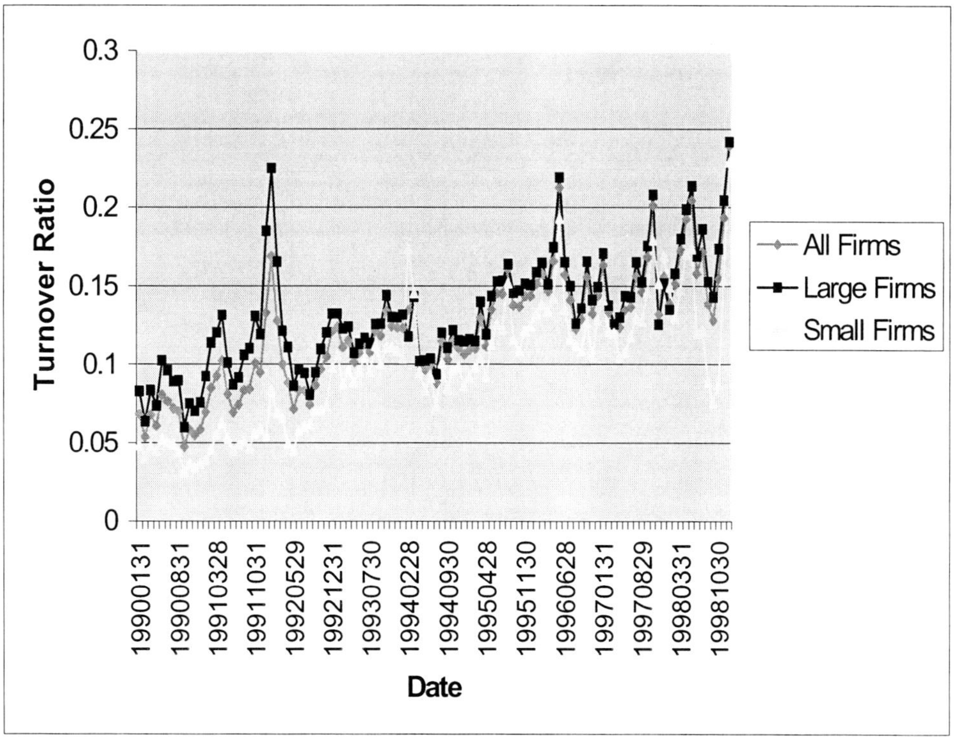

Figure 1. Monthly Average Turnover Ratios over the period January 1990 to December 1998.

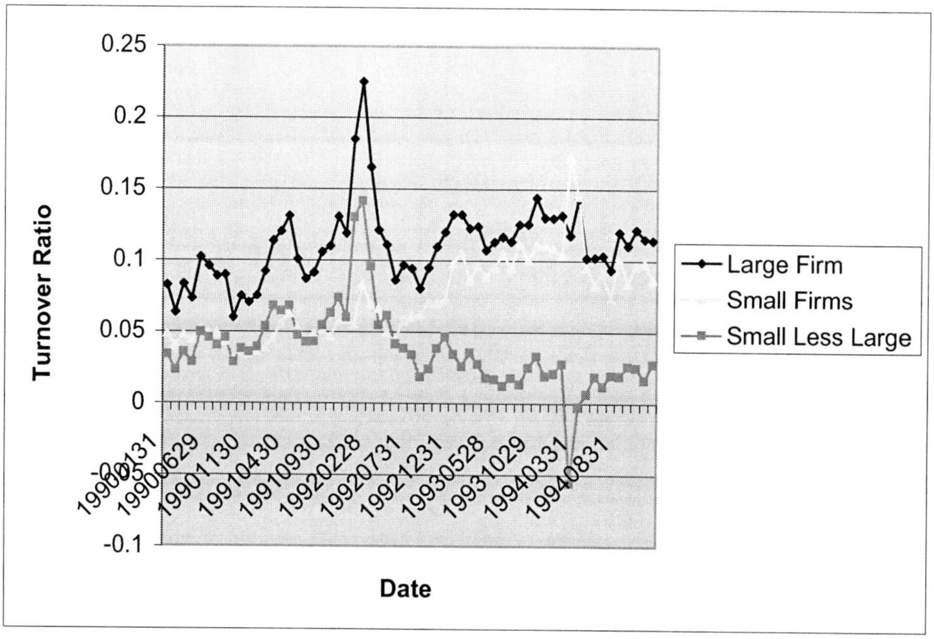

Figure 2. Monthly Average Turnover Ratios over the period January 1990 to December 1994.

The differences between "small cap" and "large cap" turnover ratios were -5.5% before 1992, and this difference declined to -2.4% after 1992. The differences in excess turnover are statistically significant at a 1% level of confidence. Therefore, controlling for other contributors to market liquidity, the 1992 SEC "trade reporting" rule has been accompanied by a net increase in the market liquidity of the targeted firms — i.e, the Nasdaq "regular" or "small cap" firms. To the extent that the increase in market liquidity is a reflection of the increased level of disclosure and market transparency, one could argue that market liquidity enhances the secondary equity market's ability to deliver the type of governance services we have discussed above.

These results are also confirmed when we make the comparison over an equal period of time before and after the promulgation of the rule to control for other factors that may explain the changes in turnover. In comparing the average turnover over the two and half years from January, 1990 through June, 1992 against the average turnover over the two and half years after the enactment of the rule from July, 1992 through December, 1994, we find that market liquidity has dramatically increased in the latter period, more markedly for small 'cap' firms. While turnover increased from 8 percent to 11 percent for all firms, it jumped from 5 percent to 10 percent for small firms, the target group of the rule, during this period (not shown on the Table). These differences are statistically significant at 1 pecent level. The gap between the market liquidity of "small cap" firms and 'large cap" firms narrowed significantly over this period. The differences between "small cap" and "large cap" turnover ratios were –5 percent before June, 1992, and this difference declined to -1.8 percent over the two and half years after June, 1992.

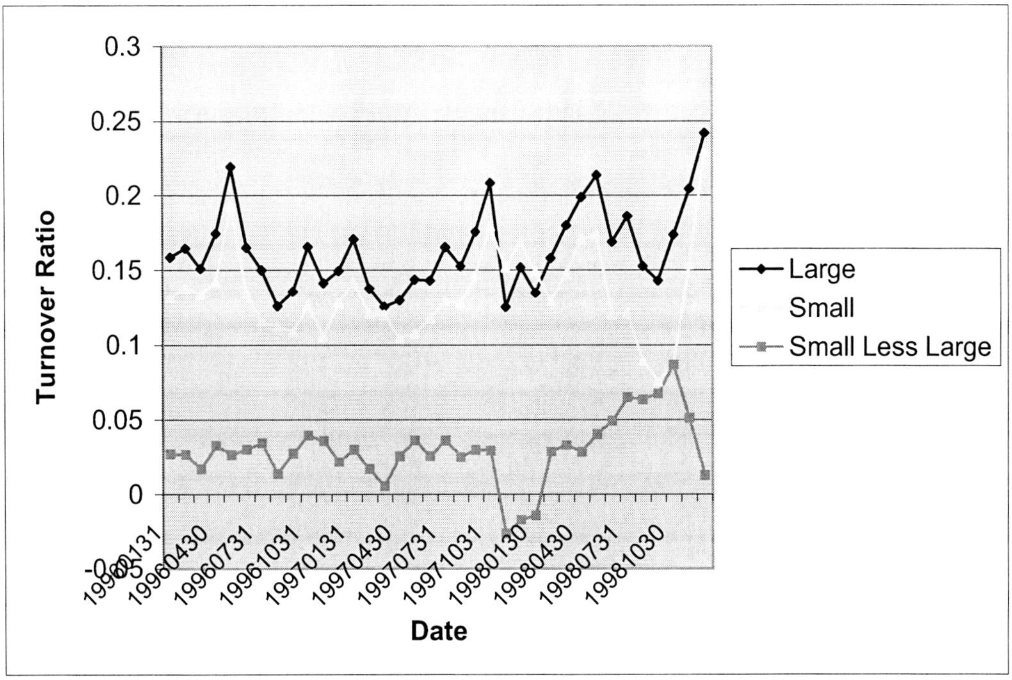

Figure 3. Monthly Average Turnover Ratios over the period January 1996 to December 1998.

Market Liquidity and the SEC "Order Handling" Rules

Historically, The Nasdaq Stock Market operated as a purely "dealer market," in which competition among dealers was presumed to assure low-trading costs to the public, thus making it unnecessary to entertain "public limit orders." The core of the 1997 SEC reforms required Nasdaq to display customer limit orders, and to disseminate the prices in private-trading venues (Electronic Communication Networks (ECNs)) throughout The Nasdaq Stock Market.

As pointed out by Barclay et al. (1999), to the extent that "public limit orders" are a feature of auction markets, such as The New York Stock Exchange, the effect of the new SEC rule can be viewed as imposing "auction market" characteristics to a traditionally "pure dealers market." This imposition of "auction market" features on a traditionally "pure dealer market" allows us to examine the alternative trading venue's impact on market liquidity and, thereby, on the degree of information aggregation and monitoring provided via the secondary equity market.

Evidence of the likely impact of the "order handling" reform is suggested in Table 4. The evidence is only suggestive in that it is based on a means comparison, without controlling for the host of factors (not related to the reform) that could have an effect on market liquidity. Nonetheless, Table 4 shows a comparison of average market liquidity before and after the 1997 SEC reform for all firms, "large cap" firms only, and "small cap" firms only. For all firms, liquidity significantly increased after the introduction of the new rule in 1997 as compared to before its introduction. The same holds true for both "large cap" firms only, and "small cap" firms only. A comprison of average turnover over equal length of periods also reveals the same patterns. Average turnover for all firms increased from 14 pecent over the two-year period from January, 1995 through December, 1996 to 16 pecent over the two-year period after the enactment of the rule, January, 1997 through December, 1998. Moreover the rise in market liquidity for small firms was more pronounced, increasing from 12 pecent to 15 percent. The rise in market liquidity could be for reasons other than the market reform, as we did not control for many known determinants of liquidity. More obviously, this was a period of stock market boom that could explain the increase in turnover. However, these results are consistent with the findings of Barclay et al. (1999) who found a significant drop in quoted and effective bid-ask spread and quoted depth (alternative measures of market liquidity) after the implementation of the "order handling" reforms.

Table 4. Market Liquidity After Introduction of SEC's "Order Handling" Rules

Variables	01/90 to 12/96	01/97 to 12/98	T-test of Difference in Means
Turnover Ratio			
All Stocks	0.112	0.159	-27.9*
Stocks in The Nasdaq Stock Market (Large Cap Stocks)	0.126	0.166	-22.4*
Nasdaq "Regular" Stocks (Small Cap Stocks)	0.087	0.137	-12.4*
Small Cap LESS Large Cap	-0.020	-0.027	1.58

* Indicates that the values in the corresponding row are statistically different from each other at the 1% level.

Note: Turnover ratio is defined as monthly dollar trading volume divided by market capitalization at the end of the month. Numbers in the Table represent monthly average turnover ratios for the category of stocks specified. The second column shows monthly averages of turnover ratios over the sample period prior to the introduction in January of 1997 of the SEC's new "order handling" requirement for Nasdaq-traded securities. The third column reports monthly averages of turnover ratios for the sample period after the implementation of the requirement. Small Cap LESS Large Cap represents cross-sectional averages of excess turnover of "small cap" stocks over the monthly average of "large cap" stocks.

CONCLUSIONS

Capital Markets Provide Corporate-Governance Services — not just Capital Formation

The importance of "going public" as a source for capital for small and emerging firms has been well recognized. As firms grow and their large-scale investment needs require more capital and risk-sharing, the natural course is to opt for equity markets. While recognizing the important role of secondary equity markets for capital formation, this paper argues that there also are other equally-important considerations.

Specifically, trading in secondary equity markets allows firms to benefit from better governance in the form of effective monitoring and control. These services include, among others, corporate monitoring and control activities, incentive-based contracts for management, and aggregation of information useful in guiding management decisions.

Market-delivered Governance Can be Measured in Terms of the Extent of Market Liquidity

The core feature of secondary equity markets from a governance perspective lies in the market's liquidity. A liquid secondary equity market promotes effective control and monitoring by enabling active shareholders to build positions where they can influence corporate policies, by facilitating value-enhancing corporate takeovers, and by enabling implementation of incentive-based compensation that aligns the interests of management and its outside shareholders. A liquid market also provides greater information efficiency, which leads to market prices that reflect information about the firm and its investment prospects more accurately.

The paper offers evidence that these market-based governance services have real economic value. Market-based governance, as measured by market liquidity, was found to have a positive relationship to growth in output and productivity improvements.

Public Policies that Impact Market Liquidity have had the Unintended Consequence of Promoting Market-based Governance that, in Turn, has had a Positive Impact on a Company's Real Economic Performance

The paper also examines the questions of what characterizes effective market-based governance, and how public policy impacts this effectiveness. Specifically, the paper examines the impact on market liquidity of two significant SEC regulatory reforms as applied to Nasdaq. The first is the SEC's 1992 requirement that subjects Nasdaq "regular" or "small cap" firms to last-sale "trade reporting" rules. The second involves the implementation of the SEC's 1997 "order handling" reform, which requires the display of "public limit orders" on The Nasdaq Stock Market, thus imposing an "auction market" feature on a purely "dealer trading" venue.

The paper concludes by suggesting that regulatory policies that increase market transparency and efficiency — through new "trade reporting" and "order handling" rules — promote the effectiveness of the secondary equity market in providing market-based governance through increases in market liquidity.

REFERENCES

Barclay, Michael J., W.G. Christie, J.H. Harris, E. Kandel and P.H. Schultz (1999), "Effects of Market Reform on the Trading Costs and Depths of Nasdaq Stocks," *Journal of Finance*, Vol. LIV No. 1: 1-34.

Bhide, Amar (1993), "The Hidden Cost of Stock Market Liquidity," *Journal of Financial Economics,* 34:31-51.

Christie, William, and Roger Huang (1994), "Market Structures and Liquidity: A Transactions Data Study of Exchange Listings," *Journal of Financial Intermediation*, 3:300-326.

Handa, Puneet, R. Schwartz and A. Tiwari (1998), "The Economic Value of the AMEX Trading Floor," Working Paper, University of Iowa.

Holmstom, Bengt, and Jean Tirole (1993), "Market Liquidity and Performance Monitoring," *Journal of Political Economy*, 10:678-709.

Kihlstrom, Richard and Steven Matthews (1990), "Managerial Incentives in an Entrepreneurial Stock-Market Model," *Journal of Financial Intermediation*, 1:57-79.

Levine, Ross and Sara Zervos (1998), "Stock Markets, Banks, and Economic Growth," *American Economic Review* 88, 537-58.

La Porta, Rafael, Florenciao Lopez-de-Silanes, Andrei Shleifer, and Robert Vishny (1996), "Law and Finance," NBER Working Paper No. 5661.

Maug, Ernst (1998), "Large Shareholders as Monitors: Is There a Tradeoff between Liquidity and Control," *Journal of Finance*, 53:65-98.

Shleifer, Andrei and Robert Vishny (1997), "A Survey of Corporate Governance," *Journal of Finance*, 52:737-783.

In: Stock Exchanges, IPO's and Mutual Funds
Editor: E. Klein, pp. 79-96

ISBN 1-59454-173-6

Chapter 5

CAN COGNITIVE ERROR EXPLAIN THE IPO PARTIAL ADJUSTMENT PHENOMENON?

Steven Dolvin
Butler University, Indianapolis, IN

ABSTRACT

As an explanation for the historically positive level of initial returns, the theory of partial adjustment of offer prices with respect to both private and public information has held up relatively well. Previous theorists and researchers examining this theory have implicitly assumed that underwriters *purposefully* fail to fully adjust offer prices; however, I consider an alternative explanation that is also consistent with partial adjustment: underwriters are affected by unconscious, rational biases that create a downward influence on offer prices.

I test six hypotheses related to the cognitive errors of conservatism and anchoring biases, finding that evidence in the IPO market is consistent with this alternative explanation. Specifically, I find that the original estimate of the offer price (i.e., the midfile price) is set at a relatively low level and adjustments to this file price, particularly upward adjustments, are insufficient, which implies that offer prices are also downward biased. I also find that the bias is inversely related to issuer involvement and positively related to market volatility, suggesting that issuing firms should take active involvement in the issuance process and attempt to go public during periods of low market volatility.

INTRODUCTION

Many possible explanations for IPO underpricing exist; however, one that has held up relatively well is the notion that underwriters only partially adjust offer prices to reflect new information. Benveniste and Spindt (1989) theorize that underwriters, in exchange for private information regarding the market demand for an issue, only partially adjust offer prices. Thus, investors are compensated for truthfully revealing private information and, as a result, offer prices are partially adjusted with respect to private information, an outcome that is empirically confirmed by Lowry and Schwert (2001). In another empirical extension, Bradley and Jordan (2002) find that underpricing can be highly explained by information that is publicly available at issuance, and they conclude that offer prices are partially adjusted with respect to public information as well.

The rationale for partial adjustment with respect to private information is understandable; however, the failure of underwriters to adjust offer prices to public information is not as straightforward. Some possible existing explanations include: a lack of negotiation (or a lack of negotiating power) by the issuer [e.g., Bradley, Cooney, Jordan, and Singh (2003)]; the willingness of issuers to accept lower offer prices in exchange for post issuance gains [e.g., the prospect theory of Loughran and Ritter (2002)]; or, the desire of underwriters to build future business through allocating high return, "hot" new issues to potential clients (i.e., "spinning").

The underlying assumption to these existing explanations is that underwriters *purposefully* desire to set the offer price relatively low. The purpose of this chapter is to consider an alternative explanation: underwriters are plagued by cognitive errors (i.e., rational, unconscious biases) that create a downward influence on offer prices. Specifically, I consider the cognitive errors of conservatism (i.e., beliefs are updated slowly) and anchoring (i.e., adjustments are insufficient and are made relative to a fixed point).

Using extant research on conservatism and anchoring, I develop numerous hypotheses designed to test for the existence of cognitive errors in the IPO pricing process. I test these hypotheses by replicating previous empirical results from the IPO market, as well as by examining some previously unresearched characteristics. Conservatism suggests that initial file prices are set too low, which implies that additional adjustments will be asymmetric.[1] I find this to be true in that downward amendments tend to be smaller in absolute value than upward amendments. Conservatism also suggests that adjustments will be asymmetric across time, which I find to be true as amendments that take place closer to the offer date are larger in absolute value. Conservatism also suggests that both midfile prices and offer prices are slow to reflect more recent market information, and, as a result, both should exhibit time series stationarity, which I find to be true.

Anchoring suggests that adjustments to midfile prices, whether upward or downward, are insufficient to capture the true adjustment needed. As such, I find that initial return is higher for those issues that have an upward amendment and lower for those that have a downward amendment. I also find, consistent with both conservatism and anchoring, that upward adjustments have a more significant effect on initial returns. If underwriters are indeed influenced by the anchoring bias, then higher market volatility and less issuer involvement in the IPO process would both increase the bias. I find evidence consistent with these expectations, and I conclude that the partial adjustment of offer prices is consistent with cognitive errors on the part of underwriters.

The remainder of this chapter proceeds as follows: Section 2 presents background on the conservatism and anchoring biases, as well as develops the hypotheses related to underwriters' potential biases; Section 3 describes my data; Section 4 presents the tests of the given hypotheses; and, Section 5 concludes.

---

1 Throughout this chapter adjustments refer to amended file prices. Unless otherwise noted, initial file prices and adjusted (amended) file prices refer to the midpoint.

BACKGROUND

Tversky and Kahneman (1974) provide the seminal work on broad classes of cognitive errors, i.e. biases in thinking. Although these biases are referred to as errors, they should not be considered irrational, as decisions are still made in a manner thought to be consistent with rational expectations. The problem occurs in that most decisions, because of complexity, must be made on limited information and with a limited amount of time. Thus, decisions are more often based on beliefs, probabilities, and heuristics (i.e., "rules of thumb") rather than on actual information, and, although the heuristics are generally useful, they are the cause of potential systematic errors (biases).

Although many fields, such as law and economics, have been quick to apply behavioral concepts, finance professionals have been slow to respond. However, given that numerous studies have cast doubt on the underlying principle of rational behavior [e.g., Shiller (2000), Lamont and Thaler (2001), and Shefrin (2002)], it is apparent that behavioral aspects have a greater influence than first thought, particularly in areas where value judgments must be made. This is especially the case for pricing IPOs, particularly when the lack of relevant historical financial data is considered. Thus, an application of behavioral concepts to the IPO process seems reasonable.

Conservatism Bias

Barberis, Shleifer, and Vishny (1998) develop the related biases of representativeness and conservatism. Representativeness encourages people to overreact to recent information, but the conservatism bias acts to spread the pattern through time. Thus, the biases tend to work against each other. In other words, people tend to anchor on the way things have normally been (conservatism); but, given a long enough pattern, people may overadjust (representativeness) by weighting recent information more highly than it should be.

Based on the description of the conservatism bias, I wish to identify characteristics that would exist if underwriters were influenced by the conservatism bias. Most evidently, I would expect the offer price set by underwriters to be too low; however, determining an appropriate value of comparison is difficult. Thus, rather than examining only offer prices, I begin with an analysis of the initial midfile price, which is the original estimate of value. If conservatism bias is present, midfile prices will initially be set too low. If midfile prices are not biased, I would expect symmetric amendments since new information should come in a normal, random fashion. However, if midfile prices are set too low, then subsequent amendments would be asymmetric. Specifically, I would expect the level of upward adjustments to be greater in absolute magnitude than the level of downward adjustments since the midfile price is already downward biased.[2]

Raedy and Shane (2000) examine the influence of conservatism on analyst earnings estimates. They find that conservatism bias is present and that the bias is increasing in

---

[2] Due to the anchoring bias, even though midfile prices are adjusted, they are done so insufficiently, which also implies that offer prices are conservative. Additionally, the level of downward adjustments may be lower than upward adjustments since issuers may withdraw IPOs if the market is not as receptive as they desire; however, the number of issues withdrawn is likely insufficient to account for the differences I find.

forecast horizon, i.e. the farther away the period being forecasted the more the conservatism bias. Thus, initial estimates are low, and any amendment to the estimate is incomplete (anchored). Also, the farther away the period being forecasted the less complete the revision. They also find that even though analysts are subject to the bias, investors as a whole are not. These results suggest that if conservatism bias is present in the underwriting process, any amendments that underwriters make close to the offer date should be larger in absolute percentage terms than those made earlier on.

Conservatism bias suggests that past levels and information are given excessive weights in creating current estimates. Thus, current information, even if more applicable, is discounted or ignored. If underwriters are affected by conservatism in setting midfile and offer prices, then these prices should be relatively stationary over time; therefore, I hypothesize that both midfile and offer prices should exhibit time series stationarity. However, because Raedy and Shane (2000) find that the market as a whole is typically unaffected by the conservatism bias, I expect that closing aftermarket prices will not exhibit time series stationarity.

Anchoring Bias

A specific cognitive error addressed by Tversky and Kahneman (1974) is the anchoring and adjustment bias. They describe this cognitive error as insufficient adjustments to a given starting value. Anchoring can occur when the starting value is some given random number or even when the initial value is based on some calculated estimate. Relating this description to the IPO market, the original midfile price is the initial value estimate, and the amended midfile price and offer price represent adjusted values.

Anchoring suggests insufficient adjustments, which implies those issues that are adjusted upward should have higher initial returns and those issues that are adjusted downward should have lower initial returns. When conservatism and anchoring are combined, upward adjustments should be more insufficient than downward adjustments. Thus, I expect an asymmetric relationship between adjustment levels and initial returns. Specifically, upward adjustments should be of greater significance in increasing initial returns than downward adjustments are at decreasing initial returns.

Various studies present evidence regarding characteristics that affect the severity of the anchoring bias. For example, Chapman and Johnson (2002) find that items of uncertain value are more subject to the anchoring bias, which is consistent with Shefrin and Statman (1994), who suggest that noisy markets increase cognitive error. Therefore, I conjecture that increased market volatility around the time of the final offer price selection, in addition to increasing pricing uncertainty, may increase the anchoring bias, where the midfile price represents the initial anchor. Chapman and Johnson (2002) also find that considering values different from the anchor reduces bias, which for the IPO market suggests that if the management of an issuing firm is selling a larger percentage of its shares (i.e., secondary shares as a percentage of total shares offered) in the IPO, then additional value considerations (due to pressure from the issuer) may result, thereby reducing the anchoring bias.[3]

---

[3] This effect may also be captured by the use of pure integer values for file and offer prices, as is evidenced by Bradley, Cooney, Jordan, and Singh (2002) who conclude that pricing on the integer is reflective of reduced

Hypotheses

Based on the previous discussion of the conservatism and anchoring biases, I consolidate my hypotheses to the following lists:

Conservatism in Prices Set by the Underwriter:

H1: The average level of downward adjustments, in absolute value, is lower than the average level of upward adjustments.

H2: Adjustments that take place earlier are smaller in absolute percentage than those that take place closer to the issue date.

H3: Midfile and offer prices exhibit time series stationarity, but aftermarket prices do not.

Anchoring in the Adjustment Process:

H4 Adjustments are insufficient. Therefore, positively adjusted issues exhibit higher initial returns, and negatively adjusted issues exhibit lower initial returns. When combined with conservatism, upward adjustments are more insufficient than downward adjustments and are, therefore, of greater significance in predicting initial returns.

H5: Increased issuer involvement reduces anchoring and, therefore, increases the offer price.

H6: Higher market volatility increases anchoring and, therefore, reduces the offer price.

Using the given hypotheses, I design tests to evaluate whether underwriters are affected by cognitive error, finding that evidence in the IPO market is consistent with these hypotheses.

Data and Descriptive Statistics

I collect data on all original firm commitment equity IPOs over the period 1990-1998 from Thomson Financial's Securities Data Company (SDC) database. I also collect first day closing prices from the Center for Research in Security Prices (CRSP). I focus on the specified period for two reasons. First, 1999-2000 is typically considered to be anomalous due to the general market bubble. Eliminating the "market bubble" period allows me to separate this behavioral phenomenon from those of primary interest in this chapter, i.e. the conservatism and anchoring biases. Second, most tests require the use of amendment information, which SDC begins reporting in 1989.

Once I eliminate unit issues, American depositary receipts, real estate investment trusts, closed end funds, spin-offs, mutual for stock conversions, and issues with offer prices below $5, my collection results in a final sample of 3,200 IPOs, which is relatively consistent with

negotiation by issuing managers. Also, the existence of a venture capitalist for a specific issue may reduce an underwriter's bias. Lower levels of overhang imply increased secondary sales, which may also be indicative of increased management involvement. Additionally, Chen and Ritter (2000) find that the gross spread is the number of issues reported in other studies examining similar time periods. As a general overview, Table 1 presents descriptive statistics for the sample.

Table 1. Firm and Offering Characteristics

Variable	N	Mean	Std. Dev.
Offer	3,200	11.96	4.40
Aftermarket	2,950	13.98	6.50
Initial	2,950	15.13	24.08
Proceeds	3,200	43.97	55.84
Secondary	3,200	11.94	19.19
VC	3,200	0.41	0.49
HT	3,200	0.38	0.49
CM Rank	3,200	7.00	2.17
NYSE	3,200	0.12	0.32
Share	3,200	3.44	4.72
Lockup	3,003	211.55	113.27
Spread	3,197	7.19	0.92

Note: This table provides firm and offering characteristics for the full sample of IPOs over the period 1990 to 1998. *Offer* is the average offer price. *Aftermarket* is the closing market price on the first day of trading. *Initial* is initial return in percent, calculated as the change in price from offer to end of first trading day. *Proceeds* represents the size of the offer in millions. *Secondary* is the percentage of shares offered that are secondary shares. *VC* is a dummy variable equal to one if the offer is venture capital backed, thus the value reported represents the percent of the firms that have venture capital backing. HT is a dummy variable equal to one if the issuer is considered a high-technology firm. *CM Rank* is based on the Carter and Manaster (1990) ranking system, where the rank ranges from 1 (lowest) to 9 (highest). *NYSE* is a dummy variable equal to one if the issue is listed on the New York Stock Exchange. *Share* is the market share in percent of the lead underwriter. *Lockup* is the number of days spent in lockup. *Spread* is the spread charged by the underwriter, in percent. Data are from Thomson Financial's Securities Data Company database and the Center for Research in Security Prices database.

On average, IPOs have an offer price of $11.96 and a first day closing price of $13.98, which leads to an average initial return of 15.13 percent. Approximately forty percent of issues are VC-backed, and about the same proportion are high-technology firms. The average firm is taken public by an underwriter with a Carter and Manaster (1990) rank of 7 and a market share of 3.44 percent. Approximately 12 percent of issues initially trade on the New York Stock Exchange. The average spread of 7.19 percent is consistent with the findings of Chen and Ritter (2000). All of these values are generally in line with previous studies.

relatively fixed at 7 percent; thus, I consider a spread of less than 7 percent to indicate increased involvement/negotiation by issuing management.

RESULTS

The majority of IPO studies focus on the overall level of initial returns; however, I conjecture that decomposing initial returns can lead to additional insights. Thus, in addition to examining initial returns, I also evaluate the influence of variables on the offer price and on the closing market price. Doing so enables me to determine if initial returns are primarily driven by actions of the underwriter or the market. In addition, I also examine the relation of midfile prices and amended prices to the variables of interest.

Conservatism

H1 Downward v. Upward Adjustments

If underwriters are indeed influenced by the conservatism bias, then the original midfile price will be relatively low. This implies that additional amendments should be asymmetric, with upward amendments being larger in absolute value than downward amendments. This follows from the notion that additional information enters the market in a normal, random fashion. Thus, positive information is equally as likely as negative information. However, if midfile prices are artificially low, then there will not be as much room for downward adjustments from negative information as there is for upward adjustments from positive information.

As a test of this hypothesis, I calculate absolute percentage changes from the original midfile price to the amended midfile price for those issues adjusted upward and those issues adjusted downward. Table 2 reports the means for these adjustments, as well as difference of means tests between upward and downward adjustments. Because issue sizes or initial midfile prices may play a role in the adjustments [e.g., Viscusi (2000) and Pogarsky and Babcock (2000)], I also report the adjustments by proceeds amount and midfile price level, with the classification being those firms with issue sizes or midfile prices above the median ($31.2 million for proceeds and $12.00 for initial midfile) and those with issue sizes or midfile prices below the median.[4]

Table 2. Downward versus Upward Adjustments

	Adjusted Up	Adjusted Down	*t*-statistic
Whole Sample	18.14	12.06	6.00
Above Median Proceeds	18.21	9.78	6.76
Below Median Proceeds	18.00	13.87	2.39
Above Median Midfile	13.16	10.68	2.50
Below Median Midfile	21.33	13.13	5.47

Note: This table presents a comparison of the absolute adjustment levels (i.e., amended midfile price relative to the original midfile price) for those IPOs that had positive adjustments to the original midfile price versus those that had negative adjustments to the original midfile. This comparison is also done for those firms above and below the median proceeds level ($31.2 million), as well as for

[4] I use the midfile price rather than the offer price to avoid the partial adjustment bias. However, for robustness I conduct the analysis based on the median offer price and find similar results.

firms above and below the median initial midfile price ($12.00). Means and *t*-statistics from a difference of means test assuming unequal variances are reported. Data are from Thomson Financial's Securities Data Company database from 1990 to 1998.

Examining Table 2, I find that the differences between upward and downward adjustments are statistically significant at any conventional level. Upward adjustments are larger in absolute value than downward adjustments, and this result is robust to both size and price levels. Thus, I conclude that the evidence on adjustment levels and direction is consistent with underwriters being influenced by the conservatism bias in their selection of prices and, therefore, is consistent with hypothesis one. Also consistent with conservatism, in unreported results I find that for issues adjusted downward, even though the adjustment is smaller in absolute average, the adjustments are larger in number. Thus, even though there is more space for upward adjustments, underwriters appear to be more willing to make downward adjustments, which is consistent with the conservatism bias.

H2 Early v. Later Adjustments

Raedy and Shane (2000) find that conservatism bias increases with forecast horizon, i.e. adjustments that take place earlier are lower in absolute value. If underwriters are affected by the conservatism bias, then amendments to midfile prices that come closer to the offer date should be larger in absolute value. As a test of this hypothesis, Table 3 reports the results from a difference test between the absolute percent changes for those midfile prices that were amended prior to three days (the median adjustment date) before the actual offer date versus those that were amended within three days of the actual offer date. Similar to Table 2, I also conduct robustness checks based on proceeds amounts and initial midfile prices.[5]

Table 3. Early versus Later Adjustments

	Adjusted Early	Adjusted Late	*t*-statistic
Whole Sample	11.34	14.15	-5.46
Above Median Proceeds	10.26	12.79	-3.98
Below Median Proceeds	13.06	16.86	-5.45
Above Median Midfile	10.67	11.45	-2.98
Below Median Midfile	12.75	17.20	-6.09

Note: This table presents a comparison of the absolute adjustment levels (i.e., amended midfile price relative to the original midfile price) for those that had adjustments that took place prior to three days before the actual offer date (Adjusted Early) versus those that had adjustments that took place within three days of the actual offer date (Adjusted Late). This comparison is also reported for those firms above and below the median proceeds level ($31.2 million) and for firms above and below the median initial midfile price ($12.00). Means and *t*-statistics from a difference of means test assuming unequal variances are reported. Data are from Thomson Financial's Securities Data Company database from 1990 to 1998.

---

5 It is possible that larger amendments occur closer to the offer date since more relevant information (on the firm and the market) is available; however, the cutoff period of 3 days prior to offering rules this out as playing a large part in the explanation of the differences found here. As a robustness check, I conduct the analysis using various days (i.e., 1 to 20) as the cutoff for determination of early versus later adjustment. Results are consistent with those reported.

The results reported in Table 3 indicate amendments that take place closer to the actual offer date tend to be larger in absolute value, at least relative to those amendments that take place earlier in the IPO process. These results are robust to controls for proceeds amounts and midfile prices. Also consistent with conservatism, I find that the number of later adjustments is greater than the number of earlier adjustments. Thus, I conclude that IPO price adjustments are consistent with hypothesis two and, therefore, consistent with conservatism bias affecting the underwriter's choice of prices.

H3 Offer Price Stationarity

Although the midfile price is the preliminary anchor, conservatism can affect adjustment levels and final offer prices. Because the final offer price must also be selected, conservatism may result in past information being given excessive weight, implying that decision makers tend to rely more on the way things have always been rather than on more recent changes. My hypothesis is that the underwriter's choice of both midfile and offer prices is affected by this bias; however, I follow Raedy and Shane (2000) and predict that the market as a whole is unaffected by this bias. As a test of this hypothesis, I consider the time series properties of midfile prices, offer prices, closing market prices, and initial returns.[6] If underwriters are indeed biased but the market is not, then I would expect contrasting time series properties (stationarity versus nonstationarity) for these variables.

Panel A of Table 4 reports average midfile prices, offer prices, aftermarket prices, and initial returns by year for my period of study. Consistent with Loughran and Ritter (2002), I find that initial returns have increased over time, particularly the period 1990-1994 versus 1995-1998. Although not a formal test, the apparent difference in means between the two periods indicates that initial returns are nonstationary.

Based on how initial return is calculated, the increase could be attributable to a relative increase in aftermarket prices, a relative decrease in offer prices, or both. If underwriters are affected by the conservatism bias, then offer prices should not decrease, and, in fact, they should be stationary, which implies that the nonstationarity in initial returns would be due to movement in aftermarket prices.

Panels B, C, and D of Table 4 report various tests designed to determine the stationarity (or nonstationarity) of midfile prices, offer prices, aftermarket prices, and initial returns. First, Panel B of Table 4 reports results from difference of means tests between the periods 1990-1994 and 1995-1998. Time series stationarity implies that means are equal across the entire time period. As expected, initial returns and aftermarket prices appear to be nonstationary (i.e., a significant *t*-statistic), but consistent with the conservatism bias, midfile prices and offer prices appear to be stationary (i.e., an insignificant *t*-statistic).

As a more formal analysis, I consider three tests designed to detect time series stationarity: time plot, sample autocorrelation function, and unit root test. (See Enders (1995) for a discussion of stationarity tests.) Figure 1 is a time plot of the four series.[7] Consistent

---

6 In examining offer prices, the actual offer price is, in part, determined by the number of shares issued, i.e. for a given IPO more shares issued leads to a lower offer price. Thus, examining the time series stationarity of offer prices in isolation does not produce meaningful results. However, examining the offer price in comparison to the market price (which is based on the same number of issued shares) enables me to draw a more meaningful conclusion.

7 For ease of viewing and analysis, I report monthly averages over the period; however, these results are consistent with using daily values.

with the difference of means tests, only midfile prices and offer prices appear to be stationary in mean. Reviewing the sample autocorrelation function, which has a critical value of 0.20, in Panel C of Table 4, only midfile and offer prices have autocorrelations that die out quickly, indicating that they are most likely stationary, but aftermarket prices and, particularly, initial returns are not. Lastly, the coefficients and *t*-statistics from the unit root test are reported in Panel D of Table 4. Comparing the *t*-statistics to the Dickey empirical distribution critical value of –2.86, I once again conclude that midfile and offer prices are stationary, but initial returns and aftermarket prices are not. These results are consistent with underwriters being affected by conservatism bias, but the market as a whole not being affected.

Table 4. Yearly Data and Stationarity Tests

	Midfile Price	Offer Price	Aftermarket Price	Initial Return
Panel A: Yearly Averages				
1990	11.38	11.26	12.35	8.62
1991	12.21	12.33	13.67	11.56
1992	12.52	12.10	13.09	9.06
1993	12.27	12.42	13.90	11.60
1994	11.76	11.21	12.26	9.27
1995	11.90	12.49	15.42	21.80
1996	12.22	12.35	14.62	15.85
1997	12.33	12.22	14.05	13.97
1998	12.71	12.48	15.35	20.63
Panel B: Difference Test				
1990-1994	12.31	12.00	13.22	10.29
1995-1998	12.44	12.21	14.81	17.56
t-statistic	-0.96	-0.85	-7.27	-8.94
Panel C: Sample Autocorrelations				
Lag1	0.10	0.43	0.52	0.53
Lag2	0.04	0.27	0.32	0.39
Lag3	0.08	0.17	0.27	0.31
Lag4	0.18	0.09	0.13	0.29
Lag5	0.00	0.00	0.12	0.29
Lag6	0.07	0.02	0.12	0.35
Lag7	0.08	0.01	0.01	0.20
Lag8	0.27	0.02	0.09	0.21
Lag9	0.02	0.03	0.04	0.18
Lag10	0.16	0.08	0.05	0.09
Panel D: Unit Root Coefficients				
Coefficient (Lag1)	0.27	0.47	0.63	0.77
Standard Error	0.19	0.14	0.14	0.13
t-statistic	-3.84	-3.78	-2.64	-1.77
Critical value	-2.86	-2.86	-2.86	-2.86

Note: This table reports various tests of stationarity in midfile prices ($), offer prices ($), aftermarket prices ($), and initial return (%) for the period 1990 to 1998. Panel A reports yearly averages. Panel B reports difference tests between the subperiods of 1990-1994 and 1995-1998. Panel C reports the sample autocorrelation function, and Panel D reports the coefficients and *t*-statistics from a unit root test. Data are from Thomson Financial's Securities Data Company database and the Center for Research in Security Prices database from 1990 to 1998.

Extending the time series analysis, if both midfile and offer prices are conservative, then there should exist a causal relationship between midfile prices and offer prices. Thus, in unreported results I perform a multivariate time series analysis. Specifically, I conduct a Granger causality test. I find a test statistic significant at the 1 percent level, leading me to reject the null of no causality and to conclude that midfile prices cause (i.e., lead) offer prices. This result is consistent with conservatism, but, just as importantly, it is also a consistent with the results that follow on the anchoring bias.

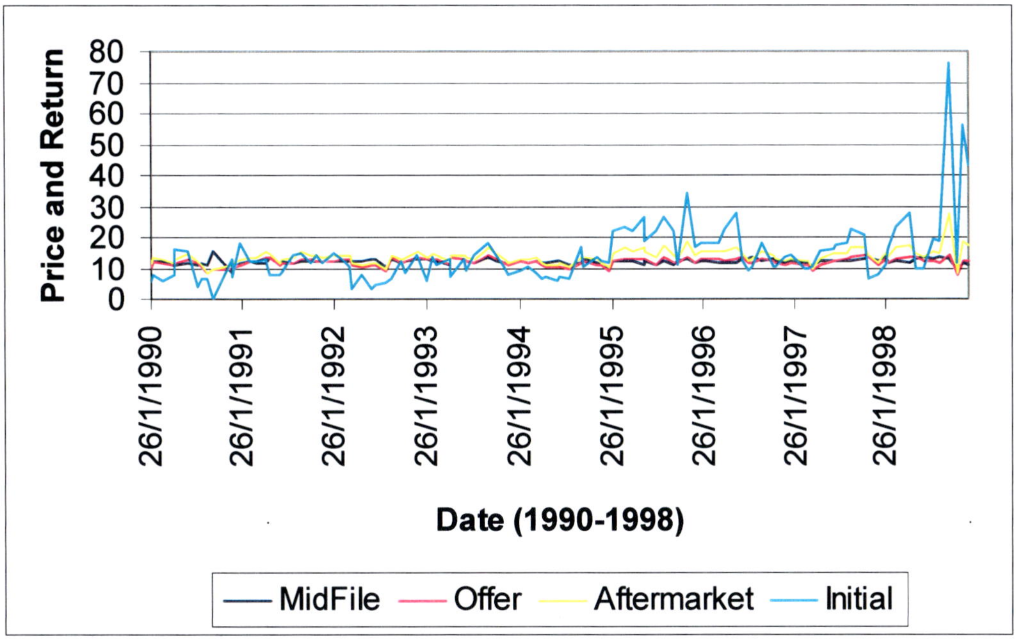

Figure 1. Time Plot. This figure plots the time series of midfile prices, offer prices, aftermarket prices, and initial return. Data are from Thomson Financial's Securities Data Company database and the Center for Research in Security Prices database from 1990 to 1998.

Anchoring

H4 Insufficient Adjustments

By definition, anchoring implies that estimated prices are insufficiently adjusted to new information. Thus, I would expect those issues that have an offer price above the original midfile price (i.e., a positive adjustment) to have greater initial returns than those issues whose offer price equals the original midfile price, which in turn should be above the initial returns of those issues with an offer price below the original midfile price (i.e., a negative adjustment).[8] To examine this potential relationship, Table 5 presents means and difference tests for initial returns by those issues adjusted upward and those issues adjusted downward,

[8] This expectation is in contrast to Benveniste and Spindt (1989) who suggest that all revealed information is rewarded. Thus, upward and downward adjustments would both lead to increased initial return.

as well as those issues that are unadjusted. Following prior tables I also report the results for those firms above and below the median proceeds amount and the median midfile price.

Table 5. Initial Return by Direction of Adjustment

	(1) Offer < Midfile	(2) Offer = Midfile	(3) Offer > Midfile	*t*-statistics (1) v. (2)	(1) v. (3)	(2) v. (3)
Whole Sample	5.32	13.05	25.69	-7.78	-22.28	-10.76
Above Median Proceeds	4.07	9.89	27.37	-5.61	-20.18	-12.75
Below Median Proceeds	5.90	14.71	22.67	-6.31	-12.67	-4.69
Above Median Midfile	3.25	9.18	22.32	-5.51	-16.98	-9.42
Below Median Midfile	6.73	14.83	27.71	-5.82	-20.49	-9.38

Note: Table 5 presents a comparison of initial return for those IPOs that had offer prices above original midfile price versus those that had offer prices equal to and below the original midfile price. This comparison is also done for those firms above and below the median proceeds level ($31.2 million), as well as for firms above and below the median initial midfile price ($12.00). Means and *t*-statistics from a difference of means test assuming unequal variances are reported. Data are from Thomson Financial's Securities Data Company database and the Center for Research in Security Prices database from 1990 to 1998.

Examining Table 5, I find that the differences between the three groups are highly significant, even after controlling for proceeds and price levels. The results are as expected, and, consistent with anchoring, those adjusted upward have the highest initial returns and those adjusted downward have the lowest initial returns. These results, however, do not account for other variables that previous studies have found to be significant in predicting initial returns. Thus, as a further test, I use a multiple regression analysis to determine if results remain consistent with the anchoring bias.

To retain consistency and comparability, I follow closely to previous literature [e.g., Bradley and Jordan (2002), Habib and Ljungqvist (2001), and Smart and Zutter (2002)] in estimating the following model for initial returns:

$$\text{Initial}_i = \alpha + \beta_1\text{LnSize} + \beta_2\text{VC} + \beta_3\text{Overhang} + \beta_4\text{HT} + \beta_5\text{Secondary} + \beta_6\text{Integer} + \beta_7\text{IPOLag} + \beta_8\text{NasLag} + \beta_9\text{Multiple} + \beta_{10}\text{Share} + \beta_{11}\text{CMRank} + \beta_{12}\text{PartialU} + \beta_{13}\text{PartialD} + \varepsilon_I \quad (1)$$

where,

Initial_i = the initial return in percent for observation i;
LnSize = natural log of the proceeds amount in millions;
VC = dummy variable equal to one if the issue is venture capital backed, zero otherwise;
Overhang = pre-IPO shares retained divided by total shares issued;
HT = dummy variable equal to one if the issuer is classified as a high technology firm, zero otherwise;
Secondary = the percentage of shares offered that are secondary shares;
Integer = dummy variable equal to one if the offer price is an integer, zero otherwise;

IPOLag	= underpricing index defined as the average initial return in percent for all IPOs in the sample on calendar days –1 to –30 before the issue date;
NasLag	= cumulative return in percent on the Nasdaq composite twenty-one trading days (one month) prior to issue;
Multiple	= dummy variable equal to one if the issue has more than one class of common shares, zero otherwise;
Share	= market share of the lead underwriter in percent;
CMRank	= underwriter prestige, as measure by the Carter and Manaster (1990) system;
PartialU	= absolute percentage difference between the offer price and the original midfile price if the adjustment is positive, zero otherwise; and,
PartialD	= absolute percentage difference between the offer price and the original midfile price if the adjustment is negative, zero otherwise.

The variables of interest for my test of the anchoring bias are *PartialU* and *PartialD*. If anchoring affects underwriters and if adjustments are indeed insufficient, then I would expect significant signs on the adjustment variables. Because I define *PartialU* and *PartialD* as absolute values, I expect a positive sign on *PartialU* and a negative sign on *PartialD*. These values would imply that (insufficient) upward adjustments lead to increased initial returns and (insufficient) downward adjustments lead to decreased initial returns. I also include a specification using dummy variables to identify if an issue was adjusted upward (*Up*) or downward (*Down*), which implies unadjusted is the omitted category, and I expect these to have similar signs to *PartialU* and *PartialD*. Also, based on the relationship between conservatism and anchoring, if both biases are present, then I expect *PartialU* (*Up*) to be of greater significance than *PartialD* (*Down*), i.e. asymmetric effects, since underwriters would be more willing to make a downward adjustment than an upward adjustment.

Table 6 reports the regression results for initial returns. Consistent with the anchoring bias, the sign on the upward adjustment variable (i.e., *PartialU* and *Up*) in both specifications is positive and significant, and the sign on the downward adjustment variable (i.e., *PartialD* and *Down*) is negative and significant. Additionally, *PartialU* (*Up*) is of higher significance than *PartialD* (*Down*). Thus, controlling for other factors, I find results that are consistent with both the anchoring bias (i.e., insufficient upward adjustments increase initial returns and insufficient downward adjustments decrease initial returns) and the conservatism bias (i.e., upward adjustments are more insufficient than downward adjustments).

H5/H6 Issuer Involvement and Market Volatility

Anchoring is a cognitive error that is unconsciously embedded in decisions; therefore, if decision makers are made aware of this error, it tends to decrease in effect. Chapman and Johnson (2002) find that making decision makers aware of additional information or encouraging consideration of different characteristics reduces anchoring. Thus, I hypothesize that if anchoring is indeed present, it can be partially mitigated through increased issuer involvement. Involvement of a third-party such as a venture capitalist may mitigate the bias; however, I primarily study secondary shares offered, since VC-backing may have confounding effects associated with certification. This follows from the notion that the larger the percentage of secondary shares offered, the higher the opportunity cost for owners from increased initial returns.

Table 6. OLS Regression of Initial Return

Variable	(1)	(2)
Intercept	11.25 (5.62)	9.21(4.29)
LnSize	-2.29 (-3.57)	-2.14 (-3.25)
VC	-1.50 (-1.75)	-0.79 (-0.88)
Overhang	0.65 (5.67)	0.92 (7.84)
HT	5.36 (6.33)	6.68 (7.64)
Secondary	-0.03 (-1.64)	-0.03 (-1.24)
Integer	3.06 (3.40)	4.23 (4.49)
IPOLag	0.15 (3.29)	0.21 (4.53)
NasLag	12.19 (7.04)	13.01 (7.22)
Multiple	0.78 (0.31)	-0.85 (-0.33)
Share	0.57 (5.67)	0.73 (6.93)
CMRank	-0.30 (-1.13)	-0.52 (-1.86)
PartialU	0.72 (21.47)	
PartialD	-0.23 (-6.25)	
Up		11.78 (9.81)
Down		-5.92 (-5.04)
N	**2,938**	**2,938**
Adj. R^2	**.2907**	**.2335**

Note: This table reports coefficients (*t*-statistics) from the regression of initial returns. Data are from Thomson Financial's Securities Data Company database and the Center for Research in Security Prices database from 1990-to 1998.

Chapman and Johnson (2002) also find that anchoring increases with variability in the item/value being determined. Thus, I expect that periods of high market volatility, as measured using the Nasdaq composite index, will be associated with higher levels of anchoring. To test these hypotheses, I use a multiple regression analysis. However, I depart from previous literature by also considering the dependent variable to be the offer price or aftermarket price rather than looking strictly at initial returns. This effectively decomposes initial return and enables me to identify different influences on underwriters and the market as a whole, rather than consolidating (and potentially confounding) effects.

In specifying the appropriate model, I begin with eq. (1); however, modifications are required. First, I add some additional variables based on findings from research on the anchoring bias. Second, when the offer price is determined, some of the variables in eq. (1) are unknown, thus I adjust the variables to include only information available at the time the offer price is set. This effectively reduces look-ahead bias. The modified model is as follows:

$$\text{Dependent}_i = \alpha + \beta_1\text{LnPre} + \beta_2\text{VC} + \beta_3\text{Overhang} + \beta_4\text{HT} + \beta_5\text{Secondary} + \beta_6\text{PreInt} + \beta_7\text{IPOLag}_{-1} + \beta_8\text{NasLag}_{-1} + \beta_9\text{Multiple} + \beta_{10}\text{Share} + \beta_{11}\text{CMRank} + \beta_{12}\text{AmUpPer} + \beta_{13}\text{AmDnPer} + \beta_{14}\text{Volatility} + \beta_{15}\text{Midfile} + \varepsilon_I \quad (2)$$

where, *VC*, *Overhang*, *HT*, *Secondary*, *Multiple*, *Share*, and *CMRank* are as previously defined. *Dependent* is either the offer price, the aftermarket price, the initial return, or the percent adjustment (*Percent*). *Percent* is defined as the absolute percentage change from the original midfile price to the offer price, and larger changes, by definition, are indicative of lower anchoring bias.[9]

LnPre is a measure of size defined as the natural log of expected proceeds, calculated as the amended midfile price (or original midfile if amended is unavailable) multiplied by the number of shares filed, in millions. *PreInt* is a dummy variable equal to one if all original and amended file prices are integers. $IPOLag_{-1}$ and $NasLag_{-1}$ are lagged one day values of the variables previously defined. This insures availability of the information at the time the offer price is set. *AmUpPer* is the absolute percent change from the original midfile to the amended midfile price if the adjustment is positive and is done at least one day prior to offer, zero otherwise. *AmDnPer* is the absolute percent change from the original midfile to the amended midfile price if the adjustment is negative and is done at least one day prior to offer, zero otherwise.

Volatility is the variance of daily returns for the Nasdaq composite index one-month prior to offer. If volatility does, in fact, increase underwriter anchoring bias, I would expect to see a negative relation between *Volatility* and offer price, but a positive (or less significant negative) relation between *Volatility* and initial returns. Lastly, I include the original *Midfile* price, as this is the initial estimate of value, i.e. the anchor. If underwriters anchor on the midfile, then *Midfile* should be positively related to the offer price and, in fact, should be of greater significance in predicting the offer price than in predicting the aftermarket price. Table 7 reports the results from these regressions.

Consistent with my expectations, issuer involvement, as measured by the percentage of secondary shares offered, is positively related to the offer price, as well as to the amendment percentage, which is consistent with issuer involvement reducing the anchoring bias. Even though *Secondary* is also positively related to the aftermarket price, the significance levels are almost twice as high for the offer price and percentage change regressions, and *Secondary* is not significant in predicting initial returns.[10]

Volatility is negatively related to the offer price and the percentage amendment, which is consistent with underwriters being influenced by the anchoring bias. In periods of high market volatility, amendments (and offer prices) are likely to be smaller. Additionally, volatility is positively, but marginally, related to initial returns, which is also consistent with anchoring and with the results of Raedy and Shane (2000), who find that the market as a whole is unaffected by the conservatism and anchoring biases.

Various researchers [e.g., Pogarsky and Babcock (2000)] have shown that the level of anchoring bias is related to the initial value of the anchor. They find that for higher levels of the initial value, anchoring bias tends to be stronger. This implies that, although the actual dollar adjustment may be larger, the percentage change for high initial value observations should be lower. If this is correct and underwriters are biased, then there should be a negative

---

9 In unreported results I use the percent change from the original midfile price to the amended midfile price and find similar results on the anchoring variables.

10 Following Bradley, Cooney, Jordan, and Singh (2002) the integer variable could also be a possible measure of issuer involvement. If this is the case, then I would expect a negative relation between PreInt and offer price and/or I would also expect a more positive relation between PreInt and aftermarket prices. The relation on integer file prices is somewhat as expected, and the relation of VC-backing is insignificant, even after accounting for potential endogeneity. However, *Secondary* is a much more straightforward proxy. As an additional measure of involvement, I also consider a dummy variable equal to one for firms with a spread less than 7 percent. I find a relation on this variable consistent with anchoring—larger adjustments and lower initial

relation between *Midfile* and the percent adjustment. I find this to be the case; thus, IPOs with higher initial midfile prices tend to have lower percentage adjustments, which is consistent with underwriters being affected by the anchoring bias.

Table 7. OLS Regressions

Variable	Offer	Aftermarket	Initial	Percent
Intercept	-0.13 (-0.59)	-0.48 (-0.97)	12.09 (4.97)	-4.90 (-2.46)
LnPre	0.02 (0.28)	-0.24 (-1.31)	-1.15 (-1.27)	0.55 (0.72)
VC	0.03 (0.34)	0.11 (0.55)	-0.47 (-0.49)	-0.30 (-0.37)
Overhang	0.06 (5.31)	0.23 (9.03)	0.93 (7.34)	0.56 (5.32)
HT	0.31 (3.53)	1.29 (6.58)	6.67 (6.93)	2.50 (3.11)
Secondary	0.01 (7.25)	0.02 (4.56)	0.03 (1.41)	0.14 (7.34)
PreInt	0.30 (3.22)	0.90 (4.29)	3.56 (3.44)	3.21 (3.72)
$IPOLag_{-1}$	0.03 (7.26)	0.07 (6.66)	0.26 (5.12)	0.36 (8.44)
$NasLag_{-1}$	1.25 (6.78)	3.93 (9.49)	19.66 (9.63)	11.00 (6.45)
Multiple	0.37 (1.43)	0.65 (1.13)	2.12 (0.75)	2.93 (1.23)
Share	0.09 (8.18)	0.25 (10.60)	1.01 (8.67)	0.99 (10.24)
CMRank	0.04 (1.53)	0.12 (1.92)	0.27 (0.88)	0.25 (0.95)
AmUpPer	0.10 (12.36)	0.14 (7.99)	0.18 (2.12)	
AmDnPer	-0.10 (-19.98)	-0.15 (-13.29)	-0.32 (-5.74)	
Volatility	-0.54 (-4.56)	-0.45 (-1.71)	1.56 (1.19)	-3.59 (-3.28)
Midfile	0.92 (49.75)	0.93 (22.40)	-0.97 (-4.74)	-1.03 (-5.99)
N	**2,764**	**2,764**	**2,764**	**2,764**
Adj. R^2	**.7827**	**.5215**	**.1629**	**.1486**

Note: This table reports coefficients (*t*-statistics) from OLS regressions. Data are from Thomson Financial's Securities Data Company database and the Center for Research in Security Prices database from 1990 to 1998.

Anchoring also suggests that the original value estimate (*Midfile*) plays a key role in the final determination of value. If underwriters do exhibit the anchoring bias, but the market does not, then midfile prices would be of greater significance in determining final offer prices than in determining aftermarket prices. I find this to be the relationship exhibited in Table 7 (*t*-statistic of 49.75 versus 22.40). Thus, I, once again, conclude that characteristics of the underwriter, and the IPO process in general, are consistent with anchoring bias on the part of the underwriter.[11]

CONCLUSION

Of the existing theories that attempt to explain IPO underpricing, one that has been confirmed in multiple studies is the partial adjustment phenomenon. Although the original theory of Benveniste and Spindt (1989) predicts partial adjustment to private information,

return. Also, the overhang coefficient is consistent with anchoring. Thus, the majority of issuer involvement variables are consistent with the presence of the anchoring bias.

11 To account for potential time series dependence, I also conduct a robustness check using year dummy variables, but I find results to be unchanged.

Bradley and Jordan (2002) have found partial adjustment to public information as well. Most explanations for the partial adjustment phenomenon, whether to public or private information, implicitly assume that underwriters *purposefully* set the offer price too low, thereby resulting in the positive levels of underpricing observed. However, Booth and Smith (1986) develop a theory that suggests underwriters have an incentive to maintain reputational capital by pricing appropriately. Thus, I drop the assumption of purposefully setting the offer price too low and consider an alternative explanation more consistent with Booth and Smith (1986): underwriters are affected by cognitive errors, which leads to downward biased estimates of value.

I specifically consider the errors of conservatism and anchoring. I find evidence that is consistent with conservative file prices, and I provide evidence showing asymmetric adjustments in level and time. Additionally, I find time series stationarity in midfile and offer prices, which is also consistent with the conservatism bias. Related to anchoring, I find that increased market volatility and reduced issuer involvement lead to lower offer prices and percentage amendments, both of which are consistent with the anchoring bias. Additionally, I find that adjustments (both upward and downward) are insufficient, resulting in higher initial returns for those IPOs adjusted upward and lower initial returns for those adjusted downward.

Based on the evidence, I concur with previous literature in that partial adjustment of offer prices does occur. However, my contribution is that I provide an alternative explanation as to the rationale for *why* partial adjustment exists. I conclude that the evidence is consistent with rational, unconscious biases (i.e., conservatism and anchoring) on the part of the underwriter. In order to minimize these biases, issuers should be more involved in the pricing process and, if possible, attempt to issue shares at times of low market volatility. Doing so will, potentially, reduce cognitive error and increase proceeds to issuing firms.

REFERENCES

Barberis, N., A. Shleifer, and R. Vishny. 1998. A Model of Investor Sentiment. *Journal of Financial Economics* 49: 307-343.

Benveniste, L. and P. Spindt. 1989. How Investment Bankers Determine the Offer Price and Allocation of New Issues. *Journal of Financial Economics* 15: 343-361.

Booth, J. and R. Smith. 1986. Capital Raising, Underwriting and the Certification Hypothesis. *Journal of Financial Economics* 15: 261-281.

Bradley, D., J. Cooney, S. Dolvin, and B. Jordan. 2003. Penny Stock IPOs. Working paper.

Bradley, D., J. Cooney, B. Jordan, and A. Singh. 2002. Negotiation and the IPO Offer Price: A Comparison of Integer versus Non-integer IPOs. Working paper.

Bradley, D. and B. Jordan. 2002. Partial Adjustment to Public Information and IPO Underpricing. *Journal of Financial and Quantitative Analysis* 37: 595-617.

Carter, R. and S. Manaster. 1990. Initial Public Offerings and Underwriter Reputation. *Journal of Finance* 45: 1045-1067.

Chapman, G. and E. Johnson. 2002. Anchoring, Confirmatory Search, and the Construction of Values. Working paper.

Chen, H. and J. Ritter. 2000. The Seven Percent Solution. *Journal of Finance* 55: 1105-1131.

Enders, W. 1995. *Applied Econometric Time Series*. New York: Wiley.

Habib, M. and A. Ljungqvist. 2001. Underpricing and Entrepreneurial Wealth Losses in IPOs: Theory and Evidence. *Review of Financial Studies* 58: 577-608.

Hanley, K. 1993. The underwriting of initial public offerings and the partial adjustment phenomenon. *Journal of Financial Economics* 34: 231-250.

Lamont, O. and R. Thaler. 2001. Can the market add and subtract? Mispricing in tech stock carve-outs. Working paper.

Lee, P. and S. Wahal. 2002. Grandstanding, Certification and the Underpricing of Venture Capital Backed IPOs. Working paper.

Loughran, T. and J. Ritter. 2002. Why Don't Issuers Get Upset About Leaving Money on the Table in IPOs? *The Review of Financial Studies* 15: 413-443.

Lowry, M. and G. Schwert. 2001. Is the IPO Pricing Process Efficient. *Journal of Financial Economics*, forthcoming.

Pogarsky, B. and L. Babcock. 2000. Damage Caps, Motivated Anchoring, and Bargaining Impasse. Working paper.

Raedy, J. and P. Shane. 2000. Horizon-Dependent Conservatism Bias in Financial Analysts' Earnings Forecasts. Working paper.

Shefrin, H. 2002. Beyond Greed and Fear (chapter 17). Oxford University Press.

Shefrin, H. and M. Statman. 1994. Behavioral Capital Asset Pricing Theory. *Journal of Financial and Quantitative Analysis* 29: 323-349.

Shiller, R. 2000. *Irrational Exuberance*. New York: Broadway Publishers.

Smart, C. and S. Zutter. 2002. Control as a Motive for Underpricing: A Comparison of Dual- and Single-class IPOs. *Journal of Financial Economics*, forthcoming.

Tversky, A. and D. Kahneman. 1974. Judgment Under Uncertainty: Heuristics and Biases. *Science* 185: 1124-1131.

Viscusi, W. 2000. The Challenges of Punitive Damages Mathematics. Harvard Law and Economics Discussion Paper No. 307.

In: Stock Exchanges, IPO's and Mutual Funds
Editor: E. Klein, pp. 97-127
ISBN 1-59454-173-6

Chapter 6

LIQUIDITY CONSEQUENCES OF LOCKUP EXPIRATIONS

Charles Cao,* Laura Casares Field and Gordon Hanka
Department of Finance, Smeal College of Business, Penn State University, University Park, PA

ABSTRACT

A principal purpose of an IPO is to gain access to a liquid market. However, post-IPO liquidity may be impaired by the information asymmetry between outsiders and the firm's founders and early investors. Consequently most IPOs feature "lockups" that prohibit insider share sales for six months. In this paper we present the first detailed analysis of the liquidity consequences of lockups, by examining liquidity changes around the expirations of 1,497 IPO lockups in the period 1995-1999. We find substantial increases in market depth as measured by quote depth, average trade size, and number of trades. As predicted by asymmetric information models, we find a statistically significant increase in trading costs as measured by effective bid-ask spreads. However, this effect has small magnitude and dissipates within a week. We find no material increase in the asymmetric information component of the spread, nor do we find other expected signatures of information asymmetry. Overall, these data show that a large body of well informed, block-holding insider traders can enter a market from which they had previously been absent, and substantially change trading volume and share price, without reducing market depth or causing more than a small, temporary widening of bid-ask spreads. A practical implication is that market liquidity probably cannot be enhanced by strengthening the current legal restrictions on trading by insiders, even in young, growth firms with potentially high information asymmetry.

---

* Contact author charles@loki.smeal.psu.edu. Thanks to Wilson Kong for excellent research assistance. This paper has benefited from the comments of Ian Domowitz, Heather Hulburt, Michelle Lowry, Harold Mulherin, Chris Muscarella, Dennis Sheehan, and the participants of the Penn State Finance workshop.

INTRODUCTION

Insider trading is now legally restricted in the U.S. and most other Western countries (Bhattacharya and Daouk (2001)).[1] These restrictions are justified partly by the hypothesis that insiders are "informed traders" who will impair market liquidity by creating a lemons problem that deters other investors from trading. This prediction flows from any of several popular microstructure models, including Copeland and Galai (1983), Glosten and Milgrom (1985), Kyle (1985), and Leland (1992).

The problem of insider trading is likely to be particularly acute in the period immediately following the firm's Initial Public Offer (IPO). Newly public firms tend to be young, high-growth firms with limited historical data. In most cases a majority of the shares are owned by founders and early investors who have a particularly sharp information advantage. Thus, asymmetric information costs could be severe, potentially defeating the IPO's purpose of creating a liquid market for the firm's shares. To mitigate this problem, the insiders of IPO firms typically submit to a "lockup", foreswearing any share sales for some fixed period, typically six months. From the insiders' perspective, the lockup is a tradeoff, sacrificing short-term liquidity in the hope of building a deeper, more liquid market in which the insiders can ultimately realize a higher value for their shares. To date, we do not know if this tradeoff is optimal.

In this paper we provide additional information on IPOs and lockups, and on the more general problem of insider trading, by presenting the first comprehensive examination of the changes in market liquidity when lockups expire and allow insider traders to enter the market en masse. We take as a starting point the recent papers that document significant post-expiration changes in share price and trading volume, including Bradley, Bradford, Roten and Ha-Chin (2001), Brav and Gompers (2000), Ofek and Richardson (2000), and especially Field and Hanka (2001).

Like most of the recent papers on lockup expirations, Field and Hanka (2001) focus on changes in price and volume, but they also note in passing that there is little change in the closing, quoted, bid-ask spread. This result is somewhat puzzling, as a lockup expiration should sharply increase the information asymmetry between market participants. Perhaps this result indicates that information asymmetry affects quote depth rather than affecting the spread. Alternatively, closing quotes may be a poor measure of spreads, as market makers know that they are not obliged to trade at their closing quote. Indeed, the quoted spread is typically not offered by any single market maker, but is rather a composite of the bid and ask from two different market makers that are each quoting wider spreads. It is also possible that lockup expirations increase the asymmetric information component of the spread, but that this increase is masked by a reduction in the fixed-cost component, due to the post-expiration increase in trading volume.

We investigate further by examining a sample of 1,497 lockup expirations in the period 1995-1999. We use TAQ data to examine intraday quote depth and effective spreads. We find that, for a few days immediately around the expiration, effective bid-ask spreads do, in fact,

[1] In the U.S., trading on the basis of "material, non-public information" is banned under Rule 10b-5 of the Securities Exchange Act of 1934. Section 16 of the Act bans short selling by "Insiders" (officers, directors, and ten percent blockholders); allows the firm to recover any profits that insiders make on positions held for less than six months (the short-swing rule) and requires insiders to disclose their trades on Form 4 no later than the 10th day of the following month.

widen by 3-4 percent, or about 0.12 percent of share price. This widening is statistically significant, but is closed within a week. This modest increase in spreads is consistent with a temporary increase in information asymmetry, but has plausible alternative explanations, such as a temporary increase in trading urgency that reduces the price-elasticity of demand for transactions. When we search for evidence of permanently increased information asymmetry, by comparing the thirty trading days before the expiration to the thirty days after the expiration, we find no clear increase in spreads, and the spread changes that we do observe seem to be driven largely by price changes. In multivariate tests that control for share price, volatility, and trading activity, we find no abnormal changes in spreads. When we decompose the spread into adverse selection and fixed-cost components, we find that the adverse-selection component does not change after lockup expiration, though the fixed-cost component declines by about half a penny, consistent with the argument that an increase in the tradable float will reduce per-trade costs by allowing the market maker to amortize his fixed costs over a larger number of trades.

While the post-expiration increase in spreads is small and temporary, we find large and persistent increases in market depth. Average quote depth in the thirty day period after lockup expiration is twenty percent higher than in the thirty days prior to the lockup expiration, and this increase is not explained by concurrent changes in price, volatility, or trading activity. Other measures of market depth also increase substantially. The average number of trades per day increases by 32 percent, and average trade size increases by 18 percent. The effective spread for large block trades does not materially change. Bacidore (1997) and Harris (2000) suggest that changes in net market liquidity can be measured by changes in the ratio of the quoted depth to the quoted spread. In our sample, the depth-to-spread ratio increases by an average of 27 percent after the lockup expiration.

If insiders sell some of their shares after lockup expiration, the number of tradable shares will increase, and the resulting liquidity benefits may mask any increase in asymmetric information costs. However, multivariate controls for trading volume do not change the univariate result that lockup expirations result in increased quote depth without materially changing spreads. As a further test we identify a subsample of firms in which the major pre-IPO shareholders (officers, directors, and five percent blockholders) do not sell any of their shares during our event window. Since these shareholders collectively own an average of 84% (median=93%) of the locked-up shares, this subsample of firms should experience only modest increases in the number of tradable shares. In this subsample we find the same result: a substantial increase in quote depth but no clear change in spreads.

Since our data give little evidence that lockup expirations produce gross liquidity impairment, we test for more specific signatures of information asymmetry. A lockup prohibits insider sales, but it does not prohibit insider purchases, so we expect the expiration of the lockup to affect bid-side quote depth more than it affects ask-side quote depth. However, the data show no such asymmetry. We do find a predicted negative relation between spread changes and trading activity, but we do not find a predicted inverted-U shaped relation between spread changes and trade size.

Overall, these results indicate that a large body of well informed, block-holding insider traders can enter a market and substantially change trading volume and share price, without reducing market depth or causing more than a small, temporary widening of bid-ask spreads. Perhaps the simplest explanation for this result is that, even under relatively extreme conditions, expected losses to insider traders are minor compared with the other costs of making a market, and hence have little effect on liquidity. A practical implication is that market liquidity probably cannot be improved by strengthening the current legal restrictions on insider trading, either with stricter laws or by adopting voluntary constraints.

The paper is organized as follows. The next section presents an overview of lockup agreements. Section 0 surveys some of the related literature. Section 0 describes our data and methods. Section 0 presents univariate tests for the predicted gross liquidity impairment after lockup expirations. Section 0 presents multivariate and subsample tests to determine whether the predicted liquidity impairment is being masked by confounding factors. Section 0 presents detailed tests for more subtle evidence of asymmetric information costs. Section 0 concludes.

LOCKUPS

Nearly all IPOs have lockups. The only common exceptions are events such as mutual-to-stock conversions, in which there are no pre-IPO shares to lock up. Typically, two thirds of the outstanding shares are locked up, and more than 80 percent of the locked-up shares are owned by officers, directors, and five percent blockholders. In recent years, more than ninety percent of lockup agreements have a term of six months. When the lockup expires, insiders are suddenly freed to sell their shares, subject to the constraint that no individual insider may sell more than the equivalent of a week's total trading volume.[2]

Theoretically, we expect lockup expirations to result in both liquidity-motivated and information-motivated insider trades. We expect liquidity-motivated trades because the founders and early investors may have a large fraction of their personal wealth tied up in the firm. We also expect that the lockup expiration will present insiders with a strong temptation to trade based on their superior information about the firm's prospects, as it is their first opportunity to sell shares without advance disclosure, and hence it is their first opportunity to act on their private beliefs about the firm's true value without bearing the cost of price changes caused by the revelation of those beliefs. Furthermore, in the period immediately after a lockup expiration, it will be uniquely difficult to prosecute insiders for illegal, information-based selling, as an information-motivated insider seller cannot easily be distinguished from the liquidity-motivated insiders who are likely to be selling at the same time.

Empirically, lockup expirations have large and obvious effects. Average trading volume doubles in a single day and is permanently increased by 40-60 percent, while share price drops significantly (Bradley, Bradford, Roten, Ha-Chin (2001), Brav and Gompers (2000), Ofek and Richardson (2000)). In the six months between the IPO and lockup expiration, fewer than 10 percent of firms disclose insider sales, but 17 percent of firms disclose insider share sales within a week of the lockup expiration, and among these firms the abnormal price drop at the expiration is twice as large (Field and Hanka (2001)). For comparison, in a typical one-year period, about half of the exchange listed firms in the U.S. will report some insider trading (Lakonishok and Lee (2000)).

---

2 Under Rule 144 of the Securities Act of 1933, all shares issued outside of a registered offer, including shares held since before the IPO, are "Restricted shares". Rule 144 requires that such shares be held at least a year before sale (two years if prior to Feb. 1997); requires sales to be disclosed on Form 144; and limits the total quarterly sales by any individual to the greater of the average weekly trading volume or one percent of the total shares outstanding.

Lockup expirations have several nice attributes that permit clean empirical tests. The expiration event is visually obvious in time series plots of volume and price, so there is little ambiguity about the relevant event date. The lockup period is largely standardized at 180 days following the IPO, so the timing of the expiration is relatively exogenous for any given firm, and does not systematically coincide with other events like earnings announcements. The lockup applies only to insider sales and not to purchases, so the lockup expiration should have a distinctive, asymmetric effect on bid-side and ask-side depth. Finally, since lockup expirations are common and affect only one firm at a time, we can construct a sample of many hundreds of independent events.

The details of lockup expirations correspond reasonably well with the assumptions of standard, asymmetric information models of market liquidity. For example, the locked-up insiders seem likely candidates for the "informed traders" postulated by most models. Since the locked-up insiders almost always include the founders and early investors in the firm, they certainly possess detailed inside information, and their informational advantage could be especially sharp in the young, growth firms that constitute the bulk of our sample. More formally, in most models a trader is "informed" if and only if his trades tend to foreshadow subsequent price changes. By this definition there is considerable empirical evidence that insider trades are, on average, informed.[3] More specifically, the insiders who trade after lockup expirations seem to be informed, as their trades (as subsequently disclosed to the SEC) are associated with economically and statistically significant drops in share price (Field and Hanka (2001)).

Another crucial assumption is that the market maker is averse to trading losses. For Nasdaq firms (the bulk of the sample), the dominant market maker is usually the underwriting firm, which may have objectives other than maximizing trading profits (Michaely and Wolmack (1999), Ellis, Michaely and O'Hara (2000a)). However, by the time of the lockup expiration (six months after the IPO) it is reasonable to assume that market makers are averse to trading losses, as more than half of trading volume is handled by market makers who are not affiliated with the underwriter, and even the underwriter-affiliated market makers typically cease their price support activities and begin to earn positive trading profits within a month of the IPO (Aggarwal (2000), Ellis, Michaely and O'Hara (2000a)).

Finally, even though lockup expirations are predictable well in advance, we do not expect them to affect market liquidity until the actual expiration day, unlike gross price changes which (in an efficient market) we expect to occur in advance. The predicted reduction in market liquidity is caused by the probability that the next trade will be executed against an informed insider, not by the possibility that insiders may enter the market on some future date, so we may reasonably expect to observe a discrete reduction in liquidity on the day that insiders are expected to enter the market.

---

[3] Evidence that insider trades are profitable and/or foreshadow future events can be found in Damodaran and Liu (1993), Halpern (1974), Mandelker (1974), Jaffe (1974), Finnerty (1976), Baesel and Stein (1979), Keown and Pinkerton (1981), Penman (1982, 1985), Elliot, Morse and Richardson (1984), Seyhun (1988 and 1992), Hirschey (1989), Lin and Howe (1990), John and Lang (1991), Seyhun and Bradley (1997), Noe (1999), and Lakonishok and Lee (2000). Evidence that disclosures of large insider trades can move the stock price is found in Givoly and Palmon (1985). Counterexamples include Meulbroek (2000) who finds no price declines on days with sales by insiders of Internet firms, and Eckbo and Smith (2000), who find that Swedish insiders did not earn abnormal profits during a period of lax enforcement of insider trading laws .

RELATED LITERATURE

Standard models predict that informed trading will impair market liquidity, by forcing market makers to widen the spread and reduce quote depth in order to protect themselves against the adverse price changes that follow informed trades (Copeland and Galai (1983), Glosten and Milgrom (1985), Kyle (1985), Leland (1992)). However, despite the substantial welfare and policy implications of this issue, empirical research is sparse and only emerging, and many questions remain unanswered. For example, are the liquidity consequences of informed trading large enough to justify state intervention? Would liquidity be enhanced by stronger insider trading laws? Does insider trading affect liquidity at all times, or only around times of high perceived information asymmetry? Is trading by designated insiders (i.e., officers, directors and blockholders) more harmful than that of analysts and other informed parties? To date, the answers to these questions are unknown.

Direct empirical measurements of the liquidity consequences of insider trading are rare, and they tend not to find the predicted liquidity impairment. Cornell and Sirri (1992) examine insider trading around Anheuser Busch's tender offer for Campbell Taggart, using ex post court records to identify insider trades, and conclude that trading volume and liquidity increased when insiders were active. The most comprehensive empirical test of the liquidity consequences of insider trading is found in Bettis, Cole and Lemmon (2000). They examine a sample of 284 firms whose internal policies restrict insider trading, and find that effective spreads increase by about two basis points (or 0.02 percent of share price) during "trading windows" when insiders are allowed to trade. By comparison, after lockup expirations we find temporary spread increases of approximately 14 basis points, although we find no long-term spread changes.

Other tests for a relation between information asymmetry and liquidity have focused on earnings announcements, hypothesizing that information asymmetry will be unusually high just before and perhaps just after the announcement, because some traders will have advance

knowledge of earnings or will better understand their implications. Venkatesh and Chiang (1986) examine earnings and dividend announcements, and find that spreads widen only around unusual earnings announcements, those that are separated from a previous announcement by more than ten days but less than thirty days. Lee, Mucklow and Ready (1993) use intraday data and find evidence that spreads widen around earnings announcements, especially in the minutes immediately prior to the announcement, but they express doubt about whether the resulting increase in trading costs is economically significant.

The issue addressed in this study, liquidity, is one component of a broader debate on the merits of insider trading. A good overview of this debate can be found in Leland (1992). Some researchers argue that insider trading can be an efficient way to compensate managers for creating new wealth (Manne (1966), Bebchuk and Fershtman (1994), Noe (1997)). However, managers might actually destroy wealth in order to maximize their trading profits (Hirshleifer (1974), Bagnoli and Khanna (1992)). Insider trading may also accelerate price discovery, leading to more efficient allocation of resources (Bernhardt, Hollifield and Hughson (1995), Baiman and Verrecchia (1996)). However, Fishman and Hagerty (1992) argue that insider trading could actually make prices less informative, by reducing outsiders' incentive to gather information. The prospect of trading against insiders may make outsiders less willing to invest in new firms (Manove (1989)), though Leland (1992) argues the reverse.

DATA AND METHODS

Data

Our initial sample is all IPOs in the Securities Data Corporation (SDC) New Issues database, in the period 1995-1999. For a firm to be included in the sample, we require the firm to have at least 3 months of TAQ data available both prior to and after the expiration day. Thus, the earliest expiration day for our sample firm is April, 1995 and the latest expiration date is June 31, 1999. (We have TAQ data though Sep. 1999.) We exclude carveouts, stocks with issue price below $5, REIT's, ADR's, unit offers, and firms that conduct a seasoned equity offer before the lockup expires (seasoned offer dates are also from SDC). These exclusions leave a potential sample of 1,534 firms. For each firm, we obtain a complete record of trades and quotes for the period from 30 days before the lockup expiration to 30 days after, from the TAQ database distributed by the NYSE. After excluding 37 firms that have fewer than ten days with valid TAQ data in either the pre- or post-expiration windows, we have a final sample of 1,497 firms. For the TAQ data, we apply standard screens to eliminate trades and quotes flagged as opening, non-standard delivery trades, as well as all Best Bid/Offer (BBO) ineligible quotes. BBO-ineligible quotes are closing quotations, trading halts, pre-opening indications, and non-firm quotations. Our results are qualitatively unchanged if we apply more stringent screens for minimum share price or trading activity.

Table 8. Summary Statistics for Sample Firms

Year of Lockup Expiration	Number of Firms	Issue Value ($Millions)	Lockup Period (Days)	Percent of Total Shares Sold in IPO	Percent with Venture Financing
1995	165	63 [31]	210 [180]	35% [33]	39%
1996	495	72 [42]	188 [180]	33% [33]	47%
1997	406	60 [33]	196 [180]	33% [30]	36%
1998	356	78 [39]	198 [180]	39% [33]	28%
1999	75	208 [49]	218 [180]	39% [33]	24%
All Years	**1,497**	**76**	**196**	**35%**	**38%**

Note: The sample is 1,497 U.S. lockup expirations in the period April, 1995 through June, 1999. Reported below are the sample means and medians (in brackets.)

Table 1 presents summary statistics for the sample firms, by year of the lockup expiration. The typical IPO offers one third of the total outstanding shares, leaving two thirds of the shares in the hands of pre-IPO shareholders, almost all of which will be locked up. Most lockups are for 180 days, but the mean lockup period is somewhat longer, at 196 days. As measured by the offer price, the typical IPO firm has a total equity value of $76 million. All years 1995-1999 are represented in the sample, but the first and last years have fewer firms due to our mid-year sample cutoffs. The characteristics of the sample firms do not change dramatically from year to year, except for a steady decline in the proportion of firms with venture capital financing, and an increase in the mean firm value in 1999. This increase is due to a few large IPOs. The decline in the percentage of firms with venture financing may be due to the "hot" IPO market, which probably increased the number of IPOs from lower-quality firms that could not attract venture financing.

Figure 1 shows the time series of total trading volume and cumulative abnormal returns (relative to the CRSP value-weighted index return) around the lockup expiration. Previous research has shown that abnormal returns and trading volume around lockup expirations depends strongly on whether the firm is venture financed, so we show results separately for venture- and non-venture financed firms.[4] In our sample, 570 firms (38 percent) are venture financed, so the results for the full sample are roughly intermediate between those of the venture- and non-venture financed subsamples. The figures show a large increase in trading volume and concurrent decline in share price immediately around the lockup expiration, especially among venture financed firms. These effects are larger than those shown in previous papers (e.g., Bradley, Bradford, Roten, and Ha-Chin (2001), Brav and Gompers (2000), Field and Hanka (2001), and Ofek and Richardson (2000)) because the effects have grown larger over time. This result confirms that lockup expirations are meaningful events that are not rendered moot by early lockup releases or by executive hedging instrument such as collars or exchange funds. Bettis, Bizjak, and Lemmon (1999) examine executive hedging instruments, and Field and Hanka (2001) find that only a few percent of lockup agreements are released early.

For our purposes, one of the attractive features of lockup expirations is that they are relatively exogenous events, not systematically timed to coincide with confounding events like earnings announcements. To verify this claim, we obtained the dates of all earnings announcements for our sample firms in the period around the lockup expiration. Earnings announcements are obtained from First Call (for years 1995-1997) or from the Dow Jones news retrieval service (for years 1998 and 1999). When we plot the frequency of earnings announcements around the lockup expiration (results available on request) the only obvious pattern is a seven calendar day (five trading day) seasonal. Lockup expirations tend to be on Mondays, while earnings announcements are most common on Tuesday. This seasonal pattern is not materially distorted around the lockup expiration, so lockup expirations do not seem to mark periods of unusually high or low incidence of earnings announcements. We also replicate our main tests in the subsamples with and without earnings announcements in either the twenty or sixty windows surrounding the lockup expiration, and find no qualitative change in the results.

---

[4] Data on the presence of venture financing are obtained from SDC.

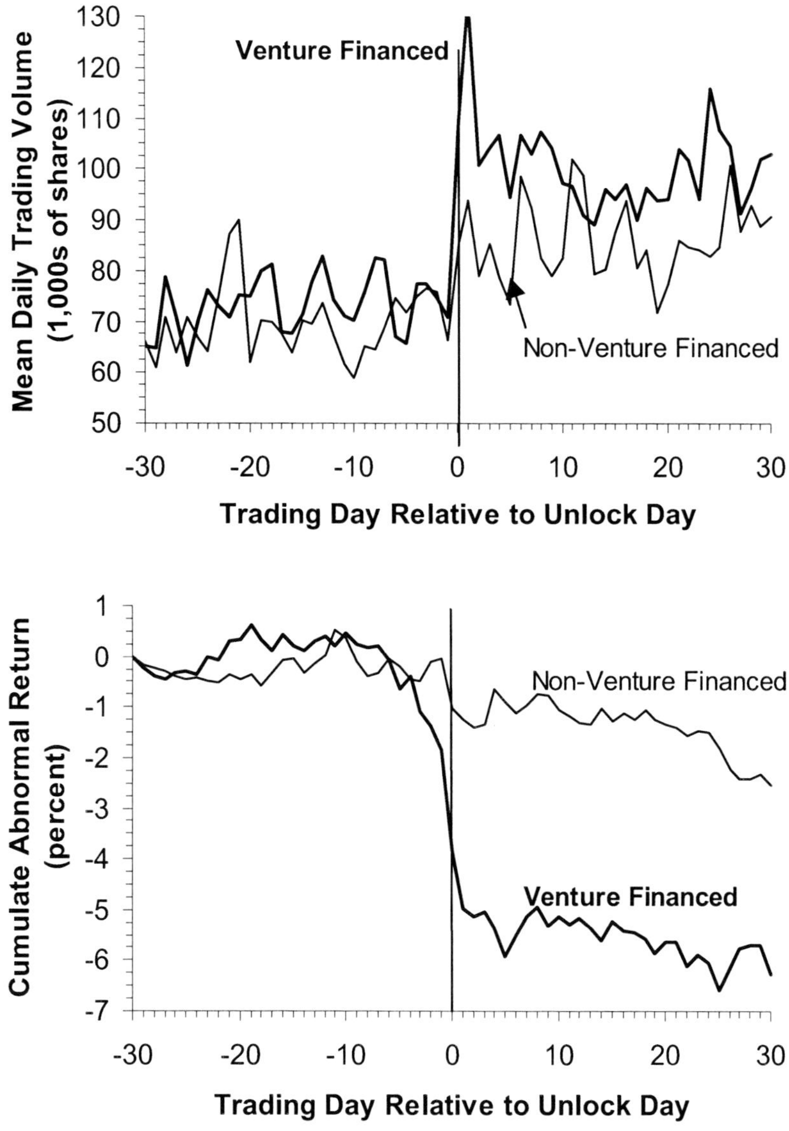

Figure 1. Volume and abnormal returns around the lockup expiration.
Cumulative abnormal returns are measured relative to the return on the CRSP value-weighted index, and are based on closing quote midpoints. The sample is 1,497 U.S. lockup expirations in the period April, 1995 through June, 1999. Data are from TAQ.

Methods

Measuring the Bid-ask Spread

We compute several measures of bid-ask spreads. The quoted spread is defined as the difference between the bid and ask, while the relative quoted spread is defined as the quoted spread divided by the midpoint of the quoted bid and ask. While quoted spreads are informative, a better measure of execution costs is given by the effective spread, defined as twice the absolute difference between the transaction price and the midpoint of the prevailing quoted spread. Most of our tests will focus on the relative effective spread (the effective spread expressed as a percentage of the quote midpoint) which we judge to be the best single measure of trading costs.

For each firm, we compute the daily average spread for each day in the pre-expiration and post-expiration windows, take the mean of the thirty daily averages, then compute the percentage difference between the means in the pre- and post-expiration windows. Our univariate tests measure the cross-sectional mean and median of these 1,497 firm-level percentage changes. Formally, each firm's spreads are computed as

$$\text{Quoted Spread} = \frac{1}{N_D}\sum_{d=1}^{N_D}\left[\frac{1}{N_{Q,d}}\sum_{q=1}^{N_{Q,d}}\left(A_{q,d} - B_{q,d}\right)\right] \quad (1)$$

$$\text{Relative Quoted Spread} = \frac{1}{N_D}\sum_{d=1}^{N_D}\left[\frac{1}{N_{Q,d}}\sum_{q=1}^{N_{Q,d}}\left(\frac{A_{q,d} - B_{q,d}}{M_{q,d}}\right)\right]\times 100\% \quad (2)$$

$$\text{Effective Spread} = \frac{1}{N_D}\sum_{d=1}^{N_D}\left[\frac{1}{N_{T,d}}\sum_{t=1}^{N_{T,d}}2\left|P_{t,d} - M_{t,d}\right|\right] \quad (3)$$

$$\text{Relative Effective Spread} = \frac{1}{N_D}\sum_{d=1}^{N_D}\left[\frac{1}{N_{T,d}}\sum_{t=1}^{N_{T,d}}2\frac{\left|P_{t,d} - M_{t,d}\right|}{M_{t,d}}\right]\times 100\% \quad (4)$$

where N_D is the number of days in the event window (usually 30). $N_{Q,d}$ is the number of quote updates on day *d*, and $N_{T,d}$ is the number of transactions on day *d*. $A_{q,d}$, $B_{q,d}$, and $M_{q,d}$ are the ask, bid, and midpoint respectively, for quote update *q* on day *d*. $P_{t,d}$, $A_{t,d}$, $B_{t,d}$, $M_{t,d}$ are the transaction price and the prevailing ask, bid, and midpoint, respectively, for transaction *t* on date *d*. While most of our results are presented for the event window [-30,+30], we also conducted our tests with the window [-60,+60] and obtained qualitatively similar results.

Measuring Market Depth and Trading Activity

We compute several measures of market depth and trading activity. Ask depth is defined as the number of shares offered for sale at the ask price. Bid depth is defined similarly, and the average of the bid and ask depth is referred to as quote depth. Average shares per transaction, average number of daily transactions, and average daily volume are defined in the obvious manner. The depth-to-spread ratio, a measure of net improvement in liquidity, is defined as the sum of the bid and ask depth divided by the quoted relative spread. These measures are averaged over firms, days, and quote updates in the same manner as spreads are averaged.

During our sample period, market-wide spreads and quote depths were trending downward, due presumably to the NASDAQ odd-eighth's quote controversy. However, the effect of this trend is small during our short sample window, so we do not control for it.

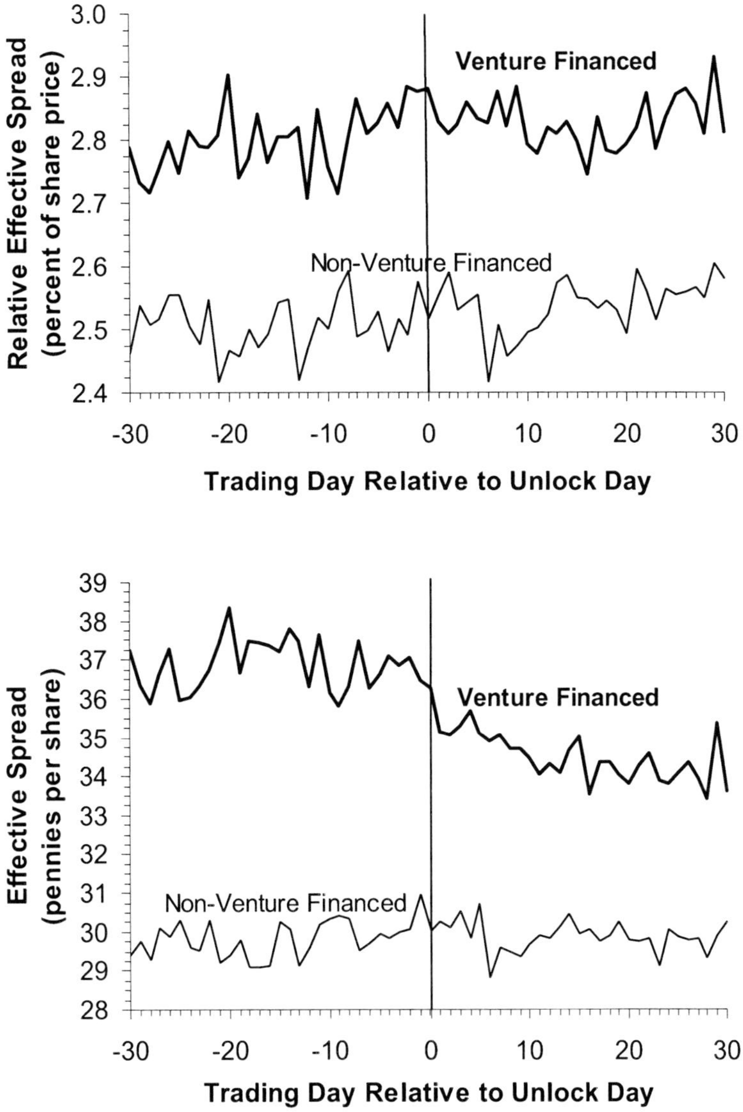

Figure 2. Average effective spreads around the lockup expiration.
Effective spreads are measures in pennies per share; relative effective spreads are measured as a percentage of the quote midpoint. The effective spread is calculated as 2×| Pt–Mt |, where Pt is the transaction price at time t and Mt is the midpoint of the bid and ask quotes in effect at time t. The sample is 1,497 U.S. lockup expirations in the period April, 1995 through June, 1999. Data are from TAQ.

Univariate Tests for Liquidity Impairment after Lockup Expirations

Changes in Bid-ask Spreads after Lockup Expirations

Figure 2 shows the time series of daily mean effective spreads for the 61-day event window centered on the lockup expiration. The upper panel shows effective spreads measured in pennies per share; the lower panel shows relative effective spreads measured as a percentage of share price. Results are shown separately for venture- and non-venture financed firms; the results for the whole sample are intermediate between these two subsamples. The upper panel shows that, after the lockup expiration, the effective spread narrows markedly in venture financed firms, but does not change much in non-venture finance firms. The drop in the spread among venture financed firms parallels the drop in their share price, so the lower panel shows no obvious change in the relative effective spread for either venture- or non-venture financed firms.

Table 9. Daily Abnormal Spreads

Day	Abnormal Relative Effective Spread	t-stat
-10	-0.5%	[-0.6]
-9	-0.4	[-0.4]
-8	1.3	[1.4]
-7	0.8	[0.9]
-6	1.0	[1.0]
-5	1.9	[1.9]
-4	1.2	[1.2]
-3	1.3	[1.4]
-2	3.1*	[3.0]
-1	4.3*	[4.2]
0	3.5*	[3.4]
1	3.9*	[2.6]
2	2.0	[1.8]
3	4.3*	[2.3]
4	2.6*	[2.4]
5	3.2*	[2.6]
6	0.2	[0.2]
7	1.9	[1.5]
8	0.5	[0.4]
9	0.9	[0.8]
10	1.0	[0.8]

* Indicates significance at the 5% level (two-tailed test).

Tabulated values represent the percentage deviation from the mean relative effective spread for the period [-30,-6]. Formally, on each day T, the tabulated value of the relative effective spread YT is calculated as:

$$Y_T = \left(\frac{S_T}{\frac{1}{25}\sum_{t=-30}^{-6} S_t} - 1 \right) \cdot 100\%$$

where St is the relative effective spread on day t, and day 0 is the lockup expiration day. The sample is 1,497 U.S. lockup expirations in the period April, 1995 through June, 1999.

Table 9 presents the time series of daily "abnormal" relative effective spreads for the period immediately around the lockup expiration. The tabulated values give the percentage deviations from the pre-expiration mean, which is measured in the period [-30,-6]. The result shows that relative effective spreads widen by 3-4 percent in the period [-2,+5], but then return to their pre-expiration levels. The temporary widening has small magnitude, but is statistically significant.

Table 3 presents formal tests for a persistent change in spreads, by comparing several measures of spreads for the thirty day periods before and after the lockup expiration. Results are shown for the whole sample and for the subsamples of firms with and without venture financing. In addition to effective spreads, results are also shown for quoted spreads. The results are consistent with the inferences drawn from Figure 2. The only significant changes in absolute spreads are in the venture-finance subsample, which shows a decline of 3-8 percent, depending on the definition of the spread and the measure of central tendency. These spread declines mirror the price declines, which are also largely confined to the venture financed subsample. The simultaneous declines in absolute spreads and share prices results in small, ambiguously-signed changes in relative spreads. The mean change in the relative effective spread is +1.9 percent, but the median change has the opposite sign, at -2.6 percent. Relative quoted spreads show similar, ambiguously-signed changes. The disagreement between the signs of the mean and median indicates that spread changes are skewed, with a majority of firms enjoying narrower spreads after the lockup expiration, while a few firms see spread increases of a somewhat larger magnitude. A detailed examination of the data (not reported) indicates that this skewness is pervasive, and is not driven by just a few extreme observations.

As robustness checks, we repeated our tests using a [-60,+60] event window, with qualitatively similar results. Also, we expect the results may depend on the exchange mechanism. Our sample is dominated by NASDAQ firms, with only 223 (15%) being traded on NYSE. In unreported tests we find no significant long-term spread changes in either the NYSE or NASDAQ subsamples.

Overall, after lockup expiration we observe a statistically significant, but small and temporary widening in bid-ask spreads. The magnitude of the change is 3-4 percent of the pre-expiration spread, and it lasts about a week.

Table 10. Tests for Persistent Univariate Changes in Bid-Ask Spreads

Variable		All Firms (n=1,497)			Venture-Backed (n=570)			Non-Venture Backed (n=927)			P-value for t-test of difference in % change for venture vs. non-venture
		Before	After	% Change	Before	After	% Change	Before	After	% Change	
Quoted Spread	*Mean*	43.8	43.4	-0.1	46.8	45.0	-3.1*	42.0	42.4	1.8	0.00
	(S.E.)	(0.5)	(0.6)	(0.6)	(0.9)	(1.0)	(0.9)	(0.6)	(0.7)	(1.2)	
	Median	38.9	38.5	-1.2	43.8	40.3	-5.1*	37.0	37.9	-0.6	
	% Positive			44%			38%			49%	
Effective Spread	*Mean*	32.7	31.9	-1.1	37.0	34.5	-5.3*	30.1	30.2	1.4	0.00
	(S.E.)	(0.5)	(0.5)	(0.6)	(0.8)	(0.8)	(1.0)	(0.6)	(0.6)	(0.8)	
	Median	28.8	27.3	-2.6	33.9	30.5	-7.7*	26.0	25.6	-1.1	
	% Positive			42%			34%			47%	
Relative Quoted Spread	*Mean*	3.6	3.7	3.4*	3.6	3.7	3.4*	3.6	3.6	3.2*	0.85
	(S.E.)	(0.1)	(0.1)	(0.7)	(0.1)	(0.1)	(1.2)	(0.1)	(0.1)	(0.9)	
	Median	3.0	3.0	-1.0	3.3	3.1	-0.0	2.9	2.9	-1.8	
	% Positive			47%			50%			46%	
Relative Effective Spread	*Mean*	2.7	2.7	1.9*	2.8	2.9	0.7	2.6	2.6	2.7*	0.16
	(S.E.)	(0.1)	(0.2)	(0.7)	(0.1)	(0.1)	(1.1)	(0.1)	(0.1)	(1.1)	
	Median	2.3	2.3	-2.6	2.6	2.4	-2.9	2.1	2.1	-2.4	
	% Positive			46%			44%			47%	

* Indicates significance at the 5% level using two-tailed t-test (for mean) or signed rank test (for median).

Note: Summary measures of bid-ask spreads for the 30-day periods before and after the IPO lockup expiration day. Spreads are measures in pennies per share; relative spreads are measured as a percentage of the quote midpoint. The quoted spread is the difference between the ask and bid quotes. The effective spread is calculated as $2\times| P_t - M_t |$, where P_t is the transaction price at time t and M_t is the midpoint of the bid and ask quotes in effect at time t. The sample is 1,497 U.S. lockup expirations in the period April, 1995 through June, 1999. Reported statistics are based on the distributions of the 1,497 firm-level means and changes. Standard errors (*S.E.*) are in parentheses. Intraday data are from the TAQ database.

Table 11. The Effect of Lockup Expiration on Market Depth

Variable		All Firms (n=1,497)			Venture-Backed (n=570)			Non-Venture Backed (n=927)			P-value for difference in % change for venture vs. non-venture
		Before	After	% Change	Before	After	% Change	Before	After	% Change	
Quote Depth	*Mean*	796	867	22*	704	785	23*	844	918	21*	0.57
	(S.E.)	(19)	(19)	(2)	(15)	(16)	(2)	(28)	(29)	(2)	
	Median	745	792	4*	692	755	6*	762	808	3*	
	% Positive			57%			59%			56%	
Depth-to- Spread Ratio	*Mean*	704	810	27*	562	666	30*	794	898	26*	0.38
	(S.E.)	(26)	(30)	(2)	(18)	(24)	(3)	(40)	(48)	(3)	
	Median	510	556	10*	480	536	12*	534	582	9*	
	% Positive			60%			63%			58%	
Effective Spreads on Trades of 10,000 Shares or More	*Mean*	1.2	1.2	3.9	1.5	1.5	7.6	1.1	1.1	1.7	0.27
	(S.E.)	(0.1)	(0.1)	(2.5)	(0.1)	(0.1)	(4.6)	(0.1)	(0.1)	(2.9)	
	Median	1.0	1.0	-2.8	1.3	1.2	-0.9	0.9	0.9	-5.2	
	% Positive			46%			49%			45%	
Number of Daily Trades	*Mean*	59	73	32*	65	74	47*	55	72	23*	0.00
	(S.E.)	(5)	(9)	(3)	(8)	(7)	(5)	(7)	(14)	(3)	
	Median	22	24	8*	24	30	16*	20	20	-4	
	% Positive			52%			61%			48%	
Trade Size (Shares)	*Mean*	1,717	1,827	18*	1,708	1,982	28*	1,722	1,731	12*	0.00
	(S.E.)	(28)	(28)	(2)	(38)	(49)	(3)	(39)	(34)	(2)	
	Median	1,438	1,560	5*	1,493	1,690	10*	1,418	1,433	-0	
	% Positive			57%			68%			50%	
Daily Volume (Shares)	*Mean*	70,105	90,171	58*	72,160	99,644	86*	68,842	84,346	41*	0.00
	(S.E.)	(3,214)	(4,980)	(4)	(4,362)	(5,568)	(7)	(4,445)	(7,271)	(4)	
	Median	37,663	43,890	14*	42,373	61,495	41*	34,180	34,013	1	
	% Positive			57%			68%			50%	

* Indicates significance at the 5% level using two-tailed t-test (for mean) or signed rank test (for median).

Note: Summary statistics for market depth and trading activity during the 30-day periods before and after the IPO lockup expiration day. The "% Change" column is based on the distribution of percentage changes. Standard errors (S.E.) are in parentheses. Quote Depth is the average of the bid and ask depth. The Depth-to-Spread Ratio is (Bid Depth + Ask Depth) / (Relative Quoted Spread). The sample is 1,497 U.S. lockup expirations in the period April, 1995 through June, 1999. Reported statistics are based on the distributions of the 1,497 firm-level means and changes. Because of the scarcity of block trades, the sample size for the block trade spread results is only 263 firms, of which 98 are venture-financed.

Changes in Market Depth after Lockup Expirations

Trading costs depend not only on bid-ask spreads, but also on market depth, roughly defined as the ability to trade large numbers of shares without seriously affecting price. Market depth is typically measured by trading activity (number and size of trades), by quote depth (the number of shares that the market maker guarantees to transact without changing the price), and by the effective spreads on block trades of 10,000 shares or more. The total cost of trading is sometimes summarized by the depth-to-spread ratio, which is the quoted depth divided by the quoted spread (Bacidore (1997), Harris (2000)). Here we test for post-expiration changes in these measures of market depth.

Table 11 presents summary measures of the pre- to post-expiration changes in quote depth, depth-to-spread ratio, effective spreads on block trades, daily number of trades, and average trade size. Results are presented for the whole sample, as well as for the venture- and non-venture financed subsamples. Comparing the thirty day periods before and after lockup expiration, the mean change in quote depth is +22 percent (median = four percent), and the mean change in the depth-to-spread ratio is +27% (median = 10 percent). Thus, we find substantial increases in quote depth after lockup expirations. A daily time series of abnormal quote depth (presented later) reveals no evidence of short-term reductions.

The changes in the effective spreads on block trades (the third row of Table 11) have the same ambiguous sign as we observed previously for the spreads on all trade sizes. The mean change in the effective spread is positive, but the median change is negative. Both the mean and median change have small magnitude, less than four percent of the pre-expiration spread, and neither is statistically significant.

Consistent with the increase in total trading volume (row 6), both the number of daily trades (row 4) and the average trade size (row 5) increase significantly after lockup expirations, especially among venture-financed firms. On average, number of trades per day increases by 32%, and average trade size increases 18%. The median changes have the same sign but smaller magnitude, and all of the mean and median changes are significantly different from zero. The changes in trading activity in the venture-financed subsample are roughly double those in the non-venture financed subsample.

Overall, our results show that trading volume and quote depth deepen by 20% or more after lockup expiration. Net trading costs, as measured by the depth-to-spread ratio, decline sharply, but the effective spreads for block trades do not change very much. These results do not support the hypothesis that market depth is impaired by the presence of insider traders.

Tests for Hidden Liquidity Impairments

Our univariate tests reveal only a small and temporary increase in spreads, and a large and persistent increase in market depth. Thus, we find no large or persistent impairment of market liquidity after lockup expirations. One potential explanation for this result is that the liquidity consequences of increased information asymmetry are masked by other consequences of lockup expirations. Here we present several tests for liquidity impairment that might be masked by confounding effects, especially changes in share price, trading activity, and the number of tradable shares. The following subsections present, in turn, multivariate regression tests, spread decomposition tests, and tests for a subsample of firms in which the number of tradable shares does not increase because insiders do not sell.

Multivariate Regression Tests

Spreads and quote depth are functions of share price, trading activity, trade size, and volatility, all of which are likely to change when the lockup expires. Price changes, in particular, seem to be important in our sample. The relative spread is known to be a declining function of share price, due to minimum tick size and other factors (Harris (1994)). Since share prices tend to fall after lockup expiration, we also expect to observe some widening of the relative spread. Table 12 shows spread changes for subsamples based on whether the average share price rises or falls between the pre- and post-expiration periods. The results show that, if the share price falls after the lockup expiration, the relative effective spread tends to widen, by an average of 12 percent (median = six percent). If the share price rises after the lockup expiration, the relative effective spread tends to narrow, by an average of 10 percent (median = 12 percent). These effects are highly statistically significant, and price changes have substantial power to predict whether the spread will widen or narrow after the lockup expiration. For example, Table 12 shows that the relative effective spread narrows in 77 percent of the 701 firms whose price rises after the lockup expiration. In unreported tests, we find that the relative effective spread narrows in 90 percent of the 185 firms whose price rises more than twenty percent, and the relative effective spread widens in 77 percent of the 192 firms whose price drops more than 20 percent.

Table 12. Percent Changes in Spreads and Quote Depth by Post-Expiration Price Change

		Price Falls (n=796)	Price Rises (n=701)
Relative Effective Spread	*Mean*	12.2*	-10.1*
	(S.E.)	(1.1)	(0.7)
	Median	6.4*	-12.4*
	% Positive	62%	23%
Quote Depth	*Mean*	24.6*	17.8*
	(S.E.)	(2.6)	(2.0)
	Median	6.0*	1.8*
	% Positive	60%	55%

* Indicates significance at the 5% level using two-tailed t-test (for mean) or signed rank test (for median)

Note: Reported statistics are based on the distribution of percentage changes between the pre- and post-expiration windows, [-30,-1] and [+1,+30]. "Price Falls" and "Price Rises" are based on the average share price over the pre- and post-expiration windows. The relative effective spread is calculated as $(2\times| Pt–Mt |) / Mt$, where Pt is the transaction price at time t and Mt is the midpoint of the bid and ask quotes in effect at time t. Quote depth is the average of the bid and ask depth, the number of shares the market maker guarantees to transact at the quoted price. Standard errors (S.E.) are in parentheses. The sample is 1,497 U.S. lockup expirations in the period April, 1995 through June, 1999. Intraday data are from the TAQ database.

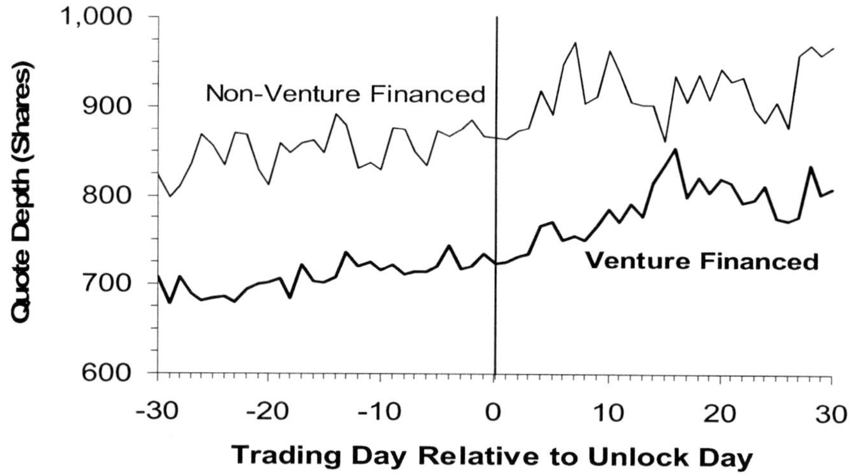

Figure 3. Average quote depth around the lockup expiration.
Quote depth is the average of the bid-side and ask-side depth, which are the minimum number of shares that the market maker guarantees to transact at the quoted price. The sample is 1,497 U.S. lockup expirations in the period April, 1995 through June, 1999. Data are from TAQ.

To test for abnormal changes in spreads and quote depth, we estimate regression models of the relative effective spread and quote depth as functions of share price, volatility, and trading activity. The sample for this test includes two observations per firm: one observation for the pre-expiration period and another for the post-expiration period. A dummy variable indicates whether the observation occurs in the pre- or post-expiration period, and the coefficient on this dummy is our primary test statistic. The dependent variables are the thirty-day means of either the relative effective spread or quote depth, as presented in the earlier tables. The explanatory variables are volatility and the thirty day means of closing share prices, daily number of trades, daily average trade size, and daily volume. We measure volatility by the standard deviation of the thirty daily returns, calculated from closing midpoints. Formally, we estimate models of the form:

$$\begin{pmatrix} Y[-30,-1]_{i=1} \\ \vdots \\ \vdots \\ Y[-30,-1]_{i=1,497} \\ \hline Y[+1,+30]_{i=1} \\ \vdots \\ \vdots \\ Y[+1,+30]_{i=1,497} \end{pmatrix} = \alpha + \beta_1 \begin{pmatrix} 0 \\ \vdots \\ \vdots \\ 0 \\ 1 \\ \vdots \\ \vdots \\ 1 \end{pmatrix} + \beta_2 \cdot Price + \beta_3 \cdot Volatility + \beta_4 \cdot Trade\,Activity + \varepsilon \quad (5)$$

where *i* indexes the 1,497 firms in the sample, *Y* is the thirty-day mean of either the relative effective spread or the quote depth (average of the bid depth and the ask depth) as presented in the earlier tables, and "Trade Activity" is either total volume, or number of trades and average trade size. In the spread model we control for the reciprocal of price, rather than price, as the dependent variable has price in its denominator.

Table 6 presents the coefficient estimates. The coefficients on the control variables are sensible and in most cases highly significant. The relative effective spread is negatively related to share price, daily volume, and daily number of trades, and is positively related to volatility and average trade size. Quote depth is negatively related to share price and volatility, and is positively related to daily volume, daily number of trades, and average trade size. Our primary test statistic is the dummy coefficient, β_1, which indicates whether the post-expiration period experiences a change in spreads or quote depth that is not explained by changes in the other variables. In the spreads model, the bulk of the explanatory power (39 percent of a maximum 43 percent) comes from the control for price changes, and the coefficient on the post-expiration dummy variable is not statistically significant in any specification. In the quote depth model, the dummy coefficient has positive sign and is always statistically significant. Thus we find no evidence for abnormal changes in spreads after controlling for price changes, but we do find significant increases in quote depth that are not explained by the concurrent changes in price, volatility, or trading activity. These results give no indication of abnormal liquidity impairment that might be attributed to asymmetric information.

Table 13. Regression Analysis of Relative Effective Spreads and Quote Depth

Model:	1	2	3	4
Panel A: Dependent Variable is Relative Effective Spread (in percentage points)				
Intercept [t-stat]	1.5 [34.5]	2.1 [31.9]	1.6 [28.2]	1.3 [17.7]
Dummy for post-expiration period	-0.05 [-0.9]	0.09 [1.5]	0.01 [0.1]	-0.05 [-0.9]
1 / Price	11.5 [44.4]		10.7 [40.0]	11.1 [40.9]
Volatility		20.6 [15.0]	5.7 [4.9]	4.3 [3.6]
Volume (in 100,000)		-0.4 [-18.5]	-0.2 [-13.7]	
Number of daily trades (in 1,000)				-0.7 [-7.4]
Trade size (in 10,000)				1.1 [5.2]
Adjusted R^2	0.39	0.13	0.43	0.41
Panel B: Dependent Variable is Quote Depth (average of bid and ask depth, in 100's)				
Intercept	8.4 [34.8]	8.3 [32.6]	9.8 [31.7]	8.2 [20.0]
Dummy for post-expiration period	0.71 [2.9]	0.53 [2.2]	0.46 [2.0]	0.60 [2.4]
Price	-0.03 [2.62]		-0.09 [-8.3]	-0.05 [-4.2]
Volatility		-26.1 [4.9]	-32.2 [-6.1]	-13.5 [-2.4]
Volume (in 100,000)		8.6 [11.0]	11.8 [13.6]	
Number of daily trades (in 1,000)				2.3 [3.9]
Trade size (in 10,000)				5.8 [5.7]
Adjusted R^2	0.01	0.04	0.06	0.02

Note: This table reports coefficient estimates from a cross sectional OLS model of the effective spread or quote depth, as a function of share price, trading volume, and volatility. The dependant variable is the mean relative effective spread or mean quote depth, as defined in the text. Price is the mean of the thirty closing midpoints. Volume is the mean of the thirty daily trading volumes. Number of Daily Trades and Average Trade Size are the means of the thirty daily averages; Volatility is the standard deviation of the thirty daily returns, computed from the closing midpoint. The sample contains two observations per firm; one observation for the pre-expiration period [-30,-1], and another for the post-expiration period [1,30], with a dummy variable taking a value of 1 in the post-expiration period. *T* statistics are given in brackets. The sample has 2,994 observations, corresponding to 1,497 U.S. lockup expirations in the period April, 1995 through June, 1999.

Changes in the Asymmetric Information Component of the Spread

Bid-ask spreads are thought to be composed of two elements: the "asymmetric information" component, which compensates the market maker for expected losses to informed traders, and the remainder or "fixed cost" component, which compensates the market maker for the other costs of making a market. The fixed cost component of the spread may fall after lockup expiration, as the increase in trading activity will allow the market maker to amortize his fixed costs over a larger number of trades. This effect should have been captured in our multivariate regression model, but as an additional test we apply a standard decomposition of the spread into an asymmetric information component, θ, and a fixed-cost component, ϕ, using the decomposition model described in Madhaven, Richardson and Roomans (1997). Formally, intraday price changes are assumed to follow:

$$p_t - p_{t-1} = a + \theta x_t - \varphi x_{t-1} + \varepsilon_t + \xi_t + \xi_{t-1} \quad (6)$$

where p_t is the share price at time t, and x_t is a trade-direction indicator that takes a value of 1 if the trade is buyer-initiated, -1 if the trade is seller-initiated, and 0 if the trade is a cross. The indicator variable is obtained using the inference procedure suggested by Lee and Ready (1991).[1] The term ε reflects the innovations in beliefs about share value, and ξ reflects errors caused by price discreteness. For each firm, parameter estimates are obtained from the pooled intraday price changes from all the days in the event window, excluding the price changes from the close to the subsequent open. For a detailed description of this decomposition, and of our GMM estimation procedure, see Madhaven, Richardson and Roomans (1997).

Table 14 summarizes the GMM parameter estimates for the thirty day periods before and after lockup expiration. The table presents the cross-sectional means and standard errors of the firm-level parameter estimates θ and ϕ for the pre- and post-expiration periods. Also presented are the implied total round trip trading cost, 2(θ+ϕ), and the proportion of trading costs due to asymmetric information. The coefficients are reasonable in the sense that they are similar to those reported elsewhere, e.g., in Glosten and Harris (1988) and Madhaven, Richardson and Roomans (1997). The main result is that the asymmetric information component, θ, does not change after the lockup expires. In the post-expiration period, the mean value of θ is 2.41 cents per share, virtually identical to the 2.40 cents in the pre-expiration period. The difference is not statistically significant. The fixed cost component, ϕ, declines from 12.03 cents to 11.57 cents, a statistically insignificant reduction of 0.46 cents per share. Thus, we find no increase in the asymmetric information component that could be

1 The trade is assumed to be seller initiated if the price is below the spread midpoint, buyer-initiated if the price is above the midpoint, and a cross if the trade is at the midpoint. Ellis, Michaely, and O'Hara (2000b) find that this procedure works well for Nasdaq stocks. We also try an alternative inference procedure suggested by Ellis *et al*, and find qualitatively similar results.

attributed to the presence of insider traders, though we do find the decline in the fixed cost component that one would expect, given the observed increase in trading activity.

The time series of abnormal effective spreads (see Table 9) suggests that the short-term effects of the lockup expiration are larger than the long-term effects. To test whether there is a significant short-term increase in asymmetric information costs, we also estimate the model in the period [+1,+10]. The results, reported in Table 14, show a slightly increased asymmetric information component and slightly reduced fixed-cost component, consistent with the changes one would predict from simultaneous increases in insider trading and total trading volume. However, once again the change in the asymmetric information components between the pre- and post-expiration periods has small magnitude and is not statistically significant.

Table 14. GMM Estimates of the Spread Components

	Period 1: [-30, -1]	Period 2: [1, 30]	Period 3: [1, 10]
θ = Asymmetric information cost per share (cents)	2.40 (0.04)	2.41 (0.07)	2.45 (0.05)
ϕ = Fixed cost per share (cents)	12.0 (0.2)	11.6 (0.2)	11.4 (0.2)
Implied Spread (cents)	28.9 (0.4)	28.0 (0.5)	27.6 (0.5)
Proportion of asymmetric information cost (%)	21.7 (0.5)	21.7 (0.5)	22.6 (0.5)

Note: This table reports cross-sectional averages of the estimated parameters of the Modhavan, Richardson and Roomans (1997) model. θ is the asymmetric information cost per share, ϕ is the fixed cost per share. The implied spread is the difference between implied bid and ask prices and is given by $2(\phi+\theta)$. $\theta/(\phi+\theta)$ is the proportion of asymmetric information cost relative to the implied spread. Standard errors are given in parentheses; all coefficients are statistically significant. The sample is 1,497 U.S. lockup expirations in the period April, 1995 through June, 1999. Day zero is the lockup expiration day.

Results in a Subsample of Firms where the Tradable Float does not Increase

The lockup expiration marks not only the arrival of new insider traders, but also the arrival of their newly-tradable shares. Any shares sold by insiders will increase the publicly tradable float, and the subsequent re-trading of these new shares could create long-term liquidity benefits that obscure the long-term costs of increased asymmetric information. Such effects should have been captured by the controls for trading activity in our multivariate model, or by our spread decomposition model, but as a robustness check we replicate our tests in a subsample where there is little or no increase in the number of tradable shares because insiders do not sell. We reason that the hypothesized liquidity impairment is caused not by actual insider sales (which are largely unobservable until after the fact) but rather by the ex ante possibility that insiders *might* sell. However, any liquidity improvements due to an increase in the number of tradable shares will be caused only by actual insider sales. Thus, if we examine a subsample with no insider selling, we should observe the costs of *potential* insider selling, unobscured by any benefits from *actual* insider selling.

Unfortunately, SEC insider trade disclosures are not reliable enough to yield a convincing determination that no insider selling occurred in a particular period, so we must use a less efficient method. We compare the share ownership disclosed in the IPO prospectus with that disclosed in the first proxy statement after the lockup expiration. When the two documents indicate no reduction in the holdings of the pre-IPO shareholders, we conclude that no significant insider sales occurred in our event window.

A weakness of this test is that the prospectus and the proxy do not itemize all shareholdings, only those of officers, directors, and five percent blockholders. On average we are able to account for 84% of the total locked-up shares (median=93%), but we cannot be certain that some or all of the remaining shares are not sold after the lockup expiration.[2] Since this test is very labor intensive, we limit our attention to a relatively small subsample. We restrict the sample to the firms whose IPOs occurred after May, 1996, the first date for which we can obtain prospectus data. We sort the sample by the year of the IPO, and then randomly select 25 percent of the firms in each year. This yields a subsample of 246 firms, of which we could obtain usable data for 216. (Our selection criteria is based on the year of the IPO, rather than the year of lockup expiration, so the sample size that is slightly smaller than one would infer from the year-by-year sample sizes in in Table 1.)

We find that, in 113 firms (52%), pre-IPO shareholders did not sell any of their shares, and in another 15 firms (7 percent), their share sales amounted to less than 0.5 percent of the shares outstanding. Thus, in 128 firms (59 percent) insiders hang on to virtually all of their shares until at least the first proxy date after the expiration window, typically about a year after the IPO. We find it somewhat surprising that only 41 percent of firms report substantial insider sales, though this result is consistent with Field and Hanka's (2001) finding that 17 percent of firms disclose insider share sales immediately after the lockup expiration.

Table 15 presents the pre- to post-expiration changes in several measures of the market depth and bid-ask spreads for the subsample of 128 firms in which we found little or no insider sales. Despite the relatively small sample, the statistical power of the tests is sufficient to reach some order-of-magnitude conclusions. The pre- to post-expiration changes in bid-ask spreads show the same ambiguous pattern that was observed in the full sample, with positive mean but negative median. The changes in quote depth have substantially positive mean and median, roughly similar to the quote depth increases we observe in the whole sample. For all the measures of trading activity, the mean change is positive but the median change is small or negative, indicating that changes in trading activity are skewed.

Overall these results indicate that, compared with our broader sample, firms with little or no insider selling experience roughly the same post-expiration changes in spreads and depth as we observe in the broader sample. These results confirm that the conclusions we draw from the broader sample are not driven by the increase in the tradable float due to insider sales.

---

2 It is conceivable that our method will miss an increase in the public float due to incentive shares that are received by insiders after the IPO and then sold at lockup expiration. However, such an event would be unusual. Incentive shares typically do not vest for at least a year (thus post-IPO incentive shares usually cannot be sold at lockup expiration) and we know of no reason for insiders to time their sale of such shares to coincide with the lockup expiration.

Table 15. Percent Changes in Spreads and Market Depth for Firms with no Insider Sales

		% change
Relative Effective Spread	*Mean*	4.2
	(S.E.)	(2.6)
	Median	-1.9
	% Positive	47%
Quote Depth	*Mean*	31.1*
	(S.E.)	(6.6)
	Median	15.6*
	% Positive	69%
Number of Daily Trades	*Mean*	11.4
	(S.E.)	(6.7)
	Median	-6.4
	% Positive	44%
Trade Size (Shares)	*Mean*	13.7
	(S.E.)	(7.5)
	Median	2.6
	% Positive	52%
Daily Share Volume	*Mean*	29.4*
	(S.E.)	(10.4)
	Median	-2.7
	% Positive	46%

* Indicates significance at the 5% level using t-test (for mean) or signed rank test (for median).

Note: Percentage changes in spreads, quote depth, and trading activity between the 30-day periods before and after the IPO lockup expiration day. Reported statistics are based on the distribution of firm-level percentage changes. Quote depth is the average of bid-side and ask-side depth. The sample is 128 U.S. firms in which insiders retained more than 99.5% of their shares until at least the first proxy date after the expiration event window. Data are from TAQ.

Tests for more Subtle Evidence of Asymmetric Information Costs

Our tests have revealed that lockup expirations produce only small and temporary changes in spreads, and no reduction of market depth. The temporary increase in spreads may be caused by temporarily increased information asymmetry, but also has plausible alternative explanations. For example, if insiders are particularly eager to sell, then market makers may temporarily widen the spread as compensation for the effort of locating additional buyers, or for taking more shares into their own inventory, or because the demand for their services is temporarily less price-elastic. To search for persuasive evidence of an increase in asymmetric information costs, here we present tests for several "signatures" of asymmetric information. The following tests search for evidence of asymmetric information in the differences between bid-side and ask-side quote depth, in the cross-sectional relation between spread changes and trade size, and in the cross-sectional relation between spread changes and pre-expiration trading activity.

Asymmetry in the Changes in Bid-side and Ask-side Quote Depth

Lockups prevent insider share sales, but not insider purchases. Consequently, the expiration of the lockup will increase the probability that any given share seller is an informed insider, but should not have a large effect on the probability that a share buyer is an informed insider. Market makers who are concerned about trading against insiders should, ceteris paribus, reduce their bid-side quote depth after the lockup expiration, but will not necessarily reduce their ask-side depth. Thus, we predict an asymmetric change in quote depth after the lockup expiration, with the bid-side depth declining more (or increasing less) than the ask-side depth.

Table 16. Daily Abnormal Bid and Ask Quote Depth

Day	Abnormal Ask Size	t-stat	Abnormal Bid Size	t-stat
-10	2.0	[1.7]	0.0	[0.01]
-9	7.2*	[4.5]	2.3	[1.8]
-8	3.9*	[3.0]	1.0	[0.8]
-7	2.4	[1.8]	-0.1	[-0.1]
-6	2.1	[1.6]	1.7	[1.3]
-5	7.1*	[3.6]	5.8*	[3.6]
-4	9.4*	[4.5]	7.9*	[4.9]
-3	8.2*	[4.0]	7.0*	[4.2]
-2	7.7*	[4.1]	6.7*	[4.0]
-1	8.9*	[3.5]	8.9*	[3.6]
0	7.7*	[4.7]	8.5*	[4.2]
1	8.1*	[4.5]	10.7*	[5.3]
2	10.8*	[5.8]	13.4*	[6.3]
3	13.4*	[6.0]	14.9*	[4.1]
4	17.8*	[6.4]	15.4*	[5.8]
5	17.9*	[8.3]	18.1*	[4.4]
6	18.4*	[8.0]	21.7*	[5.2]
7	19.6*	[7.0]	27.8*	[2.8]
8	17.2*	[6.5]	24.9*	[2.6]
9	19.0*	[8.5]	18.4*	[6.0]
10	27.6*	[8.4]	18.6*	[7.68]

* Indicates significance at the 5% level (two-tailed test).

Note: Tabulated values represent the deviation from the mean for the period [-30,-6]. Formally, on day T, the tabulated value is calculated as:

$$\left(\frac{x_T}{\frac{1}{25}\sum_{i=-30}^{-6} x_i} - 1 \right) 100\%$$

where x is the market depth measure listed in the column headings, and day zero is the lockup expiration. The sample is 1,497 U.S. lockup expirations in the period April, 1995 through June, 1999.

Table 16 presents the daily time series of abnormal bid-side and ask-side quote depth. The tabulated values represent the percentage deviation from the mean in the pre-expiration period [-30,-6]. The results show steadily increasing quote depth, beginning a week before the lockup expiration and continuing throughout the event window. The results show no evidence that bid-side depth declines relative to ask-side depth. In fact, in the days immediately around the lockup expirations, the abnormal bid depth is actually larger than the abnormal ask depth. Of the eight days in the period [-2,+5], only two show larger abnormal ask depth, while five show larger abnormal bid depth.

Table 17 tests for longer term effects by presenting summary measures of the percentage changes in bid-side and ask-side quote depth between the thirty day periods before and after the lockup expiration. Again, the results do not show the predicted asymmetry. The mean changes in bid-side and ask-side depth are nearly identical, at 21 and 22 percent, respectively. The difference is not statistically significant. The median changes are the same, at four percent, and the percent positive changes are similar, at 57 and 58 percent, respectively.

Table 17. Test for Persistent Asymmetric Changes in Bid and Ask Quote Depth

		Before	After	% Change
Ask-Side Quote Depth	*Mean*	795	875	22*
	(S.E.)	(15)	(17)	(2)
	Median	742	799	4*
	% Positive			57%
Bid-Side Quote Depth	*Mean*	797	859	21*
	(S.E.)	(23)	(21)	(2)
	Median	749	785	4*
	% Positive			58%

% level using two-tailed t-test (for mean) or signed rank test (for median).

Note: Summary statistics for percentage changes in bid and ask quote depth between the 30-day periods before and after the IPO lockup expiration day. Quote depth is the number of shares the market maker guarantees to transact at the bid or ask price. The sample is 1,497 U.S. lockup expirations in the period April, 1995 through June, 1999. Reported statistics are based on the distributions of the 1,497 firm-level means and changes.

Thus, we do not find the asymmetry between bid-side and ask-side depth changes that we would expect if quote depth is a declining function of the probability of trading against an insider. If anything, the short-term changes in quote depth seem to imply the reverse.

The Relation between Spread Changes and Trade Size

Asymmetric information may be a bigger problem for some trades than for others. We hypothesize that informed traders will want to trade enough shares to make a meaningful profit, but will not trade in such large blocks as to call attention to themselves. Consistent with this hypothesis, Barclay and Warner (1993) find that most price movements are driven by medium sized trades. Thus we predict that, if spread increases after lockup expiration are driven by asymmetric information, then spread increases should be largest for medium-sized trades, perhaps in the range from 1,000-10,000 shares.

Table 18 shows pre- to post-expiration changes in relative effective spreads for various classes of trade size. The results are not as predicted, as the spreads on medium-sized trades (1,000-5,000 shares or 5,000-10,000 shares) actually decline relative to those on smaller or larger trades. The most pronounced difference is a median eight percent decline in the spreads on trades of 5,000-10,000 shares. Thus, the relation between trade size and spread changes does not support the hypothesis that asymmetric information widens the bid-ask spread after lockup expirations.

Table 18. Changes in the Relative Effective Spreads by Trade-Size Category

Trade Size		Before	After	% Change
100-500 *(shares)*	*Mean*	2.8%	2.8%	2.1%*
	(S.E.)	(0.1)	(0.1)	(0.8)
	Median	2.5	2.4	-2.7
	% Positive			45%
501-1,000	*Mean*	2.5	2.5	2.4*
	(S.E.)	(0.1)	(0.1)	(0.1)
	Median	2.1	2.0	-2.9
	% Positive			46%
1,001-5,000	*Mean*	2.4	2.4	2.1*
	(S.E.)	(0.1)	(0.1)	(0.8)
	Median	2.0	2.0	-3.5
	% Positive			46%
5,001-10,000	*Mean*	1.6	1.5	1.7
	(S.E.)	(0.1)	(0.1)	(1.6)
	Median	1.3	1.2	-7.9*
	% Positive			41%
> 10,000	*Mean*	1.3	1.2	3.9
	(S.E.)	(0.1)	(0.1)	(2.5)
	Median	1.0	1.0	-2.8
	% Positive			46%

* Indicates significance at the 5% level, using two-tailed t-test (for mean) or signed rank test (for median).

Note: The relative effective spread is calculated as (2×| Pt–Mt |) / Mt, where Pt is the transaction price at time t and Mt is the midpoint of the bid and ask quotes in effect at time t. The "% Change" column is based on the distribution of percentage changes. Standard errors (S.E.) are in parentheses. The sample is 1,497 U.S. lockup expirations in the period April, 1995 through June, 1999. Reported statistics are based on the distribution of the firm-level means and changes.

The Relation between Spread Changes and Trading Activity

Expected asymmetric information costs should be an increasing function of the probability of trading against an insider, which depends in turn on the volume of trading by outsiders. This implies that the firms with lower trading volume before the lockup expiration should tend to experience larger spread increases after the lockup expiration, since they will tend to experience larger increases in the probability of trading against an insider. A weakness of this test is that the same prediction follows from some of the alternative hypotheses. For example, we expect the same effect if spread changes are driven by the effort required to locate buyers for the insiders' shares, or by a reduction in the price-elasticity of demand for trades, since the arrival of a large block of insider sellers will have a relatively larger effect in a thin market.

Table 19 shows changes in relative effective spreads as a function of pre-expiration trading activity. The sample is partitioned into three equal size subsamples based on the respective average daily number of trades in the [-30,-1] window. The results are as predicted, showing a strong negative relation between pre-expiration trade activity and post-expiration spread changes. The mean change in the spread is +4.5 percent for firms in the lowest third of pre-expiration trading activity, +2.1 percent for firms in the middle third of trade activity, and -0.8 percent for firms in the highest third of trading activity. The corresponding median spread changes are -0.9 percent, -3.0 percent, and -3.2 percent. The differences between the various trade activity categories are statistically significant. The same pattern is observed in the venture-financed and non-venture financed subsamples, though the pattern is somewhat more pronounced among the venture-financed firms (results not reported).

Overall, of the three signs of increased information asymmetry that we test for, we find only one, a negative relation between spread changes and pre-expiration trading activity. We do not find the predicted asymmetry between bid-side and ask-side depth changes, nor do we find the predicted inverted-U shaped relation between trade size and effective spread changes.

Table 19. Changes in Relative Effective Spreads by Pre-Expiration Trading Frequency

	N Trades < 14 499 firms	**14 ≤ N Trades < 35 499 firms**	**N Trades ≥ 35 499 firms**
Mean	4.5*	2.1	-0.8
(S. E.)	(1.3)	(1.3)	(1.2)
Median	-0.91	-3.0*	-3.2*
% Positive	48%	44%	43%

* Indicates significance at the 5% level using two-tailed t-test (for mean) or signed rank test (for median).

Note: Summary measures of the percentage changes in the relative effective spread from [-30,-1] to [1,30]. (Day 0 is the lockup expiration.) Firms are partitioned into three equal-sized groups based on average daily number of trades in the period [-30,-1]. Reported statistics are based on the distribution of firm-level percentage changes. Standard errors (S.E.) are in parentheses. The sample is 1,497 U.S. lockup expirations in the period April, 1995 through June, 1999.

CONCLUSIONS

We examine liquidity changes around the expirations of 1,497 IPO lockup agreements in the period 1995-1999. These events mark the sudden release of a near-total prohibition on insider selling, and represent the first occasion in which an extremely well informed group of insiders – the founders and early investors in a firm – can profit from their inside knowledge by selling their shares without first revealing their intention to do so. Since lockup expirations typically occur in high-growth firms with a limited public history, the information asymmetry between insiders and outsiders is potentially severe. Furthermore, in the period immediately after the lockup expiration it will be uniquely difficult to detect and prosecute insider selling on the basis of material non-public information, as information-motivated insider traders can hide amongst the liquidity-motivated insider traders.

Empirically, lockup expirations represent a material change in market conditions, as evidenced by a permanent 40-60 percent increase in average trading volume. Consistent with the assumptions of asymmetric information models, lockup expirations are also followed by significant abnormal price changes that are correlated with insider share sales. Consequently, standard microstructure models predict a decline in market liquidity, as market makers widen the spread and reduce their quote depth in order to protect themselves against the adverse price changes associated with insider trades. Consistent with this prediction, when we compare the periods before and after lockup expirations we find a statistically significant increase in the effective bid-ask spread. However, the magnitude and duration of this effect are small. Relative effective spreads widen by 3-4 percent, or about 0.12 percent of share price, for about a week. Any longer-term changes in spreads are small, however, and seem to be driven primarily by changes in share price. Meanwhile, we observe a 20 percent increase in quote depth that is not explained by the concurrent changes in price, volatility, or trading activity. More detailed tests reveal no increase in the adverse selection component of the spread, and no evidence of increased asymmetric information costs that are masked by the benefits of increased trading volume.

The simplest interpretation of this result is that expected losses to insider traders are small relative to the other costs of making a market, and hence have little effect on spreads and quote depth. A practical implication of this result is that liquidity probably cannot be improved by strengthening the current legal restrictions on insider trading, or by supplementing them with self-imposed constraints. More broadly, since our sample includes a class of insiders that one would expect to be exceptionally well informed, in young firms with potentially severe information asymmetry, and in a time period when insider trades are clearly moving share prices, the fact that we observe no material liquidity impairment casts doubt on the hypothesis that liquidity is substantially affected by information asymmetry.

Future research might further investigate the impact of insider trading on market liquidity. Under current laws, the insiders in our sample are free to trade on the basis of their general opinions about the firm's quality and prospects, but they may be reluctant to trade on the basis of their specific knowledge of impending events that might trigger large price changes and subsequent SEC investigation (Muelbroek (1992)). Future research could test whether this distinction is important, by examining the liquidity changes around lockup expirations or other significant events in countries and time periods in which insider trading is not regulated.

REFERENCES

Aggarwal, Reena, 2000, Stabilization activities by underwriters after initial public offerings, *Journal of Finance* 55, 1075-1103.

Allen, Franklin and Douglas Gale, 1992, Stock Price Manipulation, *Review of Financial Studies* 5, 503-529.

Bacidore, Jeffrey, 1997, The impact of decimalization on market quality: An empirical Investigation of the Toronto Stock Exchange, *Journal of Financial Intermediation* 6, 92-190.

Baesel, Jerome, and Garry Stein, 1979, The Value of Information: Inferences from the Profitability of Insider Trading, *Journal of Financial and Quantitative Analysis* 14, 553-571.

Bagnoli, Mark, and Naveen Khanna, 1992, Insider Trading in Financial Signaling Models, *Journal of Finance* 47, 1905-1934.

Baiman, Stanley and Robert Verrecchia, 1996, The relation among capital markets, financial disclosure, production efficiency, and insider trading, *Journal of Accounting Research* 34, 1-22.

Barclay, Michael and Jerold Warner, 1993, Stealth trading and volatility: Which trades move prices?, *Journal of Financial Economics* 34, 281-305.

Bebchuk, Lucian Arye and Christine Jolls, 1999, Managerial Value Diversion and Shareholder Wealth, *Journal of Law, Economics, and Organization* 15, 487-502.

Bebchuk, Lucian Arye, and Chaim Fershtman, 1994, Insider Trading and the Managerial Choice among Risky Projects, *Journal of Financial and Quantitative Analysis* 29, 1-14.

Bernhardt, Dan, Burton Hollifield, and Eric Hughson, 1995, Investment and Insider Trading, *Review of Financial Studies* 8, 501-543.

Bettis, J. Carr, Jeffrey Coles, and Michael Lemmon, 2000, Corporate policies restricting trading by insiders, *Journal of Financial Economics* 57, 191-220.

Bettis, J. Carr, John M. Bizjak, and Michael L. Lemmon, 1999, *Insider trading in derivative securities: An empirical examination of the use of zero-cost collars and equity swaps by corporate investors*, unpublished working paper, Arizona State University.

Bradley, Daniel, Bradford Jordan, Ivan Roten, and Ha-Chin Yi, 2001, Venture capital and IPO lockup expiration: An empirical analysis, forthcoming in *Journal of Financial Research*.

Brav, Alon and Paul Gompers, 2000, *Insider trading subsequent to initial public offerings: Evidence from expirations of lock-up provisions*, working paper, Harvard University.

Copeland, Thomas, and Dan Galai, 1983, Information effects on the bid/ask spread, *Journal of Finance* 38, 1457-1469.

Cornell, Bradford, and Erik Sirri, 1992, The Reaction of Investors and Stock Prices to Insider Trading, *Journal of Finance* 47, 1031-1059.

Damodaran, Aswath, and Crocker Liu, 1993, Insider Trading as a Signal of Private Information, *Review of Financial Studies* 6, 79-119.

Eckbo, Espen, and David Smith, 2000, The Conditional Performance of Insider Trades, *Journal of Finance* 53, 467-498.

Elliot, John, Dale Morse, and Gordon Richardson, 1984, The Association between Insider Trading and Information Announcements, *Rand Journal of Economics* 15, 521-536.

Ellis, Katrina, Roni Michaely, and Maureen O'Hara, 2000a, When the underwriter is the market maker: An examination of trading in the IPO aftermarket, *Journal of Finance* 55, 1039-1074.

Ellis, Katrina, Roni Michaely, and Maureen O'Hara, 2000b, *The accuracy of trade classification rules: Evidence from Nasdaq*, working paper, Cornell University.

Field, Laura Casares and Gordon Hanka, 2001, The Expiration of IPO Share Lockups, forthcoming in the *Journal of Finance*

Finnerty, Joseph, 1976, Insiders and Market Efficiency, *Journal of Finance* 21, pages 1141-1148.

Fishman, Michael, and Kathleen Hagerty, 1992, Insider Trading and the Efficiency of Stock Prices, *Rand Journal of Economics* 23, 106-122.

Givoly, Dan, and Dan Palmon, 1985, Insider Trading and the Exploitation of Inside Information: Some Empirical Evidence, *Journal of Business*; 58, 69-87.

Glosten, Lawrence and Paul Milgrom, 1985, Bid, ask and transaction prices in a specialist market with heterogeneously informed traders, *Journal of Financial Economics* 14, 71-100.

Glosten, Lawrence, and Lawrence Harris, 1988, Estimating the components of the bid/ask spread, *Journal of Financial Economics* 21, 123-142.

Halpern, Paul, 1974, Empirical Estimates of the Amount and Distribution of Gains to Companies in Mergers, *Journal of Business* 47, 410-428.

Harris, Lawrence, 1994, Minimum price variations, discrete bid-ask spreads, and quotation sizes, *Review of Financial Studies* 7, 149-178.

Harris, Lawrence, 2001, *Does a large minimum price variation encourage order exposure?* Working paper, University of Southern California.

Hirschey, Mark, and Janis K.Zaima, 1989, Insider Trading, Ownership Structure, and the Market Assessment of Corporate Sell Offs, *Journal of Finance* 44, 971-980.

Hirshleifer, Jack, 1974, The Private and Social Value of Information and the Reward to Inventive Activity, *American Economic Review* 61, 561-574.

Jaffe, Jeffrey, 1974, Special Information and Insider Trading, *Journal of Business* 47, 410-428.

John, Kose, and Larry Lang, 1991, Insider Trading around Dividend Announcements: Theory and Evidence, *Journal of Finance* 46, 1361-89.

Keown, Arthur, and John Pinkerton, 1981, Merger Announcements and Insider Trading Activity: An Empirical Investigation, *Journal of Finance* 36, 855-869.

Kyle, Albert, 1985, Continuous auctions and insider trading, *Econometrica* 53, 1315-1335.

Lakonishok, Josef, and Inmoo Lee, 2001, Are insiders' trades informative? Forthcoming in the *Review of Financial Studies*.

Lee, Charles, and Mark Ready, 1991, Inferring Trade Direction from Intraday Data, *Journal of Finance* 46, 733-746.

Lee, Charles, Belinda Mucklow, and Mark Ready, 1993, Spreads, depths, and the impact of earnings information: An intraday analysis, *Review of Financial Studies* 6, 345-374.

Leland, Hayne, 1992, Insider Trading: Should It Be Prohibited?, *Journal of Political Economy* 100, 859-87.

Lin, Ji Chai and John Howe, 1990, Insider Trading in the OTC Market, *Journal of Finance* 45, 1273-1284.

Madhavan, Ananth, Mathew Richardson, and Matthew Roomans, 1997, Why Do Security Prices Change? A Transaction-Level Analysis of NYSE Stocks, *Review of Financial Studies* 10, 1035-64.

Mandelker, G., 1974, Risk and Return: The Case of Merging Firms, *Journal of Financial Economics* 1, 303-335.

Manne, H.G., 1966, *Insider Trading and the Stock Market*. New York (1966).

Manove, Michael, 1989, The Harm from Insider Trading and Informed Speculation, *Quarterly Journal of Economics* 104, 823-845.

Meulbroek, Lisa, 1992, An Empirical Analysis of Illegal Insider Trading, *Journal of Finance* 47, 1661-1699.

Meulbroek, Lisa, 2001, *Does risk matter? Corporate insider transactions in internet-based firms,* Working paper, Harvard University.

Michaely, Roni and Kent Wolmack, 1999, Conflict of interest and the credibility of underwriter analyst recommendations, *Review of Financial Studies* 12, 653-686.

Noe, Christopher, 1999, Voluntary Disclosures and Insider Transactions, *Journal of Accounting and Economics* 27, 305-326

Noe, Thomas, 1997, Insider Trading and the Problem of Corporate Agency, *Journal of Law, Economics, and Organization* 13, 287-318.

Ofek, Eli and Matthew Richardson, 2001, *The IPO lock-up period: Implications for market efficiency and downward sloping demand curves*, Working paper, New York University.

Penman, Stephen, 1982, Insider Trading and the Dissemination of Firms' Forecast Information, *Journal of Business* 55, 479-503.

Penman, Stephen, 1985, A Comparison of the Information Content of Insider Trading and Management Earnings Forecasts, *Journal of Financial and Quantitative Analysis* 20, 1-17.

Seyhun, Nejat, 1988, The Information Content of Aggregate Insider Trading, *Journal of Business* 61, 1-24.

Seyhun, Nejat, 1992, Why Does Aggregate Insider Trading Predict Future Stock Returns? *Quarterly Journal of Economics* 107, 1303-1331.

Seyhun, Nejat, and Michael Bradley, 1997, Corporate Bankruptcy and Insider Trading, *Journal of Business* 70, 189-216.

Utpal, Bhattacharya, and Hazem Daouk, 2001, The World Price of Insider Trading", Forthcoming in *The Journal of Finance*

Venkatesh, P. and R. Chiang, 1986, Information asymmetry and the dealer's bid-ask spread: A case study of earnings and dividend announcements, *Journal of Finance* 41, 1089-1102.

In: Stock Exchanges, IPO's and Mutual Funds
Editor: E. Klein, pp. 129-149
ISBN 1-59454-173-6

Chapter 7

FUNDS OF HEDGE FUNDS OR INVESTIBLE HEDGE FUNDS INDICES: WHICH IS THE BEST INVESTMENT TOOL?

Daniel Capocci*
Department of Management, University of Liège, Belgium
David Capocci
Management School, the University of Edinburgh, Ireland

ABSTRACT

Hedge funds are becoming available to a broader spectrum of investors through funds of hedge funds and investible hedge funds indices. There is no formal official of the strategies applied but each database providers defines its own strategies, which can count as much as 20 different strategies. This study aims at analysing hedge fund strategies and determining so many different hedge fund strategies that exists by analysing into details the correlation patterns that exists between theses strategies. This study proves that investible hedge funds indices segregated per strategy are strongly correlated. We have also determined that the correlation between investible hedge funds indices is much higher than the average correlation between the individual funds of each hedge fund strategy. The aggregation of individual funds into indices diversifies accordingly the risk but leads also to the loss of one of the major advantage of hedge funds, which is their weak correlation. Given that hedge funds indices are constructed on a quantitative basis, a fund of hedge funds is the only vehicle that allows a trade-off between the number of funds to include into a portfolio in order to reduce the risk inherent to hedge funds investments while keeping the correlation at a low level. As long as the fund of hedge funds double-fee structure does not impact its performance and considering that the fund manager structure its investment in such a way to keep a low degree of correlation between the fund of hedge funds and traditional financial assets, such investment represents the best alternative for a traditional investor to invest in hedge funds and improve its risk-return profile.

INTRODUCTION

While the mutual funds industry is arriving at maturity, the hedge funds industry is still in a growth phase. Today, hedge funds accessibility is mainly limited to institutional investors and wealthy people. Pressure from banks is however increasing to enlarge the availability of these funds to a larger public mainly through funds of hedge funds. At the same time, an increasing number of companies propose investible hedge funds indices for each investment stratcgy availablc.

Since 1990, when around 2000 hedge funds were managing together assets of ca. $ 60 billion, the subsequent growth of number and asset base of hedge funds has never really been refuted. The industry only suffered from a relative slowdown in 1998, but has enjoyed since then a renewed vitality with an estimated size of 8400 funds managing $900 billion assets in 2004 (Van Hedge Funds Advisors International, 2002), corresponding to growth rates of respectively 10.8% and 21.3% respectively.

Hedge fund marketing is based on two pillars: superior and/or absolute performance (see for example Ackermann et al, 1999; Capocci, Corhay and Hübner, 2004) and weak correlation with traditional investment products such as shares and bonds (Schneeweis and Spurgin, 1997; Capocci and Hübner, 2004; Kat and Amin, 2003). Considering Markowitz (1952) modern portfolio's theory, such a weak correlation between an asset class and standard investment supports allow an improved risk-adjusted return for a traditional investor.

In this study we analyse the correlation between hedge fund strategies using indices returns series and using individual hedge funds data in order to determine firstly if so many strategies are needed, and secondly if it better to use individual funds grouped in funds of hedge funds from an investor point of view or if investable indices as approximated by our indices offer the same opportunities.

The vast majority of performance studies on hedge funds have not focused on their behavior under different market conditions. This is generally due to the particularly bullish period corresponding to the time window under review, as most empirical evidence reveals that data collected prior to 1994 by several data vendors displays a significant survivorship bias, as shown by Fung and Hsieh (2000), Liang (2000) and Capocci and Hübner (2004).

Few authors have attempted to estimate the behavior of hedge funds in bear markets. The periods under study do not favor this exercise, as periods of downward trends on the stock market were rare and discontinuous. For the period 1990-1998, Edwards and Caglayan (2001) find that only three hedge fund strategies (Market Neutral, Event Driven and Macro) provide protection to investors when stock markets head south. More recently, Ennis and Sebastian (2003) contend that in general, hedge funds did not provide investor protection after the market downturn of March 2000; rather, their superior performance is mostly due to the good market timing of their managers during the US stock market bubble that preceded it.

---

* Contact author, the authors would like to thank Dee Weber from CISDM for providing access to the hedge fund data. All errors are ours.

This study benefits from the fact that stock markets have experienced a long period of depression, since stock indices have been almost continuously going down for a period of three years. Thus, our analysis neither suffers from discontinuities between down periods, that preclude any analysis of persistence, nor from arbitrarily chosen definitions of a bear market, as Fabozzi and Francis (1979), Kao et al. (1998), Rao (2001), Edwards and Caglayan (2001) and Liang (2003).

This paper is organised as following. In Section II we describe the hedge fund industry. Section III reports the literature review whereas Section IV analyses the investor's portfolio structure. In Section V we analyse the data and the descriptive statistics before reporting the results in Section VI. Section VII concludes the paper.

THE HEDGE FUND INDUSTRY[1]

Hedge funds have been around for over fifty years. The first hedge fund is typically attributed to Alfred Jones, who in 1949 started a fund that simultaneously took long and short positions in equity, using leverage with an absolute return objective.[2] For seventeen years Jones managed his portfolio in absolute obscurity until Carol Loomis (1966) coined the term hedge fund in a Fortune's article. Carol described Jones' fund to have returns significantly higher than the best performing mutual funds. This led to increased interest in hedge funds and many were formed in the two subsequent years. After a quick expansion, the hedge fund industry experienced a substantial setback during the oil crises of the early 1970s, before resuming a steady pace throughout the 1980s. Over the last decade, spectacular hedge fund activities, such as the attack on the British Pound led by Georges Soros and the near collapse of Long term Capital Management in 1998, have substantially increased the public awareness.

Although the term "hedge fund" originated from the equally long and short strategy employed by managers like Alfred Jones, the new definition of hedge funds covers a multitude of different strategies. The most commonly accepted definition is that a hedge fund must:[3]

- Have an absolute return performance objective;
- Allow the manager to be active on both the long and short sides of the markets;
- Compensate the manager with performance related fees;[4]
- Allow the manager tremendous flexibility in investment style and approach.

Hedge funds are not homogenous. There are multiple strategies that span the risk/return spectrum as described in Table 1.[5]

1 For a detailed description of hedge funds history, we recommend the *Hedge Fund Genesis* of Simone S. (2002).

2 A long position consists in the holding of an asset. Short selling is a technique to profit from a stock declining in value by borrowing shares from a broker, selling them and then buying them back at a later date for a reduced price in order to return them to the broker.

3 TASS Investment Research Ltd (April 2001).

4 Hedge Fund managers traditionally charge 2% of assets as management fee and 20% of capital gains over a hurdle rate (typically 5%) as performance fee.

5 See Appendix 1 for a definion of each strategy.

Table 1. Risk-return Spectrum of Hedge Funds' Strategies

Market Risk		
Low	***Medium***	***High***
Arbitrage	**Event Driven**	**Tactical**
Convertible Arbitrage	Mergers & Acquisitions	Long/Short Selling
Equity Market Neutral	Distressed Securities	Global Macro
Fixed Income Arbitrage	Special Situations	Managed Futures

Source: S&P and Plusfund.

Today some companies propose investible indices in hedge funds strategies. MSCI, Van Hedge Fund Advisor (Van Hedge) and HFR , for example, launched investible hedge funds indices for their clients recently. In July 2002, MSCI launched family of investible hedge funds indices arguing that their clients showed strong interest in global hedge funds indices.[6]

Traditional banks claim also their share to the hedge fund growth. They are increasing pressure to enlarge the availability of hedge funds to a larger public. An increasing number of countries are issuing laws that facilitate the setting up of hedge funds. The most recent example being the German parliament which gave final approval to a bill that allows hedge funds to be sold in the country as from January 1, 2004.[7]

These laws promote the growth of the funds of hedge funds industry as these funds spread the exposure over a number of funds and consequently reduce the underlying risks of these investment products. Hedge funds are accordingly becoming available to a broader spectrum of investors through funds of hedge funds and investible hedge funds indices.

As suggested in many academic studies (Liang 1999; Ackermann et al, 1999) Investors should only invest in hedge funds if these assets have the same reward-to-risk ratio as other financial assets. Similarly, an experienced investor would only introduce hedge funds in its portfolio if this investment can improve its risk-return profile.

The performance as well as the correlation of hedge funds with traditional assets should accordingly be analysed in order to determine if an investment in hedge funds would effectively improve an investor risk-return profile. This is the purpose of the following section.

Literature Review

As one would expect, hedge fund marketing is based on two pillars: superior performance and diversification . We review the literature on these two particular aspects hereafter.

Superior Performance

Most hedge fund managers have substantial experience in capital markets. This expertise is often presented to investors as a virtual guarantee for superior performance. This may also

6 MSCI, October 2003, Hedge Invest Index, www.msci.com, p.4.
7 Nicholas (2003) describes extensively the key factors driving the funds of hedge funds growth.

be why the sons of many famous Wall Street fathers have chosen hedge fund industry to find fame and fortune.[8]

Hedge fund performance has been analysed in academic studies. Although the theoretical principle behind performance evaluation is straightforward, several articles have been written highlighting the difficulties one encounters in practice while evaluating the performance of hedge funds. Agarwal and Naik (2000) have pointed that one of the major difficulties is to formulate a benchmark to evaluate the performance of hedge funds.

Ackermann et al. (1999) and Liang (2001) have compared hedge funds performance with the performance of mutual funds and stock indices and demonstrated that hedge funds have constantly obtained a better performance than mutual funds but not than the reference market indices considered. They also indicate that the returns in hedge funds are more volatile than both the returns of mutual funds and those of market indices.

The results of Ackermann et al. (1999) are distorted by the presence of a survivorship bias in their data. They obtained a survivorship bias of 0.14% using the definition of the difference between surviving funds and dissolved funds while the definition generally used (see Fung and Hsieh, 2000 for example) is the difference in performance between the whole database and the dissolved funds. The values usually obtained are between 1.5% (Fung and Hsieh, 2000) and 3% (Liang, 2001 and Amin and Kat, 2001). As a consequence, Ackermann et al. conclude that hedge funds do not offer a superior risk return profile than market indices. These results can be considered as overestimated and this could lead to the conclusion that hedge funds do not even outperform mutual funds. Amin and Kat (2001) have concluded that stand-alone investment in hedge funds do not offer superior risk-return profile.

The issue of persistence in performance is particularly important in the case of hedge funds because these funds experience a greater attrition rate than mutual funds (Brown et al., 1999, 2001). Agarwal and Naik (2000) find evidence of persistence in hedge funds performance, while Brown and al. (1999) prove that offshore hedge funds display positive returns adjusted for risk but they attribute this performance to style effect and they conclude that there is hardly any evidence of the existence of differential manager skills.

As a conclusion, although hedge fund marketing is based on the reputation of managers, it appears from the academic papers that the presence of certain special skills from the manager does not guarantee superior performance. Hedge funds performance is more volatile than the returns of traditional investment assets and stand-alone investments in hedge funds should not offer superior risk-return profile than market indices.

Low Correlation

The second marketing argument derives from the fact that many hedge funds follow strategies with low systematic risk.[9] As a result, hedge fund returns tend to exhibit only a weak relationship with the returns on other asset classes. According to the Modern Portfolio

---

8 John Bogle for example, son of Vanguard Group founder Jack Bogle, manages the Bogle Investment fund. Financial Times (2001) enumerates other examples.

9 Systematic risk is the risk of holding the market portfolio. As the market moves, each individual asset is more or less affected. To the extent that any asset participates in by such general market moves, that asset entails systematic risk.

Theory of Markowitz (1952), a low correlation between hedge funds and traditional investment products allow investors to reach a better efficient frontier.

Fung and Hsieh (1997), Schneeweis and Spurgin (1997) proved that the insertion of hedge funds in a portfolio can significantly improve its risk-return profile thanks to their weak correlation with other financial securities. This weak correlation has also been underlined by Liang (1999) as well as Agarwal and Naik (2000). Amin and Kat (2001) found that the average correlation between the hedge funds studied and the S&P 500 was only 0.29 and that hedge funds produced an efficient payoff profile when mixed with the S&P 500. They obtained the best results when 10-20% of the portfolio value was invested in hedge funds.

Amenc and Martellini (2002) have proven that the insertion of hedge funds in a portfolio can significantly lower the volatility of the portfolio without leading to a significant variation of the return.

For the period 1990-1998, Edwards and Caglayan (2001) found however that only three hedge fund strategies (Market neutral, Event Driven and Macro) provided protection to investors when stock markets head south. More recently, Ennis and Sebastian (2003) contend that in general hedge funds did not provide investor protection after the market downturn of March 2000; rather, their superior performance was mostly due to the good market timing of their managers during the US stock market bubble that preceded it. Liang (2003) concluded that correlation structures for alternative investment vehicles are different under different market conditions.

The first problem in the above summarised scientific performance and correlation studies comes from the fact that most of the studies have focused on hedge funds' behaviour under bull market conditions (the exception is Liang, 2003). This is generally due to the particularly bullish period corresponding to the time window under review. Most of the studies include the Asian crisis period, but, as suggested by Brown et al. (1998), few hedge funds have been significantly exposed to this financial crisis. Results are accordingly not necessarily valid in case of bear period.

The second issue is of major importance. It is based on the fact that previous results were all based on hedge fund indices. These indices are either constructed by hedge fund indices providers like in Kat (2002) which leads to the presence of a selection bias or they are constructed by the researcher on the basis of a global hedge fund database and included several dozens of individual funds in a single return series. The problem is that the correlation between these indices could be completely different from the one between individual funds and this area surely needs to be investigated further. This is the aim of our analysis.

Investor's Portfolio Structure

The hedge fund industry can be split between three key players: individual independent hedge funds managers, traditional banks and other financial institutions. As detailed in the previous section, the inherent risk linked to the investment into one individual hedge fund should prevent traditional investors to seek that kind of investments. We accordingly focus our attention to traditional banks and other financial institutions. Diversification can be obtained by investing partly its assets in funds of hedge funds or in hedge fund indices. Overall, banks are generally limiting their offer to funds of hedge funds to their retail investors . These funds are particular in the hedge fund world since they combine positions in various individual funds in order to reduce the risk of the overall portfolio. In addition to the advantage of diversification of risks, funds of hedge funds save investors significant time and expenses by providing due diligence, performance evaluation and manager monitoring (Lamm, 1999). An investment in funds of hedge funds reduces also the minimum amount of investment necessary to achieve effective diversification .

This duty has a cost. In addition to the fees charged by the managers of individual funds in which the fund invests, the manager of the fund of hedge funds charges a similar fee. According to Amin and Kat (2001), funds of hedge funds performance appears to suffer badly from their double fee structure. This was also confirmed by Brown and al. (2003).

Diversification can also be obtained by investing in investible hedge fund indices. These indices are proposed by an increasing number of companies (or so-called "other financial institutions") to their clients. An index is in principle available for each major strategy. The only issue is that investible indices are usually constructed on a purely quantitative basis. The constructor usually requires the fund to provide daily or weekly liquidity and to exist for a defined period of time; finally, and most importantly, they do not perform any qualitative analysis of the fund, which could hurt performance.

Hedge Funds as a Stand-alone Investment

Van Hedge, a hedge fund advisor, claims that hedge funds, when added to a traditional portfolio of stocks and bonds, both improves returns and reduced risk.. Similarly, Lamm (1999), chief investment strategist at Bankers Trust Private Banking, Deutsche Bank Group, states that hedge funds returns are superior to equities and bonds on a risk-adjusted basis. This conclusion is confirmed by Brown and al. (1998) that used another database. Lamm (1999) suggests in his article that for aggressive investors even a 100% exposure to hedge funds might be appropriate. Based on his computations, a 100% investment in long/short selling hedge funds has an expected return of more than 21% with a systematic risk limited to 6.4%. This result spots the investment on an even better efficient frontier than the one depicted by Van Hedge!

The comparison of hedge funds efficient frontier with the one of conventional portfolios is however not valid since hedge funds database may suffer from a survivor bias. Moreover, these outcomes are not in line with the study of professors Amin and Kat (2001) that concludes that stand-alone investment in hedge funds do not offer superior risk-return profile.

The difference of the conclusions comes from the fact that, although not explicitly detailed, Lamm (1999) and Van Hedge studies have applied traditional performance measures such as Jensen's alpha, Sharpe ratios, ... to hedge funds. These methods assume hedge funds returns to be normally distributed and to be linearly related amongst themselves and with other classes. Amin and Kat (2001) have proven however that neither of these assumptions is correct. Ross and al. (2003) state also that systematic risk cannot be reduced through diversification.

As a consequence, although the hedge fund industry concludes that an investor should put all his eggs in hedge funds through indices, it appears from scientific studies that this conclusion is based on wrong arguments and the use of wrong assumptions. This use of non up to date references allows the hedge funds industry to promote hedge fund investments through wrong advertisement at the disfavour of the investors.

Combining Hedge Funds with Traditional Assets

Various authors also analyse the impact of inserting hedge funds in a traditional investment portfolio. Lamm (1999) states that a risk-preferring investor desiring 12.5% risk would weight a portfolio 87% in EAFE equities and 14% in a portfolio of hedge funds . For a 4.5% portfolio risk, the investor should allocate as much as 76% to hedge funds.

Although scientific studies generally also conclude that a combination of hedge funds and traditional financial assets improve the risk-return of an investor, the best results are obtained when 10-20% of the portfolio value is invested in hedge funds(see Amin and Kat, 2001), which is far away from the 60% and 76% advised by Van Hedge and Lamm (1999).

Inserting hedge funds in a traditional portfolio improves accordingly the risk return profile of an investor. In most of the studies, the term hedge fund generally refers to an index of hedge funds regrouping all the strategies available. Some hedge fund strategies may however be so strongly correlated so that they would be redundant. The analysis of this correlation is performed in the next section.

Funds of hedge funds' managers of the investment institution under review generally select individual hedge funds based on the results of their due diligence and taking the limits set in the placement memorandum into account. There is no specific focus on the overall level of correlation of the strategies of the fund although this is a key advantage of hedge funds for investors. In the following section, we will try to determine to what extent hedge funds strategies are correlated.

DATA, DESCRIPTIVE STATISTICS AND SURVIVORSHIP BIAS

Before reporting our results, we present our data, analyze the descriptive statistics and study the presence of survivorship bias in our datas.

The Datas

Three main hedge fund databases are available for empirical studies: 'Managed Account Reports' (MAR), 'Hedge Fund Research, Inc.' (HFR), and 'TASS Management' (TASS) (Amin and Kat, 2001). These databases are the most used in academic and commercial hedge fund studies.[10]

Data vendors do not only collect performance data. For a majority of funds, they record other useful information such as company name, start and ending date, strategy followed, assets under management, management and incentive fees, manager's name etc. There is no

10 The three databases have never been used together in a study, but Ackermann and Ravenscraft (1998) and Ackermann et al. (1999) and Capocci and Hübner (2004) used a combination of HFR and MAR while Liang (2000) uses a combination of TASS and HFR.

consensus on the definition of the strategy followed but there are similarities. MAR defines 9 strategies with a total of 16 sub-strategies. HFR defines sixteen different strategies in two categories, 12 non-directional and 5 directional strategies, plus the Funds of Funds and the Sector categories. Finally, TASS defines 15 strategies.

We use hedge fund data from MAR, as in Fung and Hsieh (1997), Schneeweis and Spurgin (1998), and Amin and Kat (2001). The database gives monthly net-of-fee individual returns and other information on individual funds and groups them in indices. We use 108 monthly returns on 2894 individual hedge funds plus 48 indices (16 investment styles with 3 indices for each investment style: onshore, offshore and a combined index). These funds include 1622 funds alive at the end of the period (56%) and 1272 dissolved funds (44%).

Hedge funds are classified in two categories. The Individual Funds category features 13 strategies: Event driven – Risk Arbitrage, Event-Driven – Distressed Securities, Global, Global Est., Global Intern., Global Emerging, US Opportunistics,[11] Macro, Market Neutral, Long Only Leveraged, Sector, Short Sales and No Category, the latter one corresponding to funds with no stated strategy and funds whose strategy does not fill in any of the above. The Funds of Funds category features 3 strategies: Niche, Diversified and Others.

Although we removed data before 1994, the returns data are likely biased upward because individual hedge funds are added to databases only when they have a demonstrated record of success. This bias is called the instant return history bias (see Capocci and Hübner, 2004 and Capocci, Corhay and Hübner, 2004). Hedge funds that fail are largely excluded from reported returns by data vendors. Furthermore, firms that fail are often dropped from existing databases, creating even more potential for upward bias as mentioned by Lamm (1999).

We use monthly returns on 2868 individual hedge funds (15 investment styles). These funds include 1530 funds alive at the end of the period (53%) and 1338 dissolved funds (47%). This confirms the high attrition rate of the industry.

The Descriptive Statistics

Table 2 reports descriptive statistics of the data used in our study and shows that the highest mean return was achieved by the Sector (1.66%) followed by Global Est. (1.29%). Average returns of funds of funds are around 0.7%, only followed by the Global (0.45%) strategy that achieves the lowest mean return.

Table 2 shows that the highest mean return was achieved by the Sector (1.66%), then the Global Est. (1.29%) and Global Emerging (1.17%) follow. Average returns of funds of funds are all around 0.70%, only followed by the Global (0.45%) strategy that achieves the lowest mean return. This pattern is similar for the mean excess returns.

[11] This strategy has been suppressed in 1999.

Table 2. Descriptive Statistics of our Hedge Fund Strategies (1/1994-12/2002)

	Hedge funds strategies					Jan.1994-December 2002 (109 months)					
	No of Funds	% of the category	% of the total	Living Funds	Dead Funds	Mean Return %	Std. Dev.%	Media %	Mi %	Ma %	Sharpe ratio
Individual Funds											
Event driven	241	10,90	8,40	148	93	0,96	1,88	1,13	-8,50	5,00	
Risk arb	135	*6,10*	4,70	94	41	0,93	1,74	0,92	-6,40	5,50	0,32
Distressed sec	106	*4,80*	3,70	70	36	0,99	2,25	1,17	-10,80	7,00	0,27
Tactical		*60,60*									
Global*	175	7,90	6,10	0	175	0,45	3,80	0,64	-25,80	13,60	0,02
Global est.	499	22,50	17,40	300	199	1,29	3,25	1,09	-9,90	12,30	0,28
Global intern.	72	3,20	2,50	46	26	0,88	2,42	0,93	-6,80	8,90	0,21
Global emerging	157	7,10	5,50	97	60	1,17	5,02	1,80	-21,70	14,30	0,16
US Opp.†	39	1,80	1,40	0	39	0,23	2,40	0,21	-5,60	7,40	-0,08
Global Macro	144	6,50	5,00	52	92	0,82	2,15	0,61	-4,10	7,00	0,2
Long only lev.	33	1,50	1,20	16	17	0,92	5,83	1,50	-17,40	13,30	0,09
Sector	190	8,60	6,60	112	78	1,66	4,43	2,07	-13,10	19,90	0,29
Short Selling	37	1,70	1,30	24	13	0,88	4,48	0,67	-13,60	13,20	0,11
Arbitrage		*28,50*									
Market neutral	634	28,50	22,10	383	251	1,04	0,97	1,05	-2,50	4,00	0,67
Individual Funds	2221	100	77	1101	1120	1,08	2,28	1,11	-25,80	19,90	0,31
Funds of Funds											
Niche	114	18	4	82	32	0,74	1,33	0,67	-4,10	5,10	0,27
Diversified	501	77	17	340	161	0,71	1,87	0,75	-7,30	7,00	0,14
Other	32	5	1	0	32	0,77	1,69	0,80	-7,30	5,80	0,23
Funds of Funds Total	647	100	23	429	218	0,72	1,77	0,71	-7,30	7,00	0,19
Total	**2868**	**100**	**100**	**1530**	**1338**	**0,99**	**2,14**	**1,11**	**-25,80**	**19,90**	**0,29**

* The Global category has been gradually suppressed and replaced by the Global Est., Global Intern. And Global Emerging category. Funds disappearance is mostly due to category transfer.

† US Opp. Funds and Funds of Funds other ended in January 1999.

Note: This Table shows the number of funds following a particular strategy (or sub-strategy), the corresponding number of living and dead funds, mean returns, mean excess returns, and Sharpe ratios for the individual hedge funds in our MAR database for the sub-periods 01:1994-03:2000 (bullish) and 04:2000-12:2002 (bearish). Sharpe ratio is the ratio of excess return and standard deviation with a risk-free rate set at 5%.

These descriptive statistics differ from the results obtained by Capocci and Hübner (2004) for the 1994-2000 period, who find that the best performers are US Opportunistics Small Caps, US Opportunistics Growth and Sector while the worst average performers are Foreign Exchange, Short Sellers the and Funds of Funds, without sub-strategy. This difference can be explained by the difference in the database used (MAR combined with HFR for Capocci and Hübner, 2004) and the different time period studied.

The Sharpe measure (the ratio of excess return and standard deviation) offers a much different picture: accounting for risk, Market Neutral funds appear to be the best performers, while the funds that achieve the highest absolute returns are only among the average risk-adjusted performers.

A look at the t-stats indicates that mean returns are significantly different from 0 at the 5% significance level for all funds and that the mean excess returns are significantly positive for all cases but the Global and Diversified funds of funds categories.

The Sharpe ratio obtained by our whole hedge fund database (0.29) is higher than the ones for the Market Proxy (0.19), and higher than for the MSCI World Excluding US (-0.15).

RESULTS

To analyse the correlation patterns between hedge funds strategies and between individual hedge funds returns, we use the classical correlation coefficient commonly used in financial papers (e.g. Liang, 1999; Amin and Kat, 2001; Agarwal and Naik, 2003; Liang 2003; Capocci and Hübner, 2004). In the first part of the section we analyse the correlations between hedge fund grouped per investment strategies. In the second section, we analyse the correlation between individual funds in various hedge funds strategies.

Correlation between Hedge Fund Indices

Funds of hedge funds' managers of the investment institution under review generally select individual hedge funds based on the results of their due diligence and taking the limits set in the placement memorandum into account. There is no specific focus on the overall level of correlation of the strategies of the fund although this is a key advantage of hedge funds for investors. In the following section, we will try to determine to what extent hedge funds strategies are correlated.

As suggested in the introduction, the traditional hedge funds literature contends that, thanks to their weak correlation between hedge funds and other securities, hedge funds are likely to improve to the risk-return trade-off when added to a traditional portfolio (see Fung and Hsieh, 1997; Schneeweis and Spurgin, 1997; Liang, 1999; Amin and Kat, 2001). It is however also important to look at the correlation between the various hedge fund strategies in order to determine the interest of dividing the industry in strategies

We first evaluate the correlation between hedge funds strategies using monthly (net-of-fees) returns reported in the database and confirm the significance of the results with the t-stat . The correlation's study is performed over the global period for which the data are relevant, i.e. from 1994 to 2002 - a time period that covers both market upturns and downturns. We also divide the sample in two sub-periods (September 1998 to March 2000 and April 2000 to December 2002) and reconduct the correlation exercise . The sub-period analysis is important as in terms of market conditions, these two sub-periods correspond respectively to a bull and a bear market. It is likely that hedge funds change their risk exposures and trading strategies over time and specifically in these specific market conditions.

A high correlation would mean that the numerous strategies available are not necessarily relevant to improve an investor's portfolio risk-adjusted return as the correlated indices would be redundant.

Table 3 summarises the correlation between the indices of hedge funds strategies constructed from our database over the global period. Figure 1 reports the average mean, median as well as the minimum and maximum correlation of each strategy compared to the others.

The results show that most of the strategies are significantly correlated except US opportunistic. This is due to the small number of returns available. Short selling funds systematically go conversely – as expected. If we consider that all coefficients above 0.6 reveal a strong correlation, we can conclude that almost all the strategies except Global, Global Emerging, US opportunistic funds and Funds of Funds (Other) are strongly correlated.

As shown in Appendix 2, results are similar for the bear and the bull period. The correlation is in fact a trend that evolves very slowly. Whatever the period analysed, results are similar. One should accordingly not expect these correlations to change substantially over time. Hedge funds strategies grouped by indices are accordingly strongly correlated. Disregarding US opportunistic funds due to the small number of data available and Global Funds due to their change of category (see table 1), on a purely correlation basis, an investor would only need Global Emerging Funds, Funds of funds – Other and a third strategy to have a benchmark representing all uncorrelated hedge funds strategies.

Given the diversity of hedge funds strategies, the high degree of correlation between the indices should in principle lead to approximately the same level of correlation between hedge funds indices and traditional financial assets. Hedge funds indices should consequently not allow an investor to improve its risk-return profile due to their high degree of correlation.

The spread between the minimum and maximum correlation is however very outstretched (see table 3). This should mean that some individual funds within each strategy are not as much correlated as the indices.

Table 3. Correlation of Hedge Funds Strategies Grouped by Indices

	RA	DS	GL	GLE	GLI	GLEM	US	GM	FN	FD	FO	MN	LO	S
RA	1,00													
DS	0,81*	1,00												
GL	0,64*	0,69*	1,00											
GLE	0,84*	0,82*	0,64	1,00										
GLI	0,71*	0,78*	0,62*	0,83*	1,00									
GLEM	0,65*	0,70*	0,77*	0,68*	0,76*	1,00								
US	0,33*	0,30*	0,23*	0,27*	0,22*	0,15	1,00							
GM	0,69*	0,71*	0,53*	0,84*	0,80*	0,62*	0,17	1,00						
FN	0,68*	0,75*	0,57*	0,76*	0,81*	0,73*	0,19*	0,74*	1,00					
FD	0,78*	0,84*	0,69*	0,88*	0,88*	0,80*	0,24*	0,88*	0,90*	1,00				
FO	0,65*	0,68*	0,59*	0,65*	0,64*	0,61*	0,24*	0,60*	0,69*	0,74*	1,00			
MN	0,80*	0,82*	0,55*	0,80*	0,79*	0,64*	0,31*	0,73*	0,80*	0,85*	0,70*	1,00		
LO	0,81*	0,77*	0,62*	0,91*	0,73*	0,66*	0,26*	0,78*	0,69*	0,81*	0,62*	0,74*	1,00	
S	0,78*	0,77*	0,57	0,94*	0,75*	0,62*	0,24*	0,80*	0,72*	0,83*	0,61*	0,75*	0,87*	1,00
SS	-0,67	-0,66*	-0,54*	-0,84*	-0,61*	-0,57*	-0,27*	-0,68*	-0,49*	-0,65*	-0,45*	-0,57*	-0,82*	-0,84

* significant at the 5% significance level.

Note: This table reports the correlation coefficients between the hedge fund indices constructed using our MAR/CISDM database over the 1:1994-12:2002 period. RA= risk arbitrage, DS= distressed securities, GL = global funds, GLE = global established funds, GLI = Global Index, GLEM= global emerging funds, US = US opportunistic funds, GM= global macro funds, FN = Fund of Funds – Niche, FD = Fund of Funds – Diversified, FO= Fund of Funds – Other, MN = market neutral, LO = long only leveraged, S = Sector, SS = short sale.

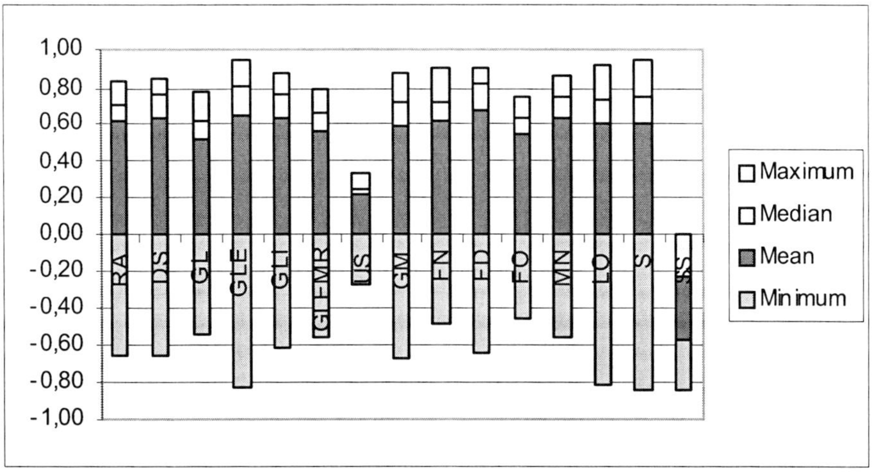

Figure 1. Mean, Median, Minimum and Maximum correlations between each hedge fund index and its peers. This figure reports the mean, median, minimum and maximum correlations between each hedge fund index and the other hedge fund indices using our MAR/CISDM database from 1:1994 to 12:2002. RA= risk arbitrage, DS= distressed securities, GL = global funds, GLE = global established funds, GLI = Global Index, GLEM= global emerging funds, US = US opportunistic funds, GM= global macro funds, FN = Fund of Funds – Niche, FD = Fund of Funds – Diversified, FO= Fund of Funds – Other, MN = market neutral, LO = long only leveraged, S = Sector, SS = short sale.

Correlation between Individual Hedge Funds

In the following section, we analyse the correlation between each individual fund of each strategy with each individual of another strategy and compute then the average correlation to compare it to the correlation of the strategies grouped by indices.

Given the high number of computations, we have limited our analysis to Risk Arbitrage Funds and Global Funds. The determination of the correlation of each individual fund from these strategies with each individual fund of the other strategies lead indeed to more than 700,000 computations.

Table 4 details the Mean, Median, Minimum and Maximum correlation between the Risk Arbitrage individual funds and the individual funds following other strategies. It appears from the figures that the mean correlation is very low, i.e. below 0.3.

Table 4. Mean, Median, Minimum, and Maximum Correlation of Risk Arbitrage Individual Funds Compared to Other Strategies

	RA-DS	RA-GL	RA-GLE	RA-GLI	RA-GLEM	RA-US	RA-GM	RA-LO	RA -S	RA -SS	RA-MN	RA-FD	RA-FN	RA-FO
Mean	0,25	0,17	0,23	0,17	0,21	0,09	0,12	0,26	0,24	-0,14	0,15	0,29	0,25	0,29
Median	0,26	0,15	0,25	0,17	0,22	0,10	0,12	0,26	0,24	-0,17	0,15	0,30	0,27	0,31
Min	-1,00	-1,00	-1,00	-1,00	-1,00	-1,00	-1,00	-1,00	-1,00	-1,00	-1,00	-1,00	-1,00	-1,00
Max	1,00	1,00	1,00	1,00	1,00	1,00	1,00	1,00	1,00	1,00	1,00	1,00	1,00	1,00

Note: This table reports the mean, median, minimum and maximum correlations between each individual risk arbitrage hedge funds and all the individual funds in the other hedge fund strategies using our MAR/CISDM database from 1:1994 to 12:2002. RA= risk arbitrage, DS= distressed securities, GL = global funds, GLE = global established funds, GLI = Global Index, GLEM= global emerging funds, US = US opportunistic funds, GM= global macro funds, FN = Fund of Funds – Niche, FD = Fund of Funds – Diversified, FO= Fund of Funds – Other, MN = market neutral, LO = long only leveraged, S = Sector, SS = short sale.

The same trend is found for the correlation between Global individual funds and the individual funds following other strategies as depicted in Table 5.

Table 5. Mean, Median, Minimum, Maximum Correlation of Global individual Funds Compared to Other Strategies

	GL-RA	GL-DS	GL-GLE	GL-GLI	GL-GLEM	GL-US	GL-GM	GL-LO	GL-S	GL-SS	GL-MN	GL-FD	GL-FN	GL-FO
Mean	0,17	0,23	0,24	0,20	0,23	0,06	0,14	0,31	0,26	-0,13	0,12	0,26	0,18	0,23
Median	0,15	0,23	0,26	0,20	0,23	0,07	0,14	0,34	0,27	-0,15	0,10	0,26	0,19	0,26
Min	-1,00	-1,00	-1,00	-1,00	-1,00	-1,00	-1,00	-1,00	-1,00	-1,00	-1,00	-1,00	-1,00	-1,00
Max	1,00	1,00	1,00	1,00	1,00	0,99	1,00	1,00	1,00	1,00	1,00	1,00	1,00	1,00

Note: This table reports the mean, median, minimum and maximum correlations between each individual global hedge funds and all the individual funds in the other hedge fund strategies using our MAR/CISDM database from 1:1994 to 12:2002. RA= risk arbitrage, DS= distressed securities, GL = global funds, GLE = global established funds, GLI = Global Index, GLEM= global emerging funds, US = US opportunistic funds, GM= global macro funds, FN = Fund of Funds – Niche, FD = Fund of Funds – Diversified, FO= Fund of Funds – Other, MN = market neutral, LO = long only leveraged, S = Sector, SS = short sale.

Both tables also indicate that at least one individual fund of each strategy (RA and GL) is perfectly correlated and at least one perfectly uncorrelated with an individual fund of another strategy. Tables 3,4 and 5 give us sufficient information to compare the average correlation between Risk Arbitrage individual funds and the individual funds of other strategies to the correlation between the Risk Arbitrage index and the other strategy indices.

The aggregation of individual funds into indices diversifies the risk but leads to the loss of one of the major advantage of hedge funds, which is their weak correlation. A trade-off must accordingly be made between the number of funds to include into a fund of hedge fund in order to reduce the risk inherent to hedge funds investment while keeping the correlation level to a low level. The determination of this trade-off is out of the scope of this assignment but could be the subject of another study.

CONCLUSION

Hedge fund marketing is based on two pillars: superior performance and weak correlation with traditional investment tools. Academic studies have proven that although hedge fund marketing is based on the reputation of managers, the presence of certain special skills from the manager does not guarantee superior performance. Hedge funds performance is more volatile than the returns of traditional investment assets and stand-alone investments in hedge funds should not offer superior risk-return profile than market indices.

When combined with traditional financial assets such as shares and bonds, an investment in hedge funds improves however the risk-return profile of the investor thanks to the weak correlation of hedge funds with the other financial assets. Amin and Kat (1999) suggest for instance that investors should invest 10 to 20% of their portfolio value in hedge funds.

We have proven that investible hedge funds indices segregated per strategy are strongly correlated. On a pure correlation basis, three hedge funds indices including at least the Global Emerging Funds index and the Funds of Funds – Other index are sufficient to have a benchmark representing all the uncorrelated hedge funds strategies.

We have also determined that the degree of correlation between individual funds is much lower than the correlation between indices which indicates that the aggregation of individual funds into indices diversifies the risk but leads also to the loss of one of the major advantage of hedge funds, which is their weak correlation.

Given that hedge funds indices are constructed on a quantitative basis, a fund of hedge funds is the only vehicle that allows a selection of individual funds. Today, funds of hedge fund managers do not consider the overall correlation of their portfolio although this is a key element for the investors. They should in the future take this element into consideration and perform a trade-off between the number of funds to include into a fund of hedge fund in order to reduce the risk inherent to hedge funds while keeping the correlation level to a low level.

Funds of hedge funds performance suffer unfortunately from a double fee structure. In this respect, funds of hedge funds managers should negotiate the fees with the individual hedge funds managers in order to reduce the impact of the double-fee structure on the performance.

In practice, this would however be difficult as only bad performing hedge funds managers or managers with little track record would welcome investments from banks given the top hedge fund managers should close their fund without having to reduce their fees.

Appendix 1: Hedge Funds Strategies[12]

Tactical - Strives to take advantage of global market trends as they relate to items such as currency, exchange rates, interest rates and other factors.

- *Long/Short selling* involves investing on both the long and short side of the market. The objective is not to be market neutral. The manager has the opportunity to shift from a net long position to a net short position. A short sale is the sale of a security not owned by the seller. This technique is used to take advantage of an anticipated price decline due to the manager's assessment of the overvaluation of the securities or the market, or in anticipation of earnings disappointments due to accounting irregularities, new competition, change of management, etc.
- *Global macro* involves investing by making leveraged bets on anticipated price movements of stock markets, interest rates, foreign exchange and commodities. Macro managers may invest in any markets using any instruments to participate in expected market movements. The positions reflect the managers' view on overall

[12] Definitions of the various hedge funds strategies can be found www.vanhedge.com.

market direction as influenced by major economic trends and/or events such as political fortunes. Global Funds include subcategories such as Global Established Funds, *Global International Funds* or Global Emerging Funds. *Global Emerging Funds* managers invest in securities issued by businesses and/or governments of countries with less developed economies (as measured by per capita Gross National Product), while *Global Established Funds* only invest in securities issued by entities from well established markets.

- *Managed futures* strives to be profitable in any type of economic climate since the manager have the flexibility to go long (buy in anticipation of rising prices) or "short" (sell in anticipation of declining prices). The Managed futures strategy is similar to the long/short selling strategy but uses higher leverage.
- *Opportunistic* Rather than consistently selecting securities according to the same strategy, the manager's investment approach changes over time to better take advantage of current market conditions and investment opportunities. *US Opportunistic* funds limit their investment in US markets.
- *Sector Funds* specialize in one sector, devoting 50% or more of their portfolio to such securities while most hedge funds are diversified among several different sectors.

Event driven involves investing in opportunities created by significant transactional events, such as *mergers and acquisitions*, bankruptcy reorganizations (*distressed securities*), spins-offs, recapitalisation and share buybacks (*special situations*). Managers buy equity, debt, or trade claims at deep discounts of companies in or facing such transactional events and expect to profit from the market's lack of understanding of the true value of the deeply discounted securities or from the inability of the majority of institutional investors to invest below investment grade securities.

Arbitrage exploits pricing discrepancies between closely related securities. There are generally three types of arbitrage:

- *Convertible arbitrage* involves purchasing a portfolio of convertible securities, generally convertible bonds, and hedging a portion of the equity risk by selling short the underlying common stock. Positions are designed to generate profits while protecting principal from directional market moves.
- *Market neutral* strategy seeks to exploit market pricing inefficiencies between related equity securities. Market neutral portfolios are designed to be either beta[13] or currency neutral or both. One example of this strategy is to build portfolios made up of long positions in the strongest companies in several industries and taking corresponding short positions in those showing signs of weakness.
- *Fixed Income Relative value/arbitrage* exploits market inefficiencies between related fixed income securities while neutralizing exposure to interest rate risk.

---

13 The beta coefficient is the amount of systematic risk present in a particular risky asset relative to that in an average risky asset. Ross, Westerfield, Jordan, 2003, *Fundamentals of Corporate Finance*, Mc Graw – Hill Higher Education, p. 431.

In addition to these strategies, there is the *Fund of funds* strategy that designs a diversified portfolio of managers with the objective of significantly lowering the volatility of investing with an individual manager. The fund of funds manager has discretion in choosing which strategies to invest in for the portfolio.

APPENDIX 2: CORRELATION BETWEEN HEDGE FUNDS STRATEGIES

Appendix 2a: Correlation of hedge fund strategies in a bull market

Table A2-1. Correlation between Hedge Fund Strategies in a Bull Market

	RA	DS	GL	GLE	GLI	GLEM	US	GM	FN	FD	FO	MN	LO	S
RA	1,00													
DS	0,89*	1,00												
GL	0,53*	0,68*	1,00											
GLE	0,82*	0,72*	0,59*	1,00										
GLI	0,76*	0,85*	0,72*	0,76*	1,00									
GLEM	0,56*	0,71*	0,68*	0,65*	0,87*	1,00								
US	0,56	0,40	-0,03	0,58	0,19	-0,20	1,00							
GM	0,89*	0,77*	0,56*	0,94*	0,79*	0,60*	0,85*	1,00						
FN	0,73*	0,78*	0,59*	0,78*	0,86*	0,75*	0,70*	0,81*	1,00					
FD	0,83*	0,85*	0,65*	0,85*	0,89*	0,77*	0,64*	0,90*	0,97*	1,00				
FO	0,73*	0,69*	0,14	0,59*	0,58*	0,37	0,86*	0,66*	0,63*	0,65*	1,00			
MN	0,78*	0,82*	0,49*	0,66*	0,68*	0,50*	0,84*	0,70*	0,80*	0,82*	0,68*	1,00		
LO	0,83*	0,74*	0,56*	0,97*	0,76*	0,64*	0,53*	0,94*	0,77*	0,84*	0,66*	0,67*	1,00	
S	0,78*	0,63*	0,37	0,87*	0,58*	0,46*	0,73*	0,89*	0,72*	0,80*	0,61*	0,61*	0,85*	1,00
SS	-0,78*	-0,65*	-0,49*	-0,91*	-0,60*	-0,49*	0,02*	-0,85*	-0,66*	-0,74*	-0,57*	-0,64*	-0,91*	-0,88*

Table A2-2. Mean, Median, Minimum and Maximum Correlation between the Hedge Funds per Strategy in a Bull Market

	Mean	**Median**	**Minimum**	**Maximum**
RA	0,64	0,77	-0,78	0,89
DS	0,63	0,73	-0,65	0,89
GL	0,43	0,56	-0,49	0,72
GLE	0,63	0,74	-0,91	0,97
GLI	0,62	0,76	-0,60	0,89
GLEM	0,49	0,62	-0,49	0,87
US	0,48	0,57	-0,20	0,86
GM	0,68	0,80	-0,85	0,94
FN	0,66	0,76	-0,66	0,97
FD	0,69	0,82	-0,74	0,97
FO	0,52	0,64	-0,57	0,86
MN	0,60	0,68	-0,64	0,84
LO	0,63	0,75	-0,91	0,97
S	0,57	0,68	-0,88	0,89
SS	-0,65	-0,65	-0,91	0,02

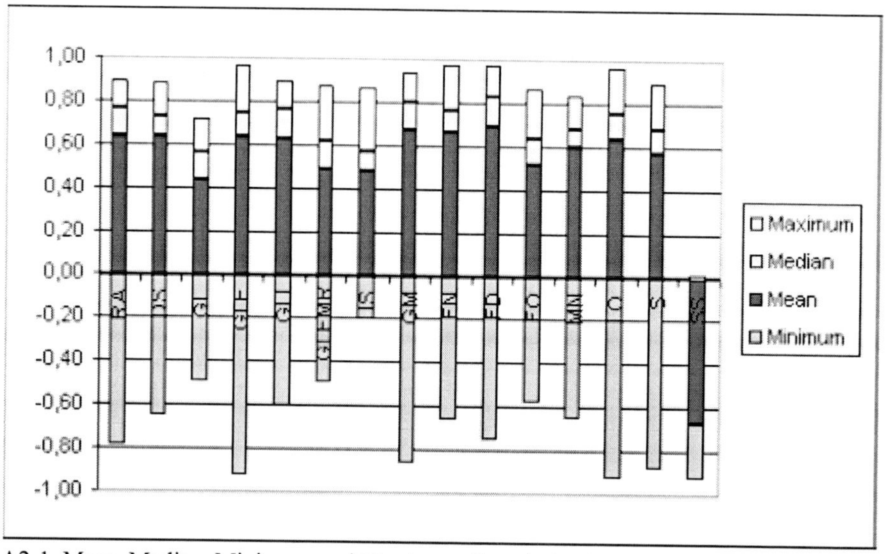

Figure A2-1. Mean, Median, Minimum and Maximum Correlation between the Hedge Funds per Strategy in a Bull Market

APPENDIX 2B: CORRELATION OF HEDGE FUNDS STRATEGIES IN A BEAR MARKET

Table A2-3. Correlation between Hedge Fund Strategies in a Bear Market

	RA	DS	GL	GLE	GLI	GLEM	US	GM	FN	FD	FO	MN	LO	S
RA	1,00													
DS	0,74*	1,00												
GL	0,46*	0,51*	1,00											
GLE	0,84*	0,79*	0,55*	1,00										
GLI	0,75*	0,65*	0,47*	0,81*	1,00									
GLEM	0,72*	0,79*	0,65*	0,88*	0,76*	1,00								
US	NA	NA	NA	NA	NA	NA	NA							
GM	0,67*	0,68*	0,45*	0,82*	0,72*	0,78*	NA	1,00						
FN	0,84*	0,73*	0,43*	0,84*	0,70*	0,73*	NA	0,78*	1,00					
FD	0,82*	0,81*	0,55*	0,92*	0,80*	0,86*	NA	0,88*	0,92*	1,00				
FO	0,65*	0,43*	0,16	0,61*	0,45*	0,45*	NA	0,50*	0,66*	0,59*	1,00			
MN	0,85*	0,64*	0,24	0,78*	0,73*	0,60*	NA	0,65*	0,79*	0,73*	0,67*	1,00		
LO	0,76*	0,72*	0,52*	0,95*	0,68*	0,84*	NA	0,72*	0,78*	0,83*	0,59*	0,67*	1,00	
S	0,74*	0,71*	0,43*	0,93*	0,70*	0,76*	NA	0,75*	0,83*	0,87*	0,52*	0,69*	0,92*	1,00
SS	-0,56*	-0,65*	-0,49*	-0,89*	-0,64*	-0,80*	NA	-0,72*	-0,65*	-0,80*	-0,41*	-0,52*	-0,90*	-0,88*

Table A2-4. Mean, Median, Minimum and Maximum Correlation between the Hedge Funds per Strategy in a Bear Market

	Mean	Median	Minimum	Maximum
RA	0,61	0,81	-0,73	0,89
DS	0,68	0,84	-0,92	0,97
GL	0,46	0,60	-0,67	0,79
GLE	0,68	0,89	-0,96	0,96
GLI	0,58	0,73	-0,83	0,90
GLEM	0,63	0,78	-0,93	0,94
US*	NA	NA	NA	NA
GM	0,62	0,78	-0,87	0,91
FN	0,67	0,78	-0,90	0,97
FD	0,70	0,86	-0,93	0,94
FO	0,47	0,59	-0,88	0,91
MN	0,58	0,73	-0,83	0,85
LO	0,62	0,72	-0,93	0,98
S	0,61	0,74	-0,88	0,93
SS	-0,69	-0,65	-0,90	-0,41

* No data are available for the bear period.

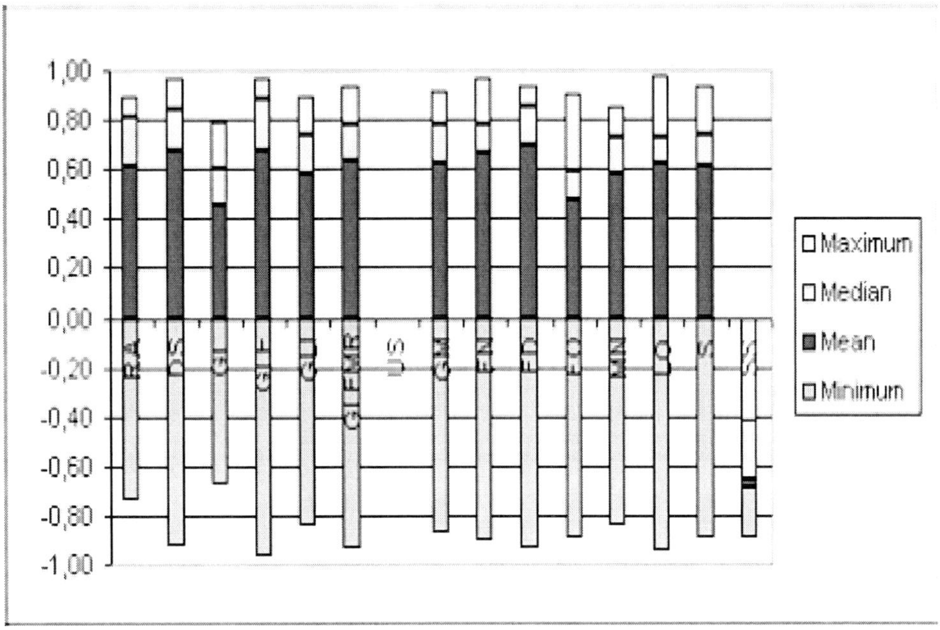

Figure A2-2. mean, median, minimum and maximum correlation between the hedge funds per strategy in a bear market.

REFERENCES

Ackermann C., Mc Enally R., Ravenscraft D., 1999, The performance of hedge funds: risk, return and incentives, *Journal of Finance* 54, pp. 833-874.

Agarwal V. and Naik N.Y., 2000, Multi-period performance persistence analysis of hedge funds, *Journal of Empirical finance and Quantitative Analysis*, 35, pp. 327-342.

Amenc N. and Martellini L., Fall 2002, Portfolio optimization and hedge fund style allocation decision, *Journal of Alternative Investment.*

Amin G.S., Kat H.M., 2001, *Hedge Fund Performance 1990-2000: Do the' money machine' really add value?*, Working paper, ISMA Centre, The University of Reading.

Brown S.J., Goetzmann, W.N., Ibboston, R.G., 1999. Offshore hedge Funds: Survival and performance 1989-1995, *Journal of Business* 72, pp. 91-118.

Brown S.J., Goetzmann, W.N., Park J., January 1998, *Conditions for survival: Changing Risk and the Performance of Hedge Fund Managers and CTAs*, NBER wording paper, www.ssrn.com.

Brown S.J., Goetzmann, W.N., Park J., Mai 1998, *Hedge funds and the Asian Currency Crisis of 1997*, Social Science Research Network Electronic Library, http://www.ssrn.com.

Brown S.J., Goetzmann, W.N., Park J., 2001, Careers and survival: Competition and risk in the hedge fund and CTA industry, *Journal of Finance* 56, pp. 1869-1886.

Brown S.J., Goetzmann, W.N., Liang B., 2003, *Fees on fees in Funds of Funds*, NBER Working paper.

Capocci D. and Hubner G., 2001, *L'Univers des Hedge Funds, une perspective empirique, Revue Bancaire et Financière*, No. 6, pp. 361-369.

Capocci D., A. Coarhay and Hubner G., 2004, Hedge Fund Performance in Bull and Bear Market, forthcoming in the *European Journal of Finance*.

Capocci D. and Hubner G., 2004, An Analysis of Hedge Funds Performance, *Journal of Empirical Finance* 11, 55-89.

Celent, 2003, The Fund of Hedge Funds Industry, *www.celent.com*, p.2.

Detnews.COM, November 29, 2003, Germany opens door to hedge funds, *www.detnews.com*, p.1.

Deutsche Bank, August 2000, *Fund of Hedge Funds – An introduction to Multi-manager Funds*, Deutsche Bank AG London, p. 54.

Edwards F.R. and CAGLAYAN M.O., 2001, Hedge Fund and Commodity Investments in Bull and Bear Markets, *Journal of Portfolio Management*, 27, No. 4.

Ennis R. M. and SEBASTIAN, M. D., 2003. A Critical Look at the Case for Hedge Funds, *Journal of Portfolio Management* 29, nr. 4.

Fabozzi F. J. and FRANCIS J. C., 1979, Mutual Fund Systematic Risk for Bull and Bear Markets: An Empirical Examination, *Journal of Finance* 34, 1243-1250.

Financial Times, June 6, 2001, Getting a little crazy in the hedge fund heat, available on *www.rjsinvestments.com.*

Fung W. and Hsieh D., 1997, Empirical characteristics of Dynamic Trading Strategies: The case for Hedge Funds, *The Review of Financial Studies*, Vol. 10, No.2, pp. 275-302.

Fung W., Hsieh, D.A., 2000, Performance characteristics of hedge funds and commodity funds: Natural vs spurious biases, *Journal of Quantitative and Financial Analysis* 35, 291-307.

Kat H.M., Amin G.S., 2002, Stocks, Bonds and Hedge Funds, *Journal of Portfolio Management*, 29, No. 4, pp. 113-120.

Kao G. W., Cheng L. T. W. and Chan K. C., 1998, International Mutual Fund Selectivity and Market Timing during Up and Down Markets, *Financial Review* 33, .

Lamm McFall.R., Winter 1999, Portfolios of Alternative Assets: Why not 100% Hedge Funds?, *The Journal of Investing*, pp. 87-96.

Liang B., 1999, On the performance of hedge funds. *Financial Analysts Journal*, pp. 72-85.

Liang B., 2000, Hedge Funds: The living and the dead, *Journal of Financial and Quantitative Analysis* 35, pp. 309-325.

Liang B., 2001, Hedge funds performance: 1990-1999, *Financial Analysts Journal. January/February*, pp. 11-18.

Liang B., Draft working paper 2003, *On the performance of Alternative Investments: CTAs, Hedge Funds, and Funds-of-Funds*, Weatherhead School of Management , p. 36.

Loomis C., April 1966, The Jones Nobody Keeps Up With, *Fortune*, p. 237-247.

Markowitz H., 1952, Portfolio Selection, *Journal of Finance* 7, pp. 77-91.

Nicholas, J.G., 2003, *Hedge Fund of Funds Investing*, Bloomberg Pr., p. 288.

Oberuc, Richard E., 1995, *Performance of Hedge Funds relative to traditional Investments*, Working Paper, LaPorte Asset Allocation System.

Ross S., Westerfield R. and Jordan B., 2003, *Fundamentals of Corporate finance – sixth edition*, McGraw-Hill Irwin, p. 774.

Schneeweis T., Spurgin R., 1997, *Managed futures, hedge funds and mutual fund return estimation: A Multi-factor approach*, CISDM Working Paper.

Simone S., 2002, Hedge Fund Genesis, *http://www.rjsinvestments.com/locked/education/hedge%20fund%20genesis.pdf, p. 3.*

Tass Investment Research Ltd, April 2001, *The case for hedge funds, 2nd edition.*

Van Chairman G., The smartest way to invest in Hedge Funds, *www.vanhedge.com*.

In: Stock Exchanges, IPO's and Mutual Funds
Editor: E. Klein, pp. 151-179
ISBN 1-59454-173-6

Chapter 8

ENTRY DECISIONS BY MUTUAL FUND FAMILIES

*Xinge Zhao**
China Europe International Business School (CEIBS), China

ABSTRACT

Due to the multiple-share-class structure of mutual funds, the entry decisions by fund families include two separate decisions: the introduction of new (single-share-class or multiple-share-class) portfolios and the introduction of new share classes for existing portfolios. The two decisions are based on very different considerations and lead to very different share class compositions. New share classes in existing portfolios are primarily the results of the expansion of traditional front-end load funds and institutional funds, and are mostly introduced in star portfolios. No-load funds rarely introduce new load share classes and no-load share classes are never observed to be added to load funds. In addition, fund families starting new multiple-share-class portfolios appear to follow a very risky introduction strategy.

Keywords: Mutual funds; Entry decisions; Multiple-share-class structure; Fund families.

INTRODUCTION

The rapid growth of the mutual fund industry is characterized not only by the dramatic increase of assets in existing funds, but also by the large number of new funds started by fund families each year. The purpose of this chapter is to study what constitutes and what determines the entry decisions—the decisions to introduce new funds—by fund families. This research aids in understanding the industrial organization of the mutual fund industry and explaining the reasons for the rapid growth of the industry, one of the most dramatic developments of financial institutions in history.

* Corresponding author: Professor Xinge Zhao, China Europe International Business School, 699 Hongfeng Road, Pudong, Shanghai, China, 201206, Tel: 011-86-21-28905601, E-mail: zxinge@ceibs.edu

Despite the importance of the entry decisions, Khorana and Servaes (1999) is the only published study dedicated to this topic. They use annual data over the period 1979-1992, and find that fund initiations are positively related to the level of assets invested in and the capital gains embedded in other funds with the same objective, the fund family's prior performance, the fraction of funds in the family in the low range of fees, and the decision by large families to open similar funds in the prior year. They also find that large families and families that have more experience in opening funds in the past are more likely to open new funds.

This chapter extends the study of Khorana and Servaes (1999) by distinguishing between the two separate decisions included in the entry decisions: the introduction of new portfolios vs. the introduction of new share classes for existing portfolios, a distinction not made in the existing literature on the evolution of the mutual fund industry. The decision to introduce new portfolios can be further separated into the decisions to introduce new single-share-class portfolios or multiple-share-class portfolios. These distinctions have significant effects on how we analyze fund families' entry decisions.

Although many funds are listed as separate funds, they are components of the same *portfolio* in a fund family. The structure of a representative mutual fund family is given in Figure 1. For example, in the Dreyfus Fund Family, the following four funds — Dreyfus Premier Aggressive Growth Fund A, Dreyfus Premier Aggressive Growth Fund B, Dreyfus Premier Aggressive Growth Fund C, and Dreyfus Premier Aggressive Growth Fund R — share the same portfolio, that of Dreyfus Premier Aggressive Growth Fund. These four funds are called *share classes* of the same portfolio.[1] Although they are listed as four separate funds, they have the same portfolio manager, the same pool of securities, and the same returns before expenses and loads. The major difference among the four funds is that they have different loads.[2] The varying load structures make them attractive to different investors, and the fund family can offer them through different brokers to reach as many investors as possible. Nanda, Narayanan, and Warther (2000) show that the existence of investor clienteles with differing liquidity and marketing needs gives rise to a variety of open-end fund structures.

The multiple-share-class structure of mutual funds complicates the study of the entry decisions by fund families, because a new fund can be either the initial share class (or one of the initial share classes) of a new portfolio (a real new fund) or just a new share class of an existing portfolio. In the above example, Fund A, the first share class of the portfolio, was started in June 1969, while the other three share classes were started in January 1996. As a result, the entry decisions by fund families include two separate decisions: the introduction of new portfolios and the introduction of new share classes for existing portfolios. The decision by a fund family to introduce new portfolios may be very different from the decision to introduce new share classes for an existing portfolio. By introducing new portfolios, the fund family adds new products to its product line of funds; while by introducing new share classes for an existing portfolio, the fund family promotes more varieties of an existing product with minimal modifications, new distribution channels, and alternative pricing structures. In this chapter, I study the introduction of new portfolios and the introduction of new share classes for existing portfolios separately and contrast the results.

---

[1] See Pozen (1998) for a detailed discussion of share classes.

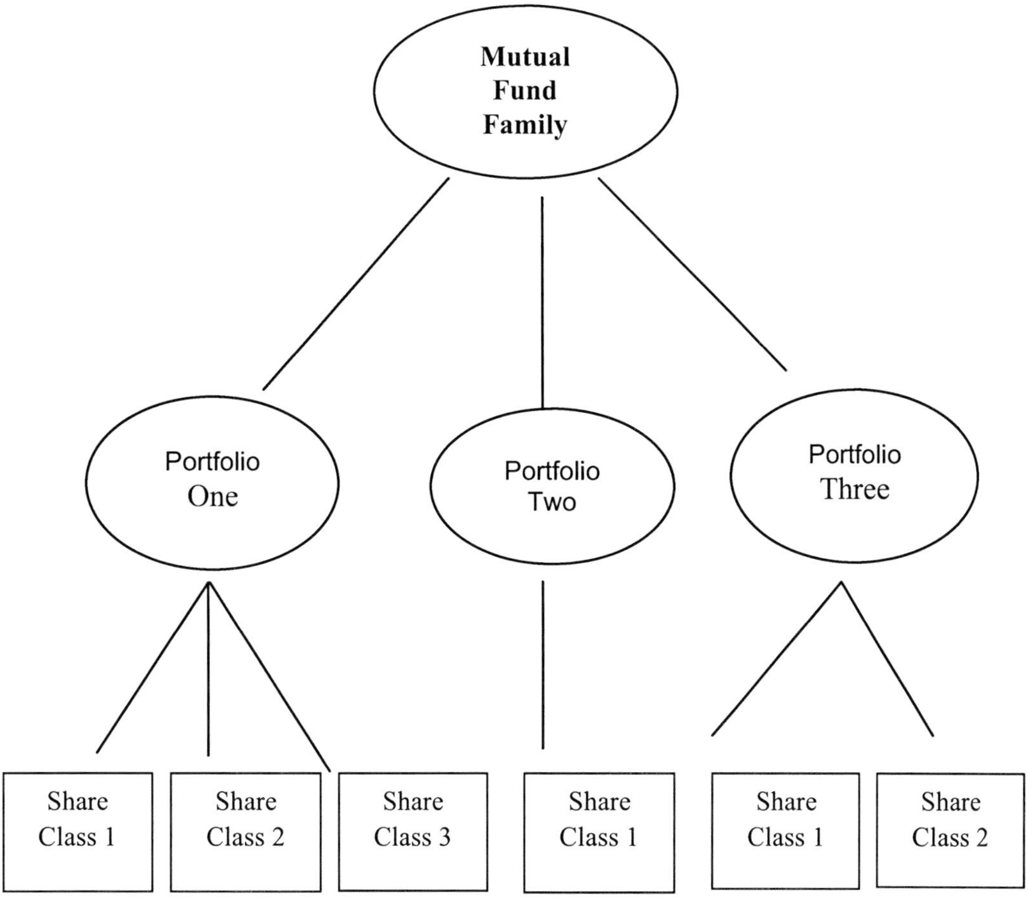

Figure 1. Structure of a representative mutual fund family. Many mutual funds are *share classes* of the same *portfolio* in a fund family. Although they are listed as separate funds, they have the same portfolio manager, the same pool of securities, and the same returns before expenses and loads. The major difference among the share classes is that they have different loads. The varying load structures make them attractive to different investors, and the fund family can offer them through different brokers to reach as many investors as possible.

I first find that the distributions across different share classes are very different for the initial share classes of new portfolios and new share classes in existing portfolios, except for the institutional share class. Besides institutional share classes, new portfolios are primarily made up of no-load share classes and front-end load share classes, while back-end load and level-load share classes account for about 50% of new share classes in existing portfolios.

When fund families introduce new portfolios, they may introduce single-share-class portfolios or multiple-share-class portfolios. Share class compositions are also quite different for new single-share-class portfolios and new multiple-share-class portfolios. Although some

[2] Fund A has a 5.75% front-end load, Fund B has a 4.00% back-end load and a 0.75% 12b-1 fee but no front-end load, Fund C also has no front-end load and a 0.75% 12b-1 fee but a low 1.00% back-end load, while Fund R has no load whatsoever.

determinants are shared in the decisions to introduce new single-share-class and multiple-share-class portfolios, such as economies of scale effect, tax effect, and objective introduction record, significant differences also exist. Fund families starting multiple-share-class portfolios appear to follow a very risky introduction strategy. They chase recent inflows, bet against market trend, and tend to add more portfolios in the same investment objective in consecutive quarters. Fund families tend to introduce both new multiple-share-class portfolios and new share classes in existing portfolios in investment objectives with poor returns, resorting to the assistance of brokers and financial advisors to attract new investments in a down market.

The two decisions to introduce new portfolios and new share classes in existing portfolios are also largely based on different considerations. Fund families with both good performance and poor performance introduce new portfolios, while new share classes are mostly introduced by fund families with unsatisfactory performance. High inflows lead families to introduce new portfolios, while low inflows entice families to introduce more share classes in existing portfolios. Although fund families are more likely to introduce new portfolios in objectives with high capital gains overhang to attract tax-sensitive investors, tax concerns do not affect fund families' decision to introduce new share classes, because new share classes are not a solution to the unrealized capital gains problem. In addition, I find that new share classes are mostly introduced in star portfolios with good performance, more assets, high expense ratio, longer history, and smaller number of share classes.

Share classes are a major innovation in the development of mutual funds, and the best-known fund families played leading roles in this process. New share classes in existing portfolios are primarily the results of the expansion of traditional front-end load funds and institutional funds. The front-end load funds expand by adding other load retail share classes and institutional share classes. Institutional funds overwhelmingly choose the load path over the no-load path to expand to the retail market. No-load funds rarely introduce new load share classes and no-load share classes are never observed to be added to load funds, both due to the reluctance of brokers and financial planners to sell any load share classes of a fund when it is also available to investors at no cost.

A comparison of my results for introduction of new portfolios and Khorana and Servaes' (1999) results shows some similarity: we both predict fund families are more likely to introduce new portfolios (funds) in objectives with high capital gains overhang and a strong introduction record. On the other hand, in terms of family returns and inflows, or objective size and returns, the results are quite different. My results for introduction of new share classes in existing portfolios, except for a strong introduction record in the family and in the investment objective, differ substantially from those of Khorana and Servaes (1999). The contradictory results underscore the importance of distinguishing between the decisions to introduce new portfolios vs. new share classes.[3]

The remainder of the Chapter is organized as follows. Section 2 describes the data and variable construction. Section 3 examines the introduction of new portfolios. Section 4 studies the initiation of new share classes for existing portfolios. Section 5 concludes.

---

[3] The data used in Khorana and Servaes (1999) end in 1992, and should include introduction of both new portfolios and new share classes in existing portfolios, considering that 95 new share classes had already been introduced in existing portfolios by the end of 1992 in my data set.

Data and Variable Construction

Data

A panel data set of quarterly data from the first quarter of 1987 to the fourth quarter of 1996 of 3,047 open-end domestic equity mutual funds is created from raw data obtained from Morningstar Inc., with some of the returns supplemented with data from Lipper and the CRSP Survivor-Bias Free US Mutual Fund Database. The data set covers all of the five Morningstar domestic equity investment objectives: Aggressive Growth, Growth, Growth and Income, Equity-Income, and Small Company.[4] The data include: fund name, fund family, portfolio name, fund share class, inception date, fund age (months), quarterly return, NAV (net asset value), expense ratio, fund loads (front-end load, back-end load, and 12b-1 fee), and total assets. For funds that exited during the sample period, a complete history of these funds until their exits is available. Therefore, the data set is free from survivorship bias.

Table 1. Fund Share Classes

Share classes	Number	Description
A	843	With a front-end load and a 12b-1 fee, no back-end load
B	470	With a back-end load and a 12b-1 fee, no front-end load
C	263	With a back-end load (much smaller than B's) and a 12b-1 fee (generally greater than B's), no front-end load; often called level-load
D	15	With a front-end load, a back-end load, and a 12b-1 fee
No-Load	681	No front-end load or back-end load, no 12b-1 fee or with a 12b-1 fee ≤ 0.25%
12b-1 Only	72	With a 12b-1 fee, but no front-end load or back-end load
Institutional	678	No load, generally with a large minimum initial purchase, for institutional investors
Advisory	21	No load in name, only available through advisors who may charge commissions or fees
Other	4	Other
Total	*3,047*	

Note: Many mutual funds are different share classes of the same portfolio. These share classes have different loads or minimum investment requirements and may be offered through different brokers. The varying load structures and minimum investment requirements make them attractive to different investors. The 3,047 funds studied in this chapter can be categorized into nine types of share classes: A, B, C, D, No-Load, 12b-1 Only, Institutional, Advisory, and Other. A (front-end load) is the largest share class in terms of number of funds, followed by No-Load, Institutional, and B (back-end load).

[4] According to Morningstar Mutual Funds User's Guide, *Aggressive Growth* funds seek rapid growth of capital. They often invest in small companies without specifying a market capitalization range and are more likely than other funds to invest in IPOs and in companies with high price/earnings and price/book ratios. *Growth* funds pursue capital appreciation by investing primarily in equity securities. Current income, if considered at all, is a secondary concern. For *Growth and Income* funds, growth of capital and current income are near-equal objectives. Investments are typically selected for both appreciation potential and dividend-paying ability. *Equity-Income* funds are expected to pursue current income by investing at least 65% of their assets in dividend-paying equity securities. *Small Company* funds seek capital appreciation by investing primarily in stocks of companies with market capitalization of less than $1 billion.

As shown in Table 1, the 3,047 funds studied in this chapter can be categorized into nine types of share classes: A, B, C, D, No-Load, 12b-1 Only, Institutional, Advisory, and Other. The description of these share classes is given in Table 1. From Table 1, we can see A (front-end load) is the largest share class in terms of number of funds, followed by No-Load, Institutional, and B (back-end load). Many funds are different share classes of the same portfolio. These share classes have different loads or minimum investment requirements and may be offered through different brokers. The 3,047 funds belong to 1,790 portfolios, as depicted in Panel A of Table 2. While the majority of portfolios, 1,111 of them, have only one share class, 679 of them are made up of at least two share classes. These 1,790 portfolios belong to 591 families, tabulated in Panel B of Table 2. While 254 families have just one portfolio, the remaining 337 families have at least two portfolios.

At the beginning of 1987, as shown in Figure 2, the composition of mutual funds was dominated by A funds and No-Load funds, each accounting for roughly 40% of all funds, while all other share classes had a combined share of about 20%. But this situation has changed dramatically after ten years. At the end of 1996, although A was still the largest share class, its share dropped to about 25%. No-Load funds and Institutional funds tied for the second place, each with a share of about 20%. Besides Institutional funds, B (back-end load) and C (level-load) funds also had dramatic growth in the ten years.

Table 2. Share Classes, Portfolios, and Fund Families

Number of Share Classes	*Number of Portfolios*
Panel A: Number of share classes in portfolios	
1	1,111
2	295
3	223
4	132
5	28
6	0
7	1
Total	1,790
Number of Portfolios	*Number of Fund Families*
Panel B: Number of portfolios in fund families	
1	254
2	121
3-5	143
6-10	48
11-20	22
21-30	2
31	1
Total	591

Note: A portfolio may have more than one share class. Many mutual funds are different share classes of the same portfolio. The 3,047 funds belong to 1,790 portfolios. While the majority of portfolios, 1,111 of them, have only one share class, 679 of them are made up of at least two share classes. The maximum number of share classes a portfolio has is seven. A fund family may have more than one portfolio. The 1,790 portfolios belong to 591 families. While 254 families have just one portfolio, the remaining 337 families have at least two portfolios.

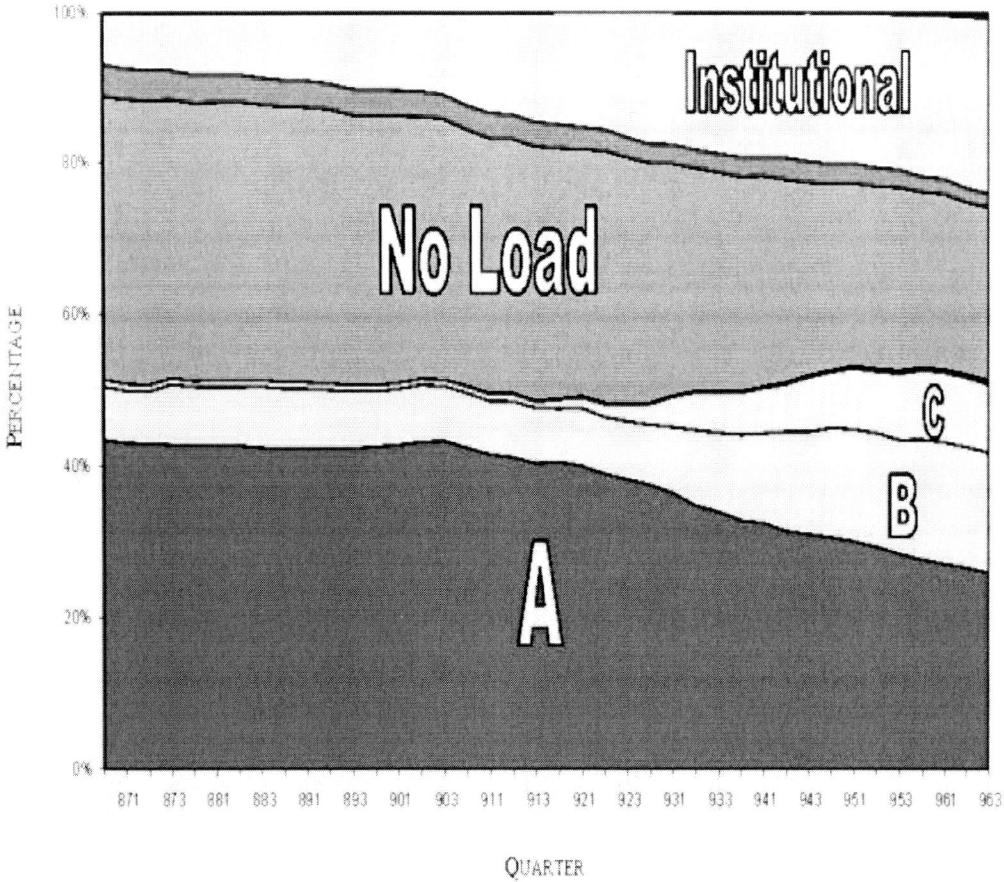

Figure 2. The evolution of fund share classes. At the beginning of 1987, the composition of mutual funds was dominated by A funds and No-Load funds, each accounting for roughly 40% of all funds, all other share classes had a combined share of about 20%. But this situation has changed dramatically after ten years. At the end of 1996, although A was still the largest share class, its share dropped to about 25%. No-Load funds and Institutional funds tied for the second place, each with a share of about 20%. Besides Institutional funds, B (back-end load) and C (level-load) funds also had dramatic growth in the ten years.

In Figure 3, at the beginning of 1987, almost all portfolios had only one share class. At the end of 1996, only about 60% of portfolios had only one share class, roughly 20%, 15%, and 4% of portfolios had two share classes, three share classes, and four share classes, respectively.

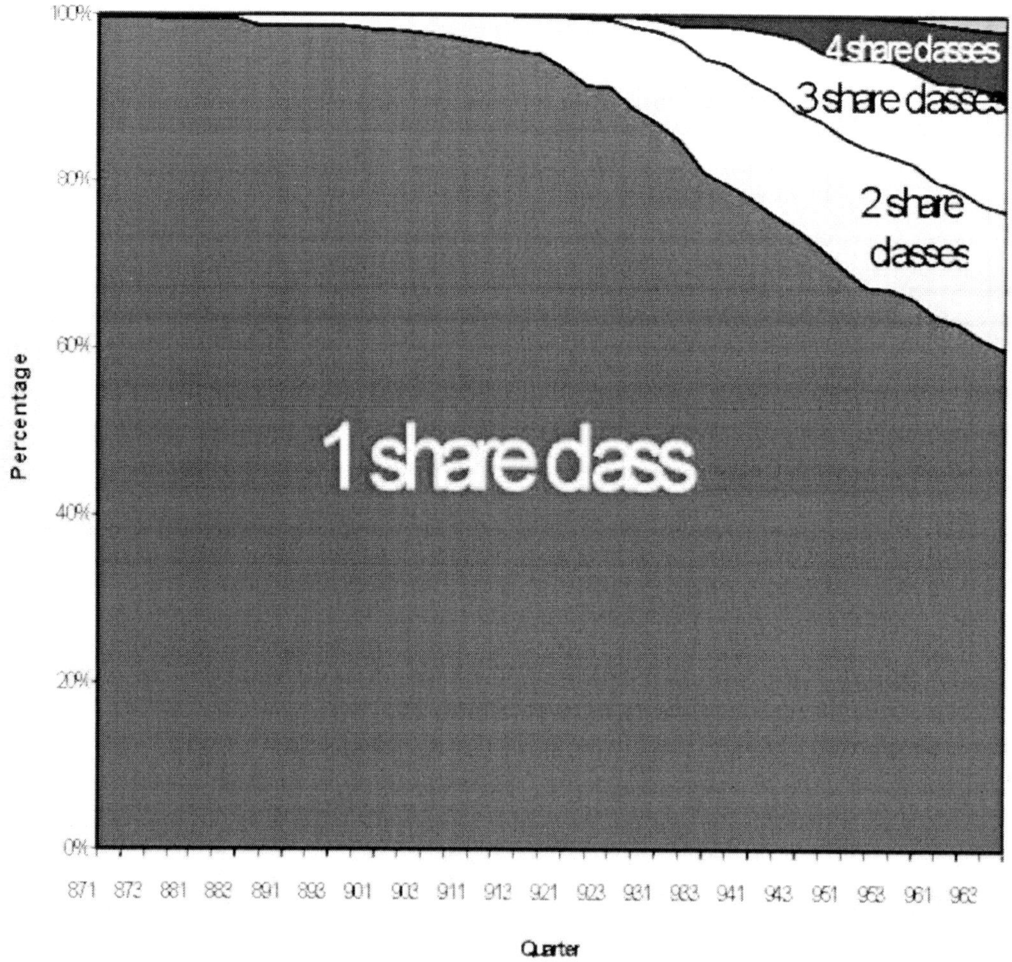

Figure 3. Number of share classes in portfolios. At the beginning of 1987, almost all portfolios had only one share class. At the end of 1996, only about 60% of portfolios had only one share class, roughly 20%, 15%, and 4% of portfolios had two share classes, three share classes, and four share classes, respectively.

As shown in Table 3, among the 3,047 funds, 2,529 funds were started in the ten-year period from 1987 to 1996. New Institutional funds and A funds were the two largest groups, each accounting for about 25% of all new funds, followed by No-Load funds, B funds, and C funds. Among these new funds, 1,576 funds were the initial share classes of new portfolios, while the remaining 953 funds were introduced as new share classes in existing portfolios.

Table 3. Distribution of Initial Share Classes in New Portfolios and New Share Classes in Existing Portfolios across Different Share Classes

	All New Funds		As Initial Share Classes in New Portfolios						As New Share Classes in Existing Portfolios					
			Single Share Class		Multiple Share Class		Sub Total		Single Share Class		Multiple Share Class		Sub Total	
Share Class	Number	%	Number	%	Number	%	Number	%	Number	%	Number	%	Number	%
A	620	24.52	282	25.99	165	33.60	447	28.36	122	18.54	51	17.29	173	18.15
B	434	17.16	36	3.22	106	21.59	142	9.01	185	28.12	107	36.27	292	30.64
C	258	10.20	14	1.29	69	14.05	83	5.27	109	16.57	66	22.37	175	18.36
D	15	0.59	2	0.18	2	0.41	4	0.25	8	1.22	3	1.02	11	1.15
No-Load	486	19.22	464	42.76	17	3.46	481	30.52	2	0.30	3	1.02	5	0.52
12b-1 Only	49	1.94	32	2.95	5	1.02	37	2.35	8	1.22	4	1.36	12	1.26
Institutional	643	25.43	253	23.32	122	24.85	375	23.79	209	31.76	59	20.00	268	28.12
Advisory	21	0.83	0	0.00	5	1.02	5	0.32	14	2.13	2	0.68	16	1.68
Other	3	0.12	2	0.18	0	0.00	2	0.13	1	0.15	0	0.00	1	0.10
Total	2,529	100.00	1,085	100.00	491	100.00	1,576	100.00	658	100.00	295	100.00	953	100.00

Note: Among the 3,047 funds, 2,529 funds were started in the ten-year period from 1987 to 1996. New Institutional funds and A funds are the two largest groups, each accounting for about 25% of all new funds, followed by No-Load funds, B funds, and C funds. Among these new funds, 1,576 funds are the initial share classes of new portfolios, while the remaining 953 funds are introduced as new share classes in existing portfolios. The distributions of these two types of new funds across different major share classes appear to be very different, except for the Institutional share class.

Table 4. Distribution of New Funds from Each Share Class across Different New Fund Categories

Share Class	Total		As Initial Share Classes in New Portfolios						As New Share Classes in Existing Portfolios					
			Single Share Class		Multiple Share Class		Sub Total		Single Share Class		Multiple Share Class		Sub Total	
	Number	%	Number	%	Number	%	Number	%	Number	%	Number	%	Number	%
A	620	100.00	282	45.48	165	26.62	447	72.10	122	19.68	51	8.22	173	27.90
B	434	100.00	36	8.29	106	24.43	142	32.72	185	42.63	107	24.65	292	67.28
C	258	100.00	14	5.43	69	26.74	83	32.17	109	42.25	66	25.58	175	67.83
D	15	100.00	2	13.33	2	13.33	4	26.66	8	53.33	3	20.00	11	73.33
No-Load	486	100.00	464	95.47	17	3.50	481	98.97	2	0.41	3	0.62	5	1.03
12b-1 Only	49	100.00	32	65.31	5	10.20	37	75.51	8	16.33	4	8.16	12	24.49
Institutional	643	100.00	253	39.35	122	18.97	375	58.32	209	32.50	59	9.18	268	41.68
Advisory	21	100.00	0	0.00	5	23.81	5	23.81	14	66.67	2	9.52	16	76.19
Other	3	100.00	2	66.67	0	0.00	2	66.67	1	33.33	0	0.00	1	33.33
All New Funds	*2,529*	*100.00*	*1,085*	*42.90*	*491*	*19.42*	*1,576*	*62.32*	*658*	*26.02*	*295*	*11.66*	*953*	*37.68*

Note: This table shows that 98.97% of No-Load funds are introduced as the initial share classes of new portfolios. In fact, 95.47% of them are introduced as the single share class of new portfolios. They are almost never introduced as new share classes in existing portfolios. More than 70% of A funds are introduced as the initial share classes of new portfolios, with 45.48% of them introduced as the single initial share class of a new portfolio. In contrast, almost 70% of B funds and C funds are introduced as new share classes in existing portfolios. Even when they are started as initial share classes of new portfolios, they are rarely started as the single initial share class but with other initial share classes instead.

The distributions of these two types of new funds across different major share classes appear to be very different, except for the Institutional share class. The most striking distinction comes from No-Load funds. No-Load funds, the largest group in the initial share classes of new portfolios with a share of 30.52%, account for a mere 0.52% of new share classes in existing portfolios. The share in the initial share classes of new portfolios is also significantly higher for A funds. On the other hand, although only 9.01% of the initial share classes of new portfolios are B funds, they account for more than 30% of new share classes in existing portfolios, the largest group in new share classes in existing portfolios. A very similar distribution can also be observed for C funds.

Table 4 exhibits the distribution of new funds from various share classes in different new fund categories. It shows that 98.97% of No-Load funds are introduced as the initial share classes of new portfolios. In fact, 95.47% of them are introduced as the single share class of new portfolios. They are almost never introduced as new share classes in existing portfolios.[1] More than 70% of A funds are introduced as the initial share classes of new portfolios, with 45.48% of them introduced as the single initial share class of a new portfolio. In contrast, almost 70% of B funds and C funds are introduced as new share classes in existing portfolios. Even though B funds and C funds have gained popularity recently, they are seldom the single share class offered for a portfolio. Even when they are started as initial share classes of new portfolios, they are rarely started as the single initial share class but are offered with other initial share classes. Once again, compared to these four share classes, Institutional funds appear to be fairly evenly distributed between new portfolios and existing portfolios, following the roughly 60/40 split between new portfolios and existing portfolios of all new funds.

As for the distribution of different share classes across the five investment objectives, no significant difference can be observed except in the Aggressive Growth objective. Institutional share classes account for more than 20% in all of the other four objectives, but only comprise 13.69% in the Aggressive Growth objective. Aggressive Growth is by far the riskiest among the five objectives. Aggressive Growth funds are most likely to invest in stocks with high price/earnings and price/book ratios, and may also use such investment techniques as heavy sector concentrations and short-selling. As a result, they may not be appropriate for many institutional investors, such as pension funds and endowments.

Variable Construction

To study fund families' decisions to introduce new portfolios and new share classes for existing portfolios, four levels of variables are created, spanning family and portfolio characteristics, as well as differences among investment objectives. Full details as to variable construction appear in Appendix A.

Objective-level variables relate to specific investment objectives, e.g., Growth or Small Company, and include the general performance, size, inflow, capital gains overhang, and

5. The five new No-Load share classes in existing portfolios are all introduced in portfolios with only Institutional share classes. Most of the 17 No-Load funds introduced as initial share classes with other initial share classes are also introduced with Institutional share classes only.

records of introduction and termination in an objective. They are created with data of funds in the same investment objective.

The general situation of the fund family, such as its performance, size, inflow, age, expense ratio, capital gains overhang, and records of introduction and termination, constitute *family-level* variables, which are created with data of funds in the same fund family.

Family-objective-level variables describe the distribution among different objectives within a family, such as shares of assets in different objectives in a family, and whether the family has many or only a few portfolios in a certain objective.

Portfolio-level variables include attributes of portfolios, such as performance, size, inflow, age, expense ratio, capital gains overhang, and records of introduction and termination of share classes. They are created with data of share classes in each portfolio.

INTRODUCTION OF NEW PORTFOLIOS BY FUND FAMILIES

In this section, I study the effects of the family level, objective level, and family-objective level variables on the introduction of new portfolios by fund families.

For each fund family in each quarter, five observations correspond to the five objectives. Each observation includes dummy variables indicating whether the family introduced new single-share-class or multiple-share-class portfolios in the objective, as well as family-level variables, and corresponding objective and family-objective variables. I use a fixed-effects logit model to study whether a fund family will introduce new portfolios. With the fixed-effects dummies for each cross-sectional unit, fund family, the model is capable of accounting for unobservable differences across fund families.

The Statistical Model

Let i = 1,2, ..., n denote each fund family, j = 1, 2, 3, 4, 5 denote each investment objective, and t = 1, 2, ..., T denote each time period. It is assumed that a family introduces a new portfolio if the benefits outweigh the costs of doing so.[2] The latent variable, y^*_{ijt}, indexes the benefit of introduction relative to cost, but is unobservable. Let y_{ijt} denote the observable dependent variable,

$$y_{ijt} = 1 \text{ if } y^*_{ijt} > 0 \qquad (1)$$
$$= 0 \text{ otherwise}$$

6. The direct costs of introducing a new portfolio include registration costs with the SEC and initial marketing costs, and direct operating costs of a new portfolio include mainly research costs and administrative costs. In terms of benefits, a new portfolio capable of attracting new investments becomes a new source of fees for a fund family since mutual funds have an assets-based compensation scheme. The fund family also benefits from economies of scale by introducing new portfolios since average operating costs can be lowered when research costs and administrative costs are spread over more portfolios.

where 1 stands for fund family i opening at least one portfolio in objective j in period t, and 0 stands for no opening. The latent variable underlying the choice is assumed to be a linear index function of the corresponding family level, objective level, and family-objective level variables,

$$y^*_{ijt} = \alpha_i + w_{it-1}\delta + z_{jt-1}\gamma + v_{ijt-1}\varphi + u_{ijt} \qquad (2)$$

where α_i is the unobservable family-specific fixed effect for the i_{th} family; $\alpha_i + u_{ijt}$ is the error term, with u_{ijt} as an idiosyncratic error; w_{it-1} is a row vector of the family level variables, z_{jt-1} is a row vector of the objective level variables, while v_{ijt-1} is a row vector of the family-objective level variables ; δ, γ, and φ are three column vectors of coefficients to be estimated. The error terms across observations within the same family are not independent relative to one another, since they share the same α_i. Details of how to estimate this model are provided in Appendix B.

Portfolio Introduction: Single-Share-Class vs. Multiple-Share-Class

When fund families introduce new portfolios, they may introduce a single-share-class portfolio or a multiple-share-class portfolio. As shown in Table 3, among the 1,576 new funds started as the initial share classes of new portfolios, about one-third of them are introduced with other initial share classes.

Among the 591 fund families, 251 introduced new portfolios. The majority of them, 181 families, only introduced new single-share-class portfolios, 25 families only introduced multiple-share-class portfolios, while the remaining 45 families introduced both. Among the fund families that only introduced new single-share-class portfolios, more than 40% of them are no-load families that only rely on direct distributions. As for the fund families that have introduced new multiple-share-class portfolios, more than 90% of them rely on brokers or financial advisors to sell shares.

Table 3 also shows that the share class compositions are quite different for new single-share-class portfolios and new multiple-share-class portfolios. Almost 70% and 25% of the share classes in new multiple-share-class portfolios belong to the three load share classes (A, B, and C) and institutional share class, respectively, while no-load share class accounts for more than 40% of new single-share class portfolios.

Considering the differences between new single-share-class and multiple-share-class portfolios, I decide to study the two decisions separately, both using the fixed-effects logit model. For each decision, I estimate two models. For flow variables such as return and inflows, Model 1 uses their quarterly values, while Model 2 is implemented with their annual values. The results for the two decisions are shown in Table 5 and Table 6, respectively.[3]

---

7. For all of the estimations in this chapter, besides using a complete list of variables, other model specifications using different sub-groups of variables are also tested. Similar qualitative results are obtained and therefore not reported.

Table 5. Fixed-effects Logit Model Estimates on Introduction of New Single-Share-Class Portfolios by Fund Families

Variables	Model 1 (Quarterly)		Model 2 (Annual)	
	Coefficients	P-values	Coefficients	P-values
Family Level				
Assets	0.007	0.211	0.008	0.169
Inflow	-0.004	0.835	0.002†	0.038
Overhang	-0.015	0.946	0.039	0.865
Age	0.005†	0.045	0.012‡	0.003
Return	-0.009	0.577	0.323	0.719
Expense ratio	-0.130	0.479	-0.141	0.551
Number of surviving portfolios	-0.334‡	0.000	-0.376‡	0.000
Number of new portfolios	0.128	0.273	0.086	0.242
Number of terminated portfolios	0.232	0.311	-0.339*	0.065
Objective Level				
Assets	0.000	0.781	-0.001	0.405
Inflow	-0.815	0.658	-0.142	0.816
Overhang	2.402‡	0.000	2.206†	0.020
Return	-0.006	0.499	-0.358	0.528
Number of new portfolios	0.054‡	0.000	0.028	0.000
Number of terminated portfolios	-0.009	0.700	-0.272*	0.052
Family-Objective Level				
Assets (share)	0.000	0.966	-0.001	0.675
Inflow	-0.157	0.311	-0.041	0.224
Overhang	0.204	0.183	0.132	0.379
Number of surviving portfolios	0.165‡	0.000	0.147‡	0.001
Number of new portfolios	-0.605†	0.049	-0.196	0.176
Pseudo R^2	0.0623		0.0782	

‡, †, and * indicate significance at the 1, 5, 10 percent confidence levels, respectively.

Note: I use a fixed-effects logit model, with each fund family as the cross-sectional unit, to study the effects of the family level, objective level, and family-objective level variables on the decisions to introduce new single-share-class portfolios by fund families. I estimate two models. For flow variables such as return and inflows, Model 1 uses their quarterly values while Model 2 is implemented with their annual values. I did not include objective level number of surviving portfolios because it is highly correlated to objective level total assets.

Table 6. Fixed-effects Logit Model Estimates on Introduction of New Multiple-Share-Class Portfolios by Fund Families

	Model 1 (Quarterly)		Model 2 (Annual)	
Variables	Coefficients	P-values	Coefficients	P-values
Family Level				
Assets	0.026	0.552	0.047	0.296
Inflow	0.189‡	0.004	-0.135	0.718
Overhang	-1.169	0.324	-0.683	0.574
Age	0.061‡	0.000	0.081‡	0.000
Return	-0.072	0.126	-3.026	0.248
Expense ratio	-0.083	0.888	-0.686	0.302
Number of surviving portfolios	-0.699	0.000	-0.983‡	0.000
Number of new portfolios	-1.196†	0.025	0.126	0.489
Number of terminated portfolios	-0.608	0.119	-0.782‡	0.002
Objective Level				
Assets	0.000	0.970	-0.002	0.315
Inflow	2.105	0.627	1.260	0.337
Overhang	3.673*	0.065	2.545	0.276
Return	-0.433*	0.084	-0.723	0.579
Number of new portfolios	0.069‡	0.000	0.026‡	0.000
Number of terminated portfolios	0.028	0.487	0.015	0.586
Family-Objective Level				
Assets (share)	0.002	0.606	0.003	0.470
Inflow	-0.071	0.392	0.006	0.920
Overhang	-0.006	0.990	-0.136	0.775
Number of surviving portfolios	-0.033	0.777	-0.086	0.497
Number of new portfolios	1.688†	0.013	0.101	0.715
Pseudo R^2	0.210		0.2103	

‡, †, and * indicate significance at the 1, 5, 10 percent confidence levels, respectively.

Note: I use a fixed-effects logit model, with each fund family as the cross-sectional unit, to study the effects of the family level, objective level, and family-objective level variables on the decisions to introduce new multiple-share-class portfolios by fund families. I estimate two models. For flow variables such as return and inflows, Model 1 uses their quarterly values while Model 2 is implemented with their annual values. I did not include objective level number of surviving portfolios because it is highly correlated to objective level total assets.

A comparison of the two tables first illustrates that some determinants are shared in the decisions to introduce new single-share-class and multiple-share-class portfolios. Nonetheless, in spite of the similarities, significant differences can also be observed in the determinants of the two decisions.

Similarities in the Introduction of Single-share-class and Multiple-Share-Class Portfolios

In both tables, the coefficients for family number of surviving portfolios are significantly negative in both models. This shows fund families with a smaller number of portfolios are more likely to introduce new portfolios. Fund families with fewer portfolios may take better advantage of the economies of scale if they introduce new portfolios. Since a fund family must start with a certain level of office space, research facilities, software, data bases, and management, research, and administrative staff, adding new portfolios may lower average operating costs, as long as the family does not have as many portfolios as can be supported by the current level of resources. I also find that fund families with a longer history are more likely to introduce new portfolios.

Fund families also are more likely to introduce new portfolios in objectives with high capital gains overhang due to a tax effect. Capital gains overhang of a portfolio is the fraction of the portfolio's total asset value consisting of unrealized capital gains. To avoid all taxes, mutual funds have to distribute at least 98% of all income and capital gains to shareholders. If the unrealized capital gains are realized and distributed to fund shareholders, shareholders' tax liabilities are increased immediately. Therefore, if current portfolios in an objective on average have high unrealized capital gains, this makes a distribution more likely in the near future and results in tax inefficiency for investors; therefore, tax-sensitive investors will be reluctant to invest in these portfolios. But new portfolios do not have unrealized capital gains problem and may be introduced to attract these investors.

Both quarterly and annual objective number of new portfolios are significantly positive, while annual family number of terminated portfolios is significantly negative. Fund families are more likely to introduce new portfolios in an objective if there has been a strong introduction record both recently and in the past year. On the other hand, a family is reluctant to introduce new portfolios if it has terminated a considerable number of portfolios in the past year.

Neither quarterly nor annual family return is significant in either table. This suggests that families with good returns or poor returns may both introduce new portfolios. Fund families with good track records are more likely to succeed in introducing new portfolios and therefore "should" introduce new portfolios. On the other hand, families with poor performance "need" to introduce new portfolios, since unsatisfactory performance leads to slow growth or even a decrease in assets and an inability to collect high management fees from current portfolios. These families need new sources of fees and an opportunity to improve the image of the family.

Differences in the Introduction of Single-Share-Class and Multiple-Share-Class Portfolios

Neither quarterly nor annual objective return is significant in Table 5, which suggests that fund families introduce new single-share-class portfolios in investment objectives with both good returns and poor returns. Fund families introduce new single-share-class portfolios in "hot" objectives to attract investors following a momentum strategy, and introduce new single-share-class portfolios in objectives with cheaper share prices to attract contrarian investors. However, fund families are more likely to start multiple-share-class portfolios in investment objectives when recent performance is poor. Considering that almost 70% of the share classes in new multiple-share-class portfolios belong to the three load share classes (A, B, and C), the fund families clearly are trying to resort to the brokers and financial advisors to attract new investors in a down market when investors are reluctant to make new investments voluntarily.

Fund families with high inflows are more likely to introduce new portfolios, not only because high inflows make it easier for new portfolios to grow, but also because new portfolios can divert inflows from existing portfolios, so that they will not grow too big to be managed efficiently. A negative relation between a fund's abnormal return and investor flows is documented in Edelen (1999). However, I find that short-term family inflows and long-term family inflows have different effects on the two decisions. High family inflows in the previous quarter only lead to the introduction of more multiple-share-class portfolios, while fund families with high inflows in the past year are more likely to only add new single-share-class portfolios. Multiple-share-class portfolios appear to be used more often by fund families to seize the opportunity of the abundant supply of money in the short run.

Economies of scale should be most significant if new portfolios are introduced in objectives in which the fund family currently has a presence, since no significant increase in research costs is necessary. But the downside would be that new portfolios may cannibalize existing portfolios. It turns out that the economies of scale effect dominates the cannibalization effect only in the introduction of single-share-class portfolios. The coefficients for family-objective number of surviving portfolios are significantly positive in both models in Table 5, but insignificant in Table 6. If a family has already had many portfolios in a certain objective, it would try to enhance its presence in that objective by introducing more single-share-class portfolios in it. Due to the multiple share classes in each portfolio, new multiple-share-class portfolios certainly cause increased concerns over cannibalization.

When many portfolios are terminated in an objective in the past year, fund families may refrain from introducing more new single-share-class portfolios in such an objective, while the introduction of multiple-share-class portfolios does not appear to be affected.

Fund families are more likely to introduce new multiple-share-class portfolios if they have not introduced many new portfolios in the previous quarter. However, when they introduce, they tend to focus on investment objectives in which they have introduced more recently. When fund families introduce new single-share-class portfolios, they have a completely different strategy on investment objective concentration. They focus on objectives in which they have not introduced many new portfolios recently.

Fund families starting multiple-share-class portfolios appear to follow a very risky introduction strategy. They chase recent inflows, bet against market trend, and tend to add more portfolios in the same investment objective in consecutive quarters. In addition, we have to notice that, introducing new multiple-share-class portfolios itself is already a fairly risky strategy, since many share classes of an untested portfolio are introduced at the same time.

INTRODUCTION OF NEW SHARE CLASSES FOR EXISTING PORTFOLIOS

I now turn to the introduction of new share classes for existing portfolios by mutual fund families. Share classes are a major innovation in the development of mutual funds, and the best- known fund families played leading roles in this process. Fidelity Advisor Funds Family appears to be the pioneer in introducing new share classes for existing portfolios.[4] Merrill Lynch Fund Group was second in line to introduce new share classes. By 1991, more fund families, such as Nations Funds, Prudential, Alliance Capital Funds, and PIMCO, had introduced new share classes in existing portfolios, the majority being adding B share classes to front-end load funds and adding A share classes to back-end load funds.

Among the 591 fund families, 191 families have multiple-share-class portfolios, and 165 families have introduced new share classes in existing portfolios. Only less than 3% of these families are no-load families that rely only on direct distributions. More than 85% of these families rely on brokers or financial advisors to sell shares, while the remaining 10% of the families focus on the institutional channels, such as pension funds or endowments.

Determinants of New Share Class Introduction

A fixed-effects logit model is applied again to study what factors affect a fund family's decision whether to add new share classes to an existing portfolio. Besides the family-level, objective-level, and family-objective-level variables used in the analysis of the introduction of new portfolios, I also include portfolio-level variables. Intuitively, whether a fund family will add new share classes to an existing portfolio also depends on the characteristics of the portfolio. For flow variables such as return and inflows, I estimate using their quarterly values in Model 1 and annual values in Model 2, as before. The results are reported in Table 7, and appear to be quite different from the results for the introduction of new portfolios.

First, new share classes are found to be introduced in star portfolios with good performance, more assets, longer history, a smaller number of share classes which makes further expansion feasible, and high expense ratio, which indicates high fee-generating ability. Table 7 shows that the coefficients for portfolio total assets, annual return, age, and expense ratio are significantly positive, while the coefficient for portfolio number of surviving share classes is significantly negative. According to industrial organization literature on differentiated products (see, e.g., Aron and Lazear, 1990; Burton, 1994; Pepall, 1990), a firm with a successful product tends to introduce more varieties of the product with limited modifications to best utilize the brand name and reach as many different clienteles as possible. Nanda, Wang, and Zheng (2003) also discuss the impacts of "stars" on a fund family.

8. In 1983, Fidelity Special Situations Fund was started as a front-end load fund. In 1986, a new share class, still with the same front-end load but a different 12b-1 fee, called Fidelity Special Situations-Plymouth was added to the original fund, whose name was changed to Fidelity Special Situations/Initial Class. Fidelity Special Situations-Plymouth is the first known new share class in an existing portfolio. In 1993, the portfolio name was changed to Fidelity Advisor Strategic Opportunities Fund. The Initial Class kept its share class name, while the Plymouth share class was renamed A. A B share class was added in 1994, and an institutional share class was added in 1995.

Table 7. Fixed-effects Logit Model Estimates on Introduction of New Share Classes for Existing Portfolios

Variables	Model 1 (Quarterly)		Model 2 (Annual)	
	Coefficients	P-values	Coefficients	P-values
Family Level				
Assets	0.004	0.779	0.000	0.977
Inflow	- 0.131	0.382	- 0.154*	0.084
Overhang	- 0.281	0.367	- 0.070	0.826
Age	0.071 ‡	0.000	0.072‡	0.000
Return	0.014	0.565	- 0.048‡	0.001
Expense ratio	- 0.554*	0.081	- 0.721*	0.051
Number of surviving portfolios	- 0.186‡	0.000	- 0.229‡	0.000
Number of new portfolios	0.191*	0.098	0.222‡	0.001
Number of terminated portfolios	- 1.384 ‡	0.000	- 0.050	0.662
Objective Level				
Assets	0.000	0.874	0.000	0.997
Inflow	- 0.957	0.650	0.439	0.516
Overhang	0.064	0.939	0.168	0.883
Return	- 0.014	0.168	- 0.012*	0.057
Number of new portfolios	0.016 ‡	0.008	0.011‡	0.001
Number of terminated portfolios	- 0.034 †	0.045	- 0.022*	0.061
Family-Objective Level				
Assets (share)	- 0.001	0.555	- 0.002	0.386
Inflow	0.022	0.596	0.004	0.872
Overhang	0.064	0.532	0.051	0.573
Number of surviving portfolios	- 0.075	0.146	- 0.091	0.116
Number of new portfolios	- 0.312	0.227	- 0.198	0.154
Portfolio Level				
Assets	0.105 ‡	0.002	0.117‡	0.001
Inflow	- 0.018	0.659	- 0.006	0.670
Overhang	- 0.045	0.311	- 0.069	0.391
Age	0.001 ‡	0.006	0.001‡	0.007
Return	0.015	0.324	0.013*	0.089
Expense ratio	0.562 ‡	0.000	0.507‡	0.000
Number of surviving share classes	- 1.323‡	0.000	- 1.290‡	0.000
Number of new share classes	0.024	0.902	- 0.243*	0.056
Number of terminated share classes	- 29.600	1.000	-31.325	1.000
Pseudo R^2	0.165		0.167	

‡, †, and * indicate significance at the 1, 5, 10 percent confidence levels, respectively.

Note: I use a fixed-effects logit model, with each fund family as the cross-sectional unit, to study the effects of the family level, objective level, family-objective level, and portfolio level variables on fund families' decisions to introduce new share classes for existing portfolios. I estimate two models. For flow variables such as return and inflows, Model 1 uses their quarterly values while Model 2 is implemented with their annual values. I did not include objective level number of surviving portfolios because it is highly correlated to objective level total assets.

Meanwhile, I also find that fund families most likely to introduce new share classes in their star portfolios are those families with unsatisfactory performance and inflows, as well as low expense ratios. Model 2 shows that the coefficients for family annual inflow, annual return, and expense ratio are all significantly negative. To promote the new share classes, the fund family only needs to rely on the good track record of the portfolio and can ignore the dismal picture of the family.

Economies of scale still appear to be a reason for fund families to introduce new share classes, since families with a smaller number of portfolios are also more likely to introduce new share classes. In fact, economies of scale are best achieved by introducing new share classes, since a new share class belongs to an existing portfolio, requiring no additional research or investment decision. Also, the cannibalization effect is minimized with new share classes, since a new share class should only attract investors not satisfied with current share classes.

Tax concerns do not affect fund families' decision to introduce new share classes, as is shown by the insignificant coefficients of capital gains overhang variables at all levels. Tax effects are not expected to play a role in a fund family's decision to introduce new share classes. This is due to SEC Rule 18f-3, requiring income, realized and unrealized capital gains and losses of multiple-share-class funds to be allocated to each share class on the basis of the net asset value of that share class in relation to the net asset value of the fund. Unlike new portfolios, which do not have capital gains overhang at initiation, new share classes are components of an existing portfolio and are also subject to the capital gains overhang in the portfolio. Therefore, new share classes are unable to attract tax-sensitive investors.

The coefficient of objective annual return is shown to be significantly negative, which suggests that new share classes are more likely to be introduced in investment objectives with poor performance. Considering that new share classes are almost all load share classes or institutional share class, as shown in Table 3, the assistance of brokers, financial advisors, and institutional investors makes it more likely for the portfolio to succeed in attracting new investments in a down market.

Strong family and objective introduction records lead a family to introduce more share classes, while termination records have the opposite effect. In both models, the coefficients for family number of new portfolios and objective number of new portfolios are significantly positive, while the coefficients for objective number of terminated portfolios are significantly negative. The coefficient for quarterly family number of terminated portfolios is also significantly negative.

It is interesting to notice that none of the family-objective level variables are significant, which suggests that the current presence in different objectives does not affect a family's decision to introduce new share classes for existing portfolios.

Expansion of Front-end Load Funds and Institutional Funds

A study of the existing share classes of portfolios that introduce new share classes shows that multiple-share-class portfolios are primarily the results of the expansion of traditional front-end load funds and institutional funds.

Single-share-class portfolios introduced about 67% of new share classes. For such single-share-class portfolios that introduced new share classes, 54.49% of them are front-end load funds, while 25.51% of them are institutional funds. If we consider all portfolios that have introduced new share classes, around 70% and 35% of them have an A share class and an institutional share class, respectively.

Among the 953 new share classes, once again, almost 70% of them are introduced in portfolios with an A share class. This reconfirms the central role of traditional front-end load funds in the development of multiple-share-class mutual funds. The front-end load funds first focus on introducing B share classes, which account for 53.54% of new share classes added by portfolios with only A share classes, to attract long-term buy-and-hold investors. Chordia (1996) indicates that a mutual fund's expected profits will increase if it can persuade investors to refrain from redeeming their holdings, and mutual funds seek to dissuade redemptions through front-end and back-end load fees. Chordia (1996) documents that back-end loads are more effective than front-end loads at dissuading redemptions, because investors will incur additional cost at redemption. This finding explains why B share classes are the top choice for traditional front-end load funds.

To attract investors who tend to trade more frequently, C share classes, which have lower back-end loads, higher 12b-1 fees, but no front-end loads, are also added. After adding a B share class, a portfolio further expands by adding a C share class, which accounts for 41.94% of new share classes added by portfolios with both A and B share classes. In the meantime, traditional front-end load funds also expand to the institutional market by adding institutional share classes, which account for 21.25% of new share classes added by portfolios with only A share classes, and 39.78% of new share classes added by portfolios with both A and B share classes. For portfolios with all three load share classes (A, B, and C), 87.23% of the new share classes introduced by them are institutional share classes.

The other major player in the development of multiple-share-class mutual funds is institutional funds. When institutional funds decide whether to choose the no-load path or the load path to expand to the retail market, they overwhelmingly selected the load path. Almost 70% of the new share classes started by portfolios with institutional shares belong to the three load share classes (A, B, and C), while only 1.56% of the new share classes are no-load.[5] A share classes are most likely the first new share class to be added by institutional funds. More than 50% of new share classes introduced by portfolios with only an institutional share are A share classes.

No-load funds only introduced 6.51% of the new share classes, almost all institutional share classes. The no-load nature restricts their options in adding more share classes. Had they introduced load share classes, brokers selling the load share classes would be ethically obliged to remind the investors of the existence of the low-cost no-load share classes. Therefore, brokers are reluctant to sell any load share classes of a portfolio that also has a no-load share class. As a result, no-load funds rarely introduce new share classes.

9. The rest of the new share classes are almost all other institutional share classes. These additional institutional share classes may target different institutions or have different features, such as different minimum initial investments.

Types of New Share Classes

When a fund family decides what new share classes to add to a portfolio, it has to consider what share classes the portfolio already has. As mentioned earlier, B share classes are the top choice for traditional front-end load funds. It turns out that 92.28% of the portfolios (89.22% of single-share-class portfolios) that introduce new B share classes already have an A share class. C share classes are also mostly started in portfolios with an A share class, which account for 88.57% of all portfolios that add new C share classes. In addition, 46.29% of the portfolios that introduce C share classes also have a B share class. It turns out that 44.57% of the portfolios that introduce C share classes have both A and B share classes. This finding reconfirms that C share classes are predominantly used in the further expansion of traditional front-end load funds.

A share classes only account for around 18% of new share classes. Among portfolios that add new A share classes, 55.81% have Institutional share classes, while 33.14% have B share classes; among single-share-class portfolios, the percentages are 57.93% and 22.76%, respectively. Considering that almost 85% of new A share classes are introduced by single-share-class portfolios, A share classes, if not introduced as the initial share class of a portfolio, are most likely to be considered first by an institutional fund trying to expand to the retail market or by a back-end load fund adding more distribution channels.

No-load share classes are almost never added as new share classes to existing portfolios. Fund families do not introduce no-load share classes to existing portfolios with load share classes, for fear that they may upset the existing distribution channels by making the portfolio also available to investors free of charge. The five no-load new share classes in existing portfolios are all introduced in portfolios with only institutional share classes.

New institutional share classes are most likely to be added by load portfolios to expand to the institutional market. Portfolios with A, B, and C share classes account for 63.50%, 30.42%, and 18.25%, respectively, of portfolios that added new institutional share classes, while 28.14% of these portfolios have both A and B share classes. New institutional share classes may also be added by no-load funds; however, this only accounts for less than 15% of new institutional share classes.

Among the 953 new share classes, 295 are added to the portfolio together with other share classes. About 70% of them are added in pairs, while the remaining 30% are added in trios. Single-share-class portfolios introduce around 85% of the pairs. Pairs of B and C share classes and pairs of B and institutional share classes, both started by front-end load funds, account for about 35% and 25% of all pairs, respectively. The third largest category, around 15% of all pairs, is pairs of A and B share classes started by institutional funds. All trios are introduced by single-share class portfolios. More than half of the trios are trios of A, B, and C share classes introduced by institutional funds, while around 25% of them are trios of B, C, and institutional share classes started by a front-end load fund.

Conclusion

This chapter examines the entry decisions by mutual fund families. Due to the multiple-share-class structure of mutual funds, the entry decisions include two separate decisions: the introduction of new portfolios and the introduction of new share classes for existing portfolios.

I find that the distributions across different share classes are very different for the initial share classes of new portfolios and new share classes in existing portfolios, except for the institutional share class. Share class compositions are also quite different for new single-share-class portfolios and new multiple-share-class portfolios. Although some determinants are shared in the decisions to introduce new single-share-class and multiple-share-class portfolios, such as economies of scale effect, tax effect, and objective introduction record, significant differences also exist. Fund families starting multiple-share-class portfolios appear to follow a very risky introduction strategy. They chase recent inflows, bet against market trend, and tend to add more portfolios in the same investment objective in consecutive quarters. Fund families tend to introduce both new multiple-share-class portfolios and new share classes in existing portfolios in investment objectives with poor returns, resorting to the assistance of brokers and financial advisors to attract new investments in a down market.

The two decisions to introduce new portfolios and new share classes in existing portfolios are also largely based on different considerations. New share classes in existing portfolios are primarily the results of the expansion of traditional front-end load funds and institutional funds. No-load funds rarely introduce new load share classes and no-load share classes are never observed to be added to load funds. In addition, I find that new share classes are mostly introduced in star portfolios with good performance, more assets, high expense ratio, longer history, and a smaller number of share classes.

The results of this research can benefit not only academicians, but also mutual fund advisors, investors, and regulators. This research aids in understanding the industrial organization of the mutual fund industry and explaining the reasons for its rapid growth. Fund advisors can better understand and learn from the entry decision process of other fund families to improve their own strategies in both product line and distribution channel expansions accordingly. Investors can use the entry behaviors of a fund family to infer the current status of the family. In the same way, fund advisors can learn about their competitors. The SEC can learn the characteristics of the fund families and funds that introduce multiple share classes, and evaluate the effect of its Rule 18f-3, which makes it easier for mutual funds to issue multiple share classes.

APPENDIX A. VARIABLE CONSTRUCTION

Four levels of variables are created, spanning family and portfolio characteristics, as well as differences among investment objectives. *Objective-level* variables relate to specific investment objectives, e.g., Growth or Small Company, and include the general performance, size, inflow, capital gains overhang, and records of introduction and termination in an objective. The general situation of the fund family, such as its performance, size, inflow, age, expense ratio, capital gains overhang, and records of introduction and termination, constitute *family-level* variables. *Family-objective-level* variables describe the distribution among different objectives within a family, such as shares of assets in different objectives in a family, and whether the family has many or only a few portfolios in a certain objective. *Portfolio-level* variables include attributes of portfolios, such as performance, size, inflow, age, expense ratio, capital gains overhang, and records of introduction and termination of share classes.

Objective-level Variables

At the objective level, variables are constructed for objective performance, objective size, objective inflow, objective capital gains overhang, number of portfolios in the objective, number of new portfolios in the objective, and number of terminated portfolios in the objective.

Quarterly objective performance is calculated by taking an asset-weighted average of the raw quarterly returns of all the portfolios in the objective. Objective size is the total assets of all of the portfolios in the objective. Since inflow is not available directly from the data, I define $Inflow_{it}$ as the net money inflow added to share class i in quarter t in excess of the capital gains due to performance,

$$Inflow_{it} = Asset_{it} - (1+r_{it})\, Asset_{it-1} - Masset_{it} \qquad (A.1)$$

where $Asset_{it}$ is the total assets of share class i at the end of quarter t, r_{it} is the raw return of share class i in quarter t, and $Masset_{it}$ is the assets added to share class i in quarter t due to acquiring other mutual funds. Quarterly objective inflow is calculated by adding the inflows of all share classes in the objective. I calculate quarterly relative objective inflow by dividing quarterly objective inflow by objective size at the end of the previous quarter.

I use measures based on Barclay, Pearson, and Weisbach (1998) to compute unrealized capital gains and overhang. For share class i in quarter t,

$$\text{Unrealized Capital Gains}_{it} = \text{Unrealized Capital Gains}_{it-1} + (NAV_{it} - NAV_{it-1}) * Shares_{it-1} + (Shares_{it} - Shares_{it-1}) * (NAV_{it} - (NAV_{it} + NAV_{it-1})/2) \qquad (A.2)$$

$$Overhang_{it} = \text{Unrealized Capital Gains}_{it} / Asset_{it} \qquad (A.3)$$

Objective overhang is calculated by dividing the sum of unrealized capital gains of all the share classes in an objective by the objective size, which describes the fraction of the total assets of an objective consisting of unrealized capital gains.

For each quarter t, I count the number of all surviving portfolios in the objective, the number of new portfolios in the objective, and the number of terminated portfolios in the objective. When I count the number of new portfolios in the objective, I ignore new share classes of existing portfolios. When I count the number of terminated portfolios in the objective, a portfolio is considered terminated if and only if all of the share classes of the portfolio are terminated.[6]

To test the effects of these variables in a longer horizon, flow variables are also computed on an annual basis. I calculate annual objective performance for each quarter by taking the compounded return of the quarterly objective returns in the last four quarters. Annual objective inflow is obtained for each quarter by adding up the quarterly objective inflows in

10. While a family can, in principle, terminate only some of the share classes in a portfolio in isolation, such an event is not very common in practice.

the last four quarters, and annual relative objective inflow is calculated by dividing annual objective inflow by objective size at the end of the t-4_{th} quarter. For the number of new portfolios in the objective, and the number of terminated portfolios in the objective in the past year, I sum the quarterly numbers in the previous four quarters. Objective size, overhang, and number of surviving portfolios are stock variables rather than flow variables, obviating the need for annual values.

Family-level Variables

At the family level, I examine family performance, family size, family inflow, family overhang, family age, family expense ratio, number of surviving portfolios in the family, number of new portfolios in the family, and number of terminated portfolios in the family.

Excess return for each portfolio in a family is obtained by subtracting the quarterly objective return from the raw return of each portfolio in the family. This measure is equivalent to the objective-adjusted return measure used in Khorana (2001), and is adopted because it measures a portfolio's performance against other portfolios with the same investment objective and tends to have the most effect on the decisions of fund families and investors among different performance measures. Quarterly family performance is calculated by taking the asset-weighted average of the excess returns of all portfolios in the family. Family size is the total assets of all portfolios in the family. Quarterly family inflow is calculated by adding the inflows of all portfolios in the family. I calculate quarterly relative family inflow by dividing quarterly family inflow by family size at the end of the previous quarter. Family overhang is calculated by dividing the sum of unrealized capital gains of all portfolios in a family by the family size, which describes the fraction of the total assets of a family consisting of unrealized capital gains. For family age, I use the age of the first portfolio in the family. Family expense ratio is calculated as the asset-weighted average of the expense ratios of all share classes in the family.

For each quarter, I count the number of all surviving portfolios in the family, the number of new portfolios in the family, and the number of terminated portfolios in the family. When I count the number of new portfolios in the family, I ignore new share classes of existing portfolios. When I count the number of terminated portfolios in the family, a portfolio is considered terminated if and only if all share classes of the portfolio are terminated.

Annual values for family performance, inflow, relative inflow, number of new portfolios, and number of terminated portfolios are computed in the same fashion as for the objective level variables. Family size, overhang, age, expense ratio, and number of surviving portfolios are stock variables rather than flow variables, obviating the need for annual values.

Family-objective-level Variables

I define family-objective asset share as the percentage of a family's total assets in an objective in the total assets of the entire family. Quarterly family-objective inflow is calculated by adding the inflows of all portfolios in an objective in the family. I calculate quarterly relative family-objective inflow by dividing quarterly family-objective inflow by family-objective size (total assets in an objective in a family) at the end of the previous quarter. Family-objective overhang is calculated by dividing the sum of unrealized capital gains of all portfolios in an objective in a family by the family-objective size. For each quarter, I count the number of all surviving portfolios, number of new portfolios, and number of terminated portfolios in an objective in the family. When I count the number of new portfolios, I ignore new share classes of existing portfolios. When I count the number of terminated portfolios, a portfolio is considered terminated if and only if all share classes of the portfolio are terminated. For all variables mentioned above, if a family does not have any portfolio in an objective yet, I set the value of the corresponding family-objective variable to zero.

It is inappropriate to set values of family-objective performance, age, and expense ratio to zero if the family does not have a portfolio in the objective. Also, since it is common that a family does not have portfolios in all five objectives, if I set these values to missing values, I lose 80% of the observations. Therefore, I do not compute family-objective level values for these three variables.

Annual values for family-objective inflow, relative inflow, number of new portfolios, and number of terminated portfolios are computed in the same fashion as for the objective level variables. Family-objective asset share, overhang, and number of surviving portfolios are stock variables rather than flow variables, obviating the need for annual values.

Portfolio-level Variables

At the portfolio level, the variables are portfolio performance, portfolio size, portfolio inflow, portfolio overhang, portfolio age, portfolio expense ratio, number of surviving share classes in the portfolio, number of new share classes in the portfolio, and number of terminated share classes in the portfolio. These variables are created in the same fashion as the family-level variables.

Appendix B. Fixed-effects Logit Model

Let i = 1, 2, …, n denote each fund family, j = 1, 2, 3, 4, 5 denote each investment objective, and t = 1, 2, …, T denote each time period. It is assumed that a family introduces a new portfolio if the benefits outweigh the costs of doing so. The latent variable, y^*_{ijt}, indexes the benefit of introduction relative to cost, but is unobservable. Let y_{ijt} denote the observable dependent variable,

$$y_{ijt} = 1 \text{ if } y^*_{ijt} > 0 = 0 \text{ otherwise} \qquad (B.1)$$

where 1 stands for fund family i opening at least one portfolio in objective j in period t, and 0 stands for no opening. The latent variable underlying the choice is assumed to be a linear index function of the corresponding family level, objective level, and family-objective level variables,

$$y^*_{ijt} = \alpha_i + w_{it-1}\delta + z_{jt-1}\gamma + v_{ijt-1}\varphi + u_{ijt} \qquad (B.2)$$

where α_i is the unobservable family-specific fixed effect for the i_{th} family; $\alpha_i + u_{ijt}$ is the error term, with u_{ijt} as an idiosyncratic error; w_{it-1} is a row vector of the family level variables, z_{jt-1} is a row vector of the objective level variables, while v_{ijt-1} is a row vector of the family-objective level variables ; δ, γ, and φ are three column vectors of coefficients to be estimated. The error terms across observations within the same family are not independent relative to one another, since they share the same α_i.

Instead of the two dimensions in a standard fixed-effects logit model, there are three dimensions: i, j, and t. I combine the j and t dimensions into one dimension, k, which stands for each objective at a certain period, so that standard fixed-effects logit model techniques can be applied.[7] The modified model works as follows. Let i = 1,2 … n denote each fund family and k = 1, 2 … K_i denote the observations for the i_{th} family. Let y_{ik} be the observable dependent variable,

$$y_{ik} = 1 \text{ if } y^*_{ik} > 0 \\ = 0 \text{ otherwise} \qquad (B.3)$$

where 1 stands for opening new portfolios in an objective at a certain period, and 0 stands for no opening, and

$$y^*_{ik} = \alpha_i + x_{ik}\beta + u_{ik} \qquad (B.4)$$

where y^*_{ik} is the latent variable; α_i is still the unobservable family-specific fixed effect for the i_{th} family; $\alpha_i + u_{ik}$ is the error term; x_{ik} is a row vector of all the variables, a combination of w_{it-1}, z_{jt-1} and v_{ijt-1}, and β is a column vector of all the coefficients to be estimated.

The nonlinearity of the decision model means that the family unobservables cannot be removed by taking deviations from unit means as in a linear fixed-effects model. I use Chamberlain's (1980) conditional probability to facilitate a solution:

$$\text{Prob}\left(y_i \middle| \sum_{k=1}^{Ki} y_{ik} = k_{1i}\right) = \frac{\exp\left(\sum_{k=1}^{Ki} y_{ik}(\alpha_i + \mathbf{x}_{ik}\beta)\right)}{\sum_{y_i \in S_i} \exp\left(\sum_{k=1}^{Ki} d_{ik}(\alpha_i + \mathbf{x}_{ik}\beta)\right)} = \frac{\exp\left(\sum_{k=1}^{Ki} y_{ik}\mathbf{x}_{ik}\beta\right)}{\sum_{y_i \in S_i} \exp\left(\sum_{k=1}^{Ki} d_{ik}\mathbf{x}_{ik}\beta\right)} \qquad (B.5)$$

where vector $y_i = (y_{i1}, \ldots, y_{iKi})$ is the opening and no opening outcomes for the i_{th} family as a whole.[8] I let $k_{1i} = \sum_{k=1}^{Ki} y_{ik}$ denote the observed number of openings in the i_{th} family, and $k_{2i} = K_i - k_{1i}$ denote the observed number of observations without opening in the i_{th} family.[9] S_i is

11. For instance, if a family needs to decide whether to start new portfolios in each of the five objectives in 10 periods, then there will be 50 observations for the family, with each observation standing for the decision by the family for each objective at a certain period.

12. For instance, $\mathbf{y_i} = (1, 0, 1)$ records openings for the 1st and 3rd observations in the i_{th} family.

13. In the example, $k_{1i} = 1 + 0 + 1 = 2$, $k_{2i} = 3 - 2 = 1$.

the set of all possible y_i *'s* which give the same k_{1i} and k_{2i}.[10] The d_{ik}'s, the elements of all possible y_i *'s*, are equal to 0 or 1 with $\sum_{k=1}^{Ki} d_{ik} = k_{1i}$. Based on equation (B5), the estimates of β are obtained by maximizing the following log-likelihood function:

$$\ln L = \sum_{i=1}^{n}\left[\sum_{k=1}^{Ki} y_{ik}\mathbf{x}_{ik}\beta - \ln\left(\sum_{\mathbf{y}_i \in S_i}\exp\left(\sum_{k=1}^{Ki} d_{ik}\mathbf{x}_{ik}\beta\right)\right)\right] \quad \text{(B.6)}$$

References

Aron, D. J., Lazear, E. P., 1990. The Introduction of new products. *American Economic Review AEA Papers and Proceedings*, 421-26.

Barclay, M., Pearson, N., Weisbach, M., 1998. Open-end mutual funds and capital gains taxes. *Journal of Financial Economics* 49, 3-43.

Berry, S. T., 1992. Estimation of a model of entry in the airline industry. *Econometrica* 60, 889-917.

Brown, S. J., Goetzmann, W. N., Ibbotson, R. G., Ross, S. A., 1992. Survivorship bias in performance studies. *Review of Financial Studies* 5, 553-80.

Burton, P. S., 1994. Product portfolios and the introduction of new products: An example from the insecticide industry. *Rand Journal of Economics* 25, 128-40.

Carhart, M. M., 1997. On persistence in mutual fund performance. *Journal of Finance* 52, 57-82.

Chamberlain, G., 1980. Analysis of covariance with qualitative data. *Review of Economic Studies* 47, 225-38.

Chevalier, J., Ellison, G., 1997. Risk taking by mutual funds as a response to incentives. *Journal of Political Economy* 105, 1167-1200.

Chodia, T., 1996. The structure of mutual fund charges. *Journal of Financial Economics* 41, 3-39.

Dunne, T., Roberts, M. J., Samuelson, L., 1988. Patterns of firm entry and exit in U.S. manufacturing industries. *RAND Journal of Economics* 19, 495-515.

Edelen, R., 1999. Investor flows and the assessed performance of open-end mutual funds. *Journal of Financial Economics* 53, 439-466.

Greene, W., 1997. *Econometric Analysis*. Prentice Hall, Inc., Upper Saddle River, New Jersey.

Khorana, A., Servaes, H., 1999. The determinants of mutual fund starts. *Review of Financial Studies* 12, 1043-1074.

Khorana, A., 2001. Performance changes following top management turnover: Evidence from open-end mutual funds. *Journal of Financial and Quantitative Analysis* 36, 371-393.

Lunde, A., Timmermann, A., Blake, D., 1999. The hazards of mutual fund performance: A Cox regression analysis. *Journal of Empirical Finance* 6, 121-52.

14. Continuing the example, $k_{1i} = 2$, $k_{2i} = 1$, so besides $\mathbf{y}_i = (1, 0, 1)$, S_i also includes $\mathbf{y}_i = (1, 1, 0)$ and $\mathbf{y}_i = (0, 1, 1)$.

Nanda, V., Narayanan, M. P., Warther, V. A., 2000. Liquidity, investment ability, and mutual fund structure. *Journal of Financial Economics* 57, 417-43.

Nanda, V., Wang, Z. J., Zheng, L. 2003. *Family values and the star phenomenon. Forthcoming in Review of Financial Studies.*

Pepall, L., 1990. Market demand and product clustering. *Economic Journal* 100, 195-205.

Pozen, R., 1998. The Mutual Fund Business. The MIT Press, Cambridge, Massachusetts.

Securities and Exchange Commission, 1995. *SEC rule 18f-3 adoption release*, release no. 33-7143, IC-20915.

Securities and Exchange Commission, 1940. *The investment company act of 1940.*

Sirri, E., Tufano, P., 1998. Costly search and mutual fund flows. *Journal of Finance* 53, 1589-1622.

ACKNOWLEDGEMENTS

I would like to thank Vladimir Atanasov, Kent Daniel, Ian Domowitz, David Dranove, Ravi Jagannathan, Erik Lie, Robert Korajczyk, Bing Liang, Charles Manski, Thomas Morrissey, George Oldfield, Robert Porter, Chris Taber, and Wanda Wallace for very helpful comments. I acknowledge the financial support of College of William & Mary. Any errors are my responsibility.

INDEX

N

O

P

Q

R

S